Study Guide

for

Siegel's

Criminology
Theories, Patterns, and Typologies
Ninth Edition

Joanne M. Ziembo-Vogl
Grand Valley State University

THOMSON

WADSWORTH

Australia • Brazil • Canada • Mexico • Singapore • Spain • United Kingdom • United States

Printer: Thomson West

ISBN 0-495-12915-1

Cover image: © Margaret Carsello/Images.com

Thomson Higher Education
10 Davis Drive
Belmont, CA 94002-3098
USA

For more information about our products, contact us at:
Thomson Learning Academic Resource Center
1-800-423-0563

For permission to use material from this text or product, submit a request online at
http://www.thomsonrights.com.
Any additional questions about permissions can be submitted by email to
thomsonrights@thomson.com.

Table of Contents

Student Introduction

It has been my experience that many students approach the topic of theory much like they do statistics, that is to say, with much trepidation. Amazingly, student attitudes at the end of the semester hardly reflect those at the beginning. This study guide is designed to assist students (those with feelings of trepidation and those without!) with the study of criminology by helping them master the important concepts and principles presented in Larry Siegel's *Criminology: Theories, Patterns, and Typologies*, 9th edition and to further stimulate their interest in studying the topics of crime and its causation. The following is a brief description of how you can make the best use of this study guide in learning the materials in the textbook and in preparing yourself for your criminology exams.

The following steps will help you to achieve the maximum benefits from this study guide. First, you should read the **Learning Objectives** to familiarize yourself with the key issues that will be presented in the chapter. Second, spend time reviewing and studying the **Keywords and Definitions;** doing so will assist you with understanding the chapter's key terms and concepts. Third, read the **Chapter Outline** and the **Chapter Summary** to obtain a general understanding of the chapter's contents. Fourth, you should diligently read the chapter in the textbook and highlight the significant points in the chapter.

Completing the **Test Bank** without using the textbook for reference is the final step. If you encounter difficulty completing some of the questions, review your textbook and try again. Repeat this process until you have answered all the questions. After completing the test bank, evaluate your accuracy by turning to the **Answer Key** at the end of the chapter. Note that there are no answers to the **Essay Questions** but the answer key provides the page numbers in the textbook containing the material that will assist you with developing responses to the essay questions. If you did not do as well on the test bank questions as you anticipated, you may wish to spend more time studying the textbook and conducting a further review of the study guide.

Also included in the study guide are **Student Exercises** that offer practical applications of the material you have studied in each chapter. Your professor may assign these exercises as outside class work or extra credit. Please note the **Criminology Web Links** that are designed to acquaint you with websites providing chapter-related material that will be of value in doing research for this course and for your other criminal justice courses.

May you find this study guide helpful in mastering the material in your textbook. Best wishes for success in this course and in all your academic pursuits. May you always be motivated to go the extra mile for it is doing so that one takes the best advantage of all that knowledge has to offer.

Joanne Ziembo-Vogl, Ph.D.
Grand Valley State University
Grand Rapids, Michigan

CRIME AND CRIMINOLOGY

OUTLINE

Chapter 1

Crime and Criminology

LEARNING OBJECTIVES

1. Understand what is meant by the field of criminology

2. Know the historical context of criminology

3. Recognize the differences among the various schools of criminological thought

4. Be familiar with the various elements of the criminological enterprise

5. Be able to discuss how criminologists define crime

6. Recognize the concepts of criminal law

7. Know the difference between evil acts and evil intents

8. Describe the various defenses to crime

9. Show how criminal law is undergoing change

10. Be able to discuss the ethical issues inherent in criminology

KEYWORDS AND DEFINITIONS

Criminology: an academic discipline that makes use of scientific methods to study the nature, extent, cause, and control of criminal behavior.

Criminologists: researchers who use scientific methods to study the nature, extent, cause, and control of criminal behavior.

Scientific Method: the gathering of data, creating of theories to explain the patterns found in the data, and testing the theories' validity by posing research questions (hypotheses) that are answered empirically.

Interdisciplinary science: a field of study that involves several disciplines; criminologists have been trained in diverse fields such as sociology, criminal justice, political science, psychology, economics, and the natural sciences.

Deviant behavior: strange, unusual behavior or any other action that departs from social norms.

Decriminalized: reducing the penalty for a criminal act but not actually legalizing it.

Utilitarianism: the philosophy that behavior occurs when the person believes it is useful, purposeful, and reasonable.

Classical criminology: the theoretical perspective suggesting that 1) people have free will to choose criminal or conventional behaviors; 2) people choose to commit crimes for reasons of greed or personal need; and 3) crime can only be controlled by the fear of criminal sanctions.

Positivism: the branch of social science that uses the scientific method of the natural sciences and suggests that human behavior is a product of social, biological, psychological, or economic forces.

Physiognomist: a scientist who studied the facial features of criminals to determine whether the shape of ears, nose, and eyes and the distance between them are associated with antisocial behavior.

Phrenologist: a scientist who studied the shape of the skull and bumps on the head to determine whether these physical attributes are linked to criminal behavior; phrenologists believed that external cranial characteristics dictate which areas of the brain control physical activity.

Psychopathic personality: a personality characterized by a lack of warmth and feeling, inappropriate behavior responses, and an inability to learn from experience. Some psychologists view psychopathy as a result of childhood trauma; others see it as a result of biological abnormality.

Atavistic anomalies: the physical characteristics (enormous jaws and strong canine teeth) of criminals that show they are throwbacks to more primitive times.

Criminal anthropology: the field of study that believes that serious offenders inherit criminal traits.

Biological determinism: the view that criminality is the result of inherited physical traits.

Biosocial theory: the theory that holds that there is a link among physical and mental traits, the social environment, and behavior.

Cartographic school of criminology: an approach developed in Europe in the early nineteenth century making use of social statistics to provide important demographic information on the population, including density, gender, religious affiliations, and wealth. Many of the relationships between crime and social phenomena identified then still serve as a basis for criminology today.

Anomie: a condition produced by normlessness; Because of rapidly shifting moral values, the individual has few guides to what is socially acceptable.

Chicago School: group of urban sociologists who studied the relationship between environmental conditions and crime.

Social ecology: the idea that social forces operate in urban areas and create criminal interactions causing some neighborhoods to become "natural" areas for crime.

Socialization: the interactions people have with the various individuals, organizations, institutions, and processes of society that help them mature and develop.

Ecological view: a belief that social forces operating in urban areas create criminal interactions; some neighborhoods become natural areas for crime.

Socialization view: process of human development and enculturation. Socialization is influenced by key social processes and institutions.

Bourgeoisie: in Marxist theory, the owners of the means of production; the capitalist ruling class.

Proletariat: a term used by Marx to refer to the working class members of society who produce goods and services but who do not own the means of production.

Criminological enterprise: the broader arena of criminology that consists of criminal statistics, sociology of the law, theory construction, criminal behavior systems, penology, and victimology.

White collar crime: term developed by Edwin Sutherland and used to describe economic crime activities.

Crime typology: research on the links between different types of crimes and criminals.

Penology: the study of the correction and control of known offenders in order to formulate strategies for crime control.

Consensus view: the belief that the majority of citizens in a society share common ideals and work toward a common good and that crimes are acts that are outlawed because they conflict with the rules of the majority and are harmful to society.

Substantive criminal law: the written code that defines crimes and their punishments.

Social harm: a view that behaviors harmful to other people and society in general must be controlled

Conflict view: the perspective that depicts society as a collection of diverse groups that are in constant and continuing conflict.

Interactionist view: the perspective that holds that (1) people act according to their own interpretation of reality, through which they assign meaning to things; (2) they observe the way others react, either positively or negatively; and (3) they reevaluate and interpret their own behavior according to the meaning and symbols they have learned from others.

Stigmatize: to label one as an outcast or deviant because they have violated social rules.

Moral entrepreneurs: those who use their influence to shape the legal process in the way they see fit.

Crime: a violation of societal rules of behavior as interpreted and expressed by a criminal legal code created by people holding social and political power. Individuals who violate these rules are subject to sanctions by state authority, social stigma, or loss of status.

Code of Hammurabi: the first written criminal code developed in Babylonia around 4,000 years ago.

Mosaic Code: the laws of the ancient Israelites, found in the Old Testament of the Judeo-Christian Bible.

Legal code: the specific laws that fall within the scope of criminal law.

Compurgation: in early English law, a process whereby an accused person swore an oath of innocence while being backed up by a group of twelve to twenty-five "oath-helpers," who would attest to his character and claims of innocence.

Ordeal: based on the principle of divine intervention and the then-prevalent belief that divine forces would not allow an innocent person to be harmed, this was a way of determining guilt involving such measures as having the accused place his or her hand in boiling water or hold a hot iron to see if God would intervene and heal the wounds. If the wound healed, the person was found not guilty; conversely, if the wound did not heal, the accused was deemed guilty of the crime for which he or she was being punished.

Common law: early English law and its use of precedents that became the basis of American law.

Mala in se **crimes**: crimes that are considered inherently evil and depraved.

Mala prohibitum **crimes**: crimes defined by the legislature, which reflect existing social conditions.

Statutory crimes: crimes defined by legislative bodies in response to changing social conditions, public opinion, and custom.

First-degree murder: the killing of another person after premeditation and deliberation.

Voluntary manslaughter: a homicide committed in the heat of passion or during a sudden quarrel; although intent may be present, malice is not.

Battery: a physical attack that includes hitting, punching, slapping, or other offensive touching of a victim.

Assault: an attack that may not involve physical contact; includes attempted battery or intentionally frightening the victim by word or deed.

Rape: unlawful sexual intercourse with a female without her consent.

Robbery: taking or attempting to take something of value by force or threat of force and/or by putting the victim in fear.

Burglary: breaking into and entering a home or structure for the purposes of committing a felony.

Arson: the intentional or negligent burning of a home, structure, or vehicle for criminal purposes such as profit, revenge, fraud, or crime concealment.

Larceny: taking for one's own use the property of another, by means other than force or threats on the victim or forcibly breaking into a person's home or workplace; theft.

Felony: any crime punishable by incarceration for one year or more, or death.

Social control function: the ability of the criminal law to control, restrain, and direct human behavior through its sanctioning power.

Actus reus: the guilty act committed by the accused.

Mens rea: the criminal intent to commit the act; referred to as a guilty mind.

Strict liability crimes: those crimes for which the law states that a person accused is guilty simply by doing what the statute prohibits; intent does not enter the picture.

Stalking: a pattern of behavior directed at a specific person that includes repeated physical or visual proximity, unwanted communications, and/or threats sufficient to cause fear in a reasonable person.

Pedophile: sexual offender who targets children.

CHAPTER OUTLINE

I. What is criminology?
   A. Criminology is the scientific approach to studying criminal behavior.
      1. Body of knowledge regarding crime as a social phenomenon
      2. Development of criminal law and its use to define crime
      3. The cause of law violation
      4. Methods used to control criminal behavior
      5. An interdisciplinary science
         a. Explains the origins, extent, and nature of crime in society
   B. Criminology and criminal justice
      1. Criminology explain the etiology (origin), extent, and nature of crime in society.
      2. Criminal justice refers to the study of the agencies of social control – police, courts, and corrections.
   C. Criminology and deviance
      1. Deviance – behavior that departs from social norms
      2. Not all crimes are deviant; not all deviant acts are illegal or criminal.
   D. Becoming deviant
      1. Criminologists study how deviant acts are criminalized and how criminal acts are decriminalized.

II. A Brief History of Criminology
   A. The study of crime and criminality is relatively recent.
   B. Classical criminology
      1. During the eighteenth century, social philosophers began to embrace the view that human behavior was a result of rational thought process.
         a. Jeremy Bentham's utilitarianism: people choose to act after weighing costs and benefits, pleasure and pain.
         b. Cesare Beccaria applied Bentham's principles to crime.
            1) To deter crime, the pain of punishment must be administered in a fair, balanced, and proportionate amount to counterbalance the pleasure obtained from crime.

C. Nineteenth-century positivism
   1. Emergence of scientific method
      a. People began using careful observation and analysis of natural phenomena to understand the workings of the world.
      b. Auguste Comte
         1) The father of sociology
         2) Applied scientific methods to sociology
         3) He and his followers became known as positivists.
   2. Two elements of positivism
      a. Human behavior is a function of forces beyond the person's control.
      b. The use of the scientific method to solve problems
   3. Biological Positivism
      a. Physiognomists – studied facial features of criminals to determine their association with antisocial behavior.
      b. Phrenologists – studied the link between the shape of the skull and bumps on the head and antisocial behavior.
      c. Concept of psychopathic personality
      d. Early research efforts shifted attention to brain functioning and personality as the keys to criminal behavior.
      e. Freud's work established the psychological basis of behavior.
   4. Cesare Lombroso
      a. Serious offenders inherit criminal traits – biological determinism
      b. Born criminals have atavistic anomalies – throwbacks to more primitive times
      c. Indirect heredity: criminogenic traits acquired from a degenerate family whose members suffered such ills as insanity, syphilis, and alcoholism
      d. Direct heredity: being related to a family of criminals
D. Foundations of sociological criminology
   1. Traced to the works of Adolphe Quetelet and Emile Durkheim
   2. Quetelet
      a. Began the use of data and statistics in criminological research
      b. Helped develop the cartographic school of criminology
      c. Uncovered the relationship of age, sex, season, climate, population composition, and poverty to criminality
      d. Quetelet's findings directly challenged Lombrosian biological determinism.
   3. Durkheim
      a. Crime is a normal and necessary social event.
      b. Impossible to imagine a society without crime
      c. Crime paves the way for social change.
      d. Crime calls attention to social ills.
      e. Coined the term anomie – norm and role confusion
E. The Development of sociological criminology
   1. Chicago School – University of Chicago – Ezra Park, Ernest Burgess, Louis Wirth
      a. Research on social ecology of the city
      b. Found some neighborhoods are "natural areas" for crime due to social forces
      b. Poverty leads to a critical breakdown in social institutions, such as schools and family.
      c. Crime is a function of where one lives rather than individual pathologies.

F. The Development of social process theories
1. During the 1930s and 1940s, a group of sociologists concluded that the individual's relationship to important social processes was the key to understanding human behavior.
    a. Edwin Sutherland – crime is a learned behavior.
    b. Walter Reckless – crime occurs when children develop an inadequate self-image that renders them incapable of controlling their own misbehavior.
2. By mid-century most American criminologists had embraced either the ecological view or the socialization view of crime.
G. The roots of conflict criminology
1. Karl Marx's *Communist Manifesto*
    a. The character of every civilization is determined by its mode of production.
    b. Described the oppressive labor conditions during the rise of industrial capitalism and the relationship between the owners of he means of production (the bourgeoisie) and the laborers (the proletariat)
    c. Marx's writings laid the foundation for a Marxist criminology developed by young sociologists who began to analyze the social conditions in the United States that promoted class conflict and crime.
H. Contemporary criminology
1. The various schools of criminology have evolved and continue to have impact.
    a. Classical theory has evolved into choice and deterrence theories.
    b. Biological positivism has evolved into biological and psychological trait theories.
    c. Quetelet and Durkheim's sociological criminology has evolved into contemporary social ecological theory.
    d. Marxist writings have evolved into critical criminology.
    e. Criminologists are now integrating theories linking personal, situational, and social forces. These are termed developmental theories.

III. What Criminologists Do: The Criminological Enterprise?
A. Criminologists are devoted to the study of crime and criminal behavior. Several subareas of criminology comprise the criminological enterprise.
1. Criminal statistics
    a. To create valid and reliable measurements of criminal behaviors
    b. Also used to make international comparisons
2. Sociology of law
    a. The role social forces play in shaping the criminal law
    b. The role of criminal law in shaping society
3. Theory construction
    a. Systematic set of interrelated statements or principles that explain some aspect of social life
    b. Theories are based on social fact and tested by constructing hypotheses and then assessing the hypotheses using empirical research.
4. Criminal behavior systems
    a. Involves research on specific criminal types and patterns
    b. Involves research on the links between different types of crimes and criminals (crime typology)
5. Penology
    a. The correction and control of known criminal offenders; subarea that most resembles criminal justice

     6.   Victimology
        a.   The study of victims and victimization
        b.   Calculating the costs of victimization.
        c.   Measuring the factors that increase the likelihood of becoming a victim
        d.   Studying the victim's role in precipitating crime
        e.   Designing services for victims of crime

IV. How Criminologists View Crime
    A. The consensus view of crime
        1.   Crimes are behaviors believed to be repugnant to all elements of society.
        2.   Social harm is what sets strange, unusual, or deviant behavior – or any action that departs from the social norms – apart from criminal behaviors.
    B. The conflict view of crime
        1.   The conflict view depicts society as a collective of diverse groups that are in constant and continuing conflict.
        2.   Groups able to assert their political power use the law and criminal justice system to advance their economic and social position.
        3.   Criminal law protects the haves from the have-nots.
        5.   Crime is a political concept designed to protect the power and position of the upper classes at the expense of the poor.
    C   The interactionist view of crime
        1.   Holds that people, institutions, and events are viewed subjectively and labeled either good or evil according to the interpretation of the evaluator.
        2.   Crime definitions reflect the preferences and opinions of people who hold social power in a particular legal jurisdiction.
        3.   Criminals are individuals society has stigmatized, or chosen to label as outcasts or deviants, because they have violated social rules.
        4.   Criminal law is seen as conforming to the benefits of moral crusaders or moral entrepreneurs who use their influence to shape the legal process in the way they see fit.
    D. Defining crime
        1.   Integrated definition: Crime is a violation of societal rules of behavior as interpreted and expressed by a criminal legal code created by people holding social and political power. Individuals who violate these rules are subject to sanctions by state authority, social stigma, and loss of status.

V. Crime and Criminal Law
    A. The concept of criminal law has been recognized for more than 3,000 years.
        1.   The Code of Hammurabi, one of the oldest, established a system of crime and punishment based on physical retaliation ("an eye for an eye").
        2.   The Mosaic Code was the foundation of Judeo-Christian moral teachings and the U.S. legal system.
        3.   German and Anglo-Saxon legal codes
            a.   Compurgation: the accused person swore an oath of innocence with the backing of twelve to twenty-five "oath-helpers," who could attest to his or her character and claims of innocence.
           b.   Trial by ordeal: based on the principle that divine forces would not allow an innocent person to be harmed.

B.   Common law
1.   Judge-made law that emerged after the Norman conquest of England in 1066, that was based on the precedents commonly applied in all similar cases.
  a.   *Mala in se* – inherently evil and depraved
  b.   *Mala prohibitum* – defined by Parliament
C.   Contemporary criminal law
1.   Crimes are divided into felonies and misdemeanors based on seriousness.
2.   Acts prohibited by the criminal law constitute behaviors considered unacceptable and impermissible by those in power.
3.   Social goals the government expects to achieve:
  a.   Enforce social control
  b.   Discourage revenge
  c.   Express public opinion and morality
  d.   Deter criminal behavior
  e.   Punish wrongdoing
  f.   Maintain social order
D.   The evolution of criminal law
1.   Criminal law is constantly evolving to reflect social and economic conditions.
2.   May change because of shifts in culture and in social conventions
3.   Future direction of criminal law remains unclear

VI.   Ethical Issues in Criminology
A.   Involves recognizing criminology's political and social consequences
B.   Major ethical issues include:
1.   What is to be studied?
  a.   Guided by criminologists' interests
  b.   Influence of governmental funding
2.   Who is to be studied?
  a.   A tendency to focus on one element of the community while ignoring others
3.   How are studies to be conducted?
  a.   Should subjects be told true purpose of a survey?
  b.   Providing special treatment to one group while depriving others
  c.   Protecting subjects from harm

CHAPTER SUMMARY

Criminology is the scientific approach to studying criminal behavior. It deals with the processes of making laws, of breaking laws, and of reacting to the breaking of laws. Research in criminology is characterized by the use of the scientific method. Criminal justice refers to describing, analyzing, and explaining the behavior of justice agencies. Although the two fields are different, they do overlap. Criminologists must know how criminal justice agencies operate and criminal justice experts must understand the nature of crime.

Classical criminology developed in the 19th century. Cesare Beccaria argued that people have free will and choose their behavior. Therefore, crime can be controlled by fear of punishment if is severe, certain, and swift. Positivism followed classical criminology and began with biological determinism and Cesare Lombroso who argued that serious offenders had inherited criminal traits. The foundations of sociological criminology developed with Adolphe Quetelet and his use of data and statistics in criminological research. Emile Durkheim followed with the idea that crime is a normal and necessary social event. He coined the term "anomie" to describe norm and role confusion. In the United States, the Chicago School pioneered research in social ecology – the ecological view – and found that some neighborhoods are "natural areas" for crime because of poverty and broken social institutions. The socialization view followed, proposing that people learn criminal attitudes or develop an inadequate self-image. The 1960s and 1970s brought conflict criminology that applied Marxist principles to the study of crime.

In contemporary criminology we find classical theory has evolved into rational choice and deterrence theories, positivism now considers how biological and psychological traits interact with the environment to influence criminality, sociological theories examine social structure, learning experiences, and socialization, conflict theorists now examine how unfair economic structures impact high crime rates, and criminologists integrate theories into developmental theories that link personal, situational, and social factors.

The criminological enterprise has six major subareas. The first subarea is criminal statistics, which describes and measures crime. Next is the sociology of the law that analyzes how society shapes the law and how the law shapes society. The third subarea is theory and theory development, which focuses on crime causation. The next subarea is criminal behavior systems, which focuses on crime typology. Fifth, is penology that deals with corrections, rehabilitation, and treatment. Last, is vicitmology that focuses on the role of victims in crime.

There are three perspectives from which criminologists view crime. The first is the consensus view which holds that the substantive criminal law reflects the values, beliefs, and opinions of society's mainstream and that there is a consensus or general agreement among a majority of citizens on what behaviors should be illegal. The second perspective is the conflict view which holds that society is a collection of diverse groups who are in constant and continuous conflict. Those groups who achieve power use the law and the criminal justice system to advance their economic and social position so that they become the haves and control the have-nots. The third perspective is the interactionist view of crime. Under this view, people act according to their own interpretation of reality. They observe how others react positively or negatively. People then reevaluate and interpret their own behavior according to the meaning and symbols they have learned from others. Therefore, good and evil is interpreted by the evaluator.

Our system of criminal law is based on English common law and the use of precedents. Crime is viewed as being of two types: 1) *mala in se* and 2) *mala prohibitum*. Crimes are classified according to the punishments allowed by law: 1) felonies are the more serious offenses and 2) misdemeanors are the less serious offenses. There are two components in every crime: 1) the guilty act or *actus reus* and 2) the guilty mind or *mens rea*. Consequently, there are three basic criminal defenses: 1) denying the *actus reus*, 2) denying the *mens rea*, or 3) providing justification for the act.

Criminology is a discipline that involves several ethical issues that fall into three categories. First, what is to be studied? Second, who is to be studied? Third, how are the studies to be conducted?

STUDENT EXERCISES

Exercise 1

Make a list of five deviant acts that are not criminal. Make a list of five criminal acts that are not deviant. Compare your list with those compiled by your classmates. Why do you think that there is not complete agreement among you and your classmates?

Exercise 2

Make a list of 15 crimes. Ask five or six colleagues (who are not in your criminology class) to rank the 15 crimes from most serious to least serious. How do the rankings provided by your colleagues compare? Overall, is there general agreement or complete disagreement? Criminologists from what perspective of crime would have predicted this result?

CRIMINOLOGY WEB LINKS

http://cj.wadsworth.com/siegel_crim9e
This website is designed exclusively for your textbook. Take a look around the website to familiarize yourself with it. Also keep in mind that this website will always have an up-to-date list of weblinks contained in the textbook.

http://www.criminology.fsu.edu/cjlinks/
This is a website maintained by Dr. Cecil Greek. It contains information pertaining to criminology-related web sites.

http://www.ncjrs.org/
This website contains a wealth of information pertaining to crime and justice. It provides you access to government documents on every aspect of crime.

http://fjsrc.urban.org/index.cfm
This web site maintains the Bureau of Justice Statistics (BJS) Federal Justice Statistics Program (FJSP) database, which contains information about suspects and defendants processed in the Federal criminal justice system. Using data obtained from Federal agencies, the FJSP compiles comprehensive information describing defendants from each stage of Federal criminal case processing.

TEST BANK

FILL-IN THE BLANKS

1. Criminology is a discipline that makes use of the _____ _____ to study the nature, extent, cause, and control of criminal behavior.

2. Criminal justice refers to the study of the _____ of social control that handle criminal offenders.

3. The earliest "scientific" studies examining human behavior were _____ oriented.

4. The Chicago School pioneered research on the _____ _____ of the city of Chicago.

5. Criminal statistics involves measuring the amount and trends of _____ _____.

6. A criminologist's choice of orientation or perspective depends, in part, on his or her _____ of crime.

7. The _____ view of crime traces its antecedents to the symbolic interaction school of sociology.

8. Inherently evil crimes are often referred to as _____ _____ _____.

9. To satisfy the requirements of actus reus, guilty actions must be _____.

10. _____ _____ _____ are crimes defined by statute that do not require mens rea, as the person is guilty simply by doing what the statute prohibits.

TRUE/FALSE QUESTIONS

1. T/F Criminology is an interdisciplinary science.

2. T/F Criminologists study how criminal acts are decriminalized.

3. T/F Deviance refers to the study of behavior that departs from the law.

4. T/F Classical criminology believes people's choice of crime may be controlled by his or her fear of punishment.

5. T/F Positivism holds that criminals are not responsible for their crimes.

6. T/F Possessing atavistic anomalies means that criminals are intellectually inferior.

7. T/F Durkheim argued that crime is not useful and it is unhealthy for society.

8. T/F The Chicago School sociologists and their contemporaries focused on the functions of social institutions.

9. T/F Conflict criminology applies Marxist principles to the study of crime.

10. T/F The sociology of law is a subarea of the criminological enterprise.

11. T/F Penology is the study of the links between different types of crimes and criminals.

12. T/F Criminal law is constantly evolving to reflect social and economic conditions.

13. T/F The consensus view of crime links illegal behavior to the concept of social harm.

14. T/F According to the conflict view of crime, "real" crimes include murder, rape, and incest.

15. T/F Criminal law has a social control function.

MULTIPLE CHOICE QUESTIONS

1. Emphasizing that behavior occurs when the actor considers it useful, purposeful, and reasonable is called:
   a. determinism
   b. hedonism
   c. utilitarianism
   d. classicism

2. Which is NOT a subarea in the field of criminology?
   a. Identifying the nature of crime
   b. Explaining the behavior of justice agencies
   c. Explaining the cause of crime
   d. Describing the extent of crime

3. The most famous classical criminologist is:
   a. Cesare Beccaria
   b. Cesare Lombroso
   c. Adolphe Quetelet
   d. Emile Durkheim

4. To control criminal behavior, punishment must be:
   a. swift
   b. severe
   c. certain
   d. all of the above

5. Those who study the shape of the skull and bumps on the head to determine whether their physical attributes were linked to criminal behavior are called:
   a. physiognomists
   b. phrenologists
   c. classical criminologists
   d. positivists

6. Lombroso held that born criminals suffer from:
   a. mental illness
   b. disease
   c. atavistic anomalies
   d. all of the above

7. The assumed link among physical and mental traits, the social environment, and behavior is called:
   a. positivism
   b. biological determinism
   c. biosocial theory
   d. criminal anthropology

8. The person who instigated the use of data and statistics in performing criminological research is:
   a. Emile Durkheim
   b. Adolphe Quetelet
   c. Robert Ezra Park
   d. Ernest W. Burgess

9. The cartographic school of criminology made extensive use of:
   a. social statistics
   b. the law
   c. skull measurements
   d. psychology

10. The interactions people have with the various individuals, organizations, institutions, and processes of society that help them mature and develop are called:
    a. cartography
    b. social ecology
    c. anomie
    d. socialization

11. Which of the following is a subarea of the criminological enterprise?
    a. penology
    b. criminal behavior systems
    c. sociology of law
    d. all of the above

12. The subarea of criminology concerned with the role social forces play in shaping criminal law is called:
    a. criminal behavior systems
    b. penology
    c. vicitimology
    d. the sociology of the law

13. The study of criminal behavior that involves research on the links between different types of crimes and criminals is known as:
    a. crime categorization
    b. crime typology
    c. victimology
    d. penology

14. The position that crimes are behaviors believed to be repugnant to all elements of society called:
    a. consensus view
    b. interactionist view
    c. conflict view
    d. criminological view

15. What sets deviant behavior apart from criminal behavior is:
    a. society's attitude
    b. the law
    c. social harm
    d. precedent

16. Depicting society as a collection of diverse groups is the position of:
    a. consensus view
    b. interactionist view
    c. conflict view
    d. criminological view

17. Those who say that those who hold social power impose their definition of right and wrong on the rest of the population hold the:
    a. consensus view
    b. interactionist view
    c. conflict view
    d. criminological view

18. The basis for the U.S. legal system is found in the:
    a. Mosaic Code
    b. Code of Hammurabi
    c. Napoleonic Code
    d. English Code

19. Which of the following pertains to common law?
    a. English parliament could not enact legislation to supplement judge-made law.
    b. Precedents would be commonly applied in all cases.
    c. They were only crimes that were mala in se.
    d. All of the above.

20. The unlawful touching of another with the intent to cause injury is called:
    a. assault
    b. battery
    c. rape
    d. solicitation

21. For a crime to occur, the state must show the accused had the intent to commit the act. The intent to commit the act is commonly called:
    a. mala in se
    b. actus reus
    c. mala prohibitum
    d. mens rea

22. If a child is sick, the parents must seek medical aid. The failure to act in this case is considered a crime for which of the following reasons?
    a. imposition by statute
    b. contractual relationship
    c. relationship of the parties based on status
    d. biological determinism

23. By arguing that they were falsely accused and that the real culprit has yet to be identified, the accused is:
    a. denying the actus reus
    b. denying the mens rea
    c. arguing justification
    d. denying the mala in se

24. Criminal law can change because of which of the following?
    a. social conditions
    b. economic conditions
    c. shifts in culture
    d. all of the above

25. A major ethical issue in criminology is that too often criminologists focus their attention on:
    a. white males
    b. poor and minorities
    c. prisoners
    d. juveniles

ESSAY QUESTIONS

1. List and describe the subareas of the criminological enterprise.

2. Explain the conflict view of crime.

3. Explain the interactionist view of crime.

4.   Discuss the social goals the government hopes to achieve by outlawing unacceptable behaviors.

5.   List and describe the three major categories of ethical issues in criminology.

MATCHING

1. _____ Deviance
2. _____ Interdisciplinary
3. _____ Emile Durkheim
4. _____ Code of Hammurabi
5. _____ Criminological Enterprise
6. _____ Anomie
7. _____ Social Theory
8. _____ Criminal Law
9. _____ Bourgeoise
10. _____ Compurgation

A. A condition produced by normlessness
B. Criminologists have been trained in diverse fields most commonly sociology, but also criminal justice, political science, psychology, economics, and the natural sciences.
C. A sworn oath of innocence backed by twelve to twenty-five oath-helpers
D. Owners of the means of production
E. Systematic set of interrelated statements or principles that explain some aspect of social life
F. Behavior that departs from social norms
G. Most famous set of written laws of the ancient world preserved on basalt rock columns.
H. Has a social control function
I. Crime is normal.
J. Subareas within the broader arena of criminology

CHAPTER 1 ANSWER KEY

Fill in the Blank Answers

1. scientific methods
2. agencies
3. biologically
4. social ecology
5. criminal behavior
6. definition
7. interactionist
8. *mala in se*
9. voluntary
10. strict liability crimes

True/False Answers

1.	T	6.	F	11.	F
2.	T	7.	F	12.	T
3.	F	8.	T	13.	T
4.	T	9.	T	14.	F
5.	F	10.	T	15.	T

Multiple Choice Answers

1.	C	11.	D	21.	D
2.	B	12.	D	22.	C
3.	A	13.	B	23.	A
4.	D	14.	A	24.	D
5.	A	15.	C	25.	B
6.	C	16.	C		
7.	C	17.	B		
8.	B	18.	A		
9.	A	19.	B		
10.	D	20.	B		

Essay Questions

1. Pages 11-13
2. Pages 16-17
3. Page 17
4. Pages 19-20
5. Pages 21-24

Matching Answers

1.	F	6.	A
2.	B	7.	F
3.	I	8.	H
4.	G	9.	D
5.	J	10.	C

THE NATURE AND EXTENT OF CRIME

OUTLINE

Chapter 2

The Nature and Extent of Crime

LEARNING OBJECTIVES

1. Be familiar with the various forms of crime data

2. Know the problems associated with collecting data

3. Be able to discuss the recent trends in the crime rate

4. Be familiar with the factors that influence crime rates

5. Be able to discuss the patterns in the crime rate

6. Be able to discuss the association between social class and crime

7. Recognize that there are age, gender, and racial patterns in crime

8. Describe the various positions on gun control

9. Be familiar with Wolfgang's pioneering research on chronic offending

10. Be able to discuss the influence the discovery of the chronic offender has had on criminology

KEYWORDS AND DEFINITIONS

Uniform Crime Report (UCR): data collected from local law enforcement agencies by the Federal Bureau of Investigation and published yearly.

Index crimes: the eight most serious crimes that are reported by the Federal Bureau of Investigation in the Uniform Crime Reports; the crimes include murder and nonnegligent manslaughter, forcible rape, robbery, aggravated assault, burglary, larceny, arson, and motor vehicle theft.

Part I crimes: the major unit of analysis of the Uniform Crime Report; the crimes include murder and nonnegligent manslaughter, forcible rape, robbery, aggravated assault, burglary, larceny, arson, and motor vehicle theft.

Part II crimes: all other crimes that are not included in the Part I offenses of the Uniform Crime Reports.

Cleared crimes: crimes are cleared 1) when at least one person is arrested, charged, and turned over to the court for prosecution; or 2) by exceptional means, when some element beyond police control precludes the arrest of an offender.

National-Incident-Based Reporting System: a new program that is attempting to provide more detailed information on individual criminal incidents by using a uniform, comprehensive program. This program requires local police agencies to provide at least a brief account of each incident and arrest within 22 crime patterns, including the incident, victim, and offender information.

Sampling: selecting for study a limited number of subjects who are representative of entire groups sharing similar characteristics.

Population: an entire group sharing similar characteristics.

Cross-sectional survey: a type of survey that is representative of all members of society.

Self-report survey: type of survey in which participants describe their recent and lifetime criminal activity.

National Crime Victimization Survey (NCVS): a national survey sponsored by the Bureau of Justice Statistics of the U.S. Department of Justice. Households are asked to report on the frequency, characteristics and consequences of criminal victimization for such crimes as rape, sexual assault, robbery, assault, theft, household burglary, and motor vehicle theft.

Victimization survey: type of survey in which people describe their experience as crime victims.

Cohort: a group of people who share a like characteristic over time.

Retrospective cohort study: a study that uses an intact cohort of known offenders and looks back into their early life experiences by checking their education, family, police, and hospital records.

Meta-analysis: gathering data from a number of previous studies.

Systematic review: collecting the findings from previously conducted scientific studies that address a particular problem, appraising and synthesizing the evidence, and using the collective evidence to address a particular scientific question.

Data mining: a criminological technique that uses multiple advanced computational methods, including artificial intelligence (the use of computers to perform logical functions), to analyze large data sets usually involving one or more data sources.

Crime mapping: computerized crime maps that allow criminologists to analyze and correlate a wide array of date to create immediate, detailed visuals of crime patterns – the spatial geography of crime.

Instrumental crimes: those crimes committed for the purpose of obtaining desired goods and other services that cannot be obtained through conventional means.

Expressive crimes: crimes that are committed as a means of expressing rage, frustration, and anger against society.

Aging out: the process by which offenders reduce the frequency of their offending behavior as they age.

Masculinity hypothesis: the view that women who commit crimes have biological and psychological traits similar to men.

Chivalry hypothesis: the view that female criminality is hidden because of the culture's generally protective and benevolent attitude toward women.

Liberal feminist theory: the theory that suggests that the traditionally lower crime rate for women could be explained by their "second class" economic and social position.

Career criminal: a person who repeatedly violates the law and organizes his or her lifestyle around criminality.

Chronic offender: according to Wolfgang, a delinquent offender who is arrested five or more times before he or she is 18 and who stands a good chance of becoming an adult criminal; such offenders are responsible for more than half of all serious crimes.

Early onset: the exposure to a variety of personal and social problems at an early age that makes on most at risk to repeat offending.

Persistence: the idea that those who started their delinquent careers early and who committed serious violent crimes throughout adolescence were the most likely to persist as adults.

Continuity of crime: the view that crime begins early in life and continues throughout the life course. Thus, the best predictor of future criminality is past criminality.

Three strikes: policies whereby people convicted of three felony offenses receive a mandatory life sentence.

CHAPTER OUTLINE

I. Primary Sources of Crime Data
    A. Official record research
        1. The Uniform Crime Report (UCR)
            a. Includes crimes reported to local police departments and number of arrests made by police agencies.
            b. Index or Part I crimes: murder and nonnegligent manslaughter, forcible rape, robbery, aggravated assault, burglary, larceny, arson, and motor vehicle theft
        2. Compiling the Uniform Crime Report
            a. Monthly reports of known crime from law enforcement agencies
            b. Monthly reports of crimes cleared
            c. Also reported
                1) Data on the number of clearances involving the arrest of juvenile offenders
                2) Data on the value of property stolen and recovered in connection with Part I crimes
                3) Detailed information on homicides
            d. Three methods to express crime data
                1) Number of crimes reported and arrests made

    2) Crime rates per 100,000
    3) Changes in the number and rate of crime over time
3. Validity of the Uniform Crime Report
    a. Reporting practices
        1) Not all crimes are reported.
        2) Victim surveys indicate less than 40 percent are reported.
    b. Law enforcement practices
        1) Changes in how reporting is done
        2) Law enforcement interpretation of the definitions of index crimes
        3) Systematic errors
        4) Some may deliberately alter their reports to improve image.
        5) Boosting efficiency may increase crime rates.
        6) Higher crime may result from improved technology or better-qualified personnel.
    c. Methodological problems
        1) No federal crimes are reported.
        2) Reports are voluntary and vary in accuracy and completeness.
        3) Not all police departments submit reports.
        4) The FBI uses estimates in its total crime projections.
        5) If an offender commits multiple crimes, only the most serious is recorded.
        6) Each act is listed as a single offense for some crimes but not for others.
        7) Incomplete acts are lumped together with completed ones.
        8) Important differences exist between the FBI's definition of certain crimes and those used in a number of states.
4. NIBRS: The future of the Uniform Crime Report
    a. National Incident-Based Reporting System – a program that collects data on each reported crime incident
    b. Includes a brief account of each incident and arrest
    c. Information provided on 46 specific offenses
    d. Hate and bias crime information provided
    e. Over twenty states have implemented NIBRS
B. Survey research
    1. Used to measure attitudes, beliefs, values, characteristics, and behavior
        a. Sampling: a representative group
        b. Population: the entire group from which a representative sample is taken
        c. Cross-sectional survey: representative of all members of society
    3. Self-report surveys
        a. Participants asked to describe their recent and lifetime participation in criminal activity; asked about attitudes, values, and behaviors
        b. Most focus on juvenile delinquency and youth crime
        c. Also used with prison inmates and drug users
    4. Self-report patterns
        a. Monitoring the Future study – University of Michigan Institute for Social Research
            1) Annually since 1978; asks 2,500 high school seniors about their substance abuse
            2) Data indicate the number of people who break the law is far greater than the number projected by official statistics.

      5.   Validity of self-reports
- a. Responses accurately reflect respondents' true life experiences
- b. Critics disagree
  - 1) Cannot expect respondents to candidly admit illegal acts
  - 2) May exaggerate criminal acts, forget, or be confused
  - 3) Many trivial offenses in self-reports
- c. "Missing cases" phenomenon is a problem
- d. Reporting accuracy differs among racial, ethnic, and gender groups
- e. The "known group method" used to verify self-report data

C. The National Crime Victimization Survey (NCVS)
1. Designed to address non-reporting issue
   - a. Large nationally representative sample – 84,000 households, 149,000 people age 12 or older
   - b. People report victimization experiences
   - c. High completion rate
   - d. Considered relatively unbiased, valid estimation of victimizations
   - e. Finds many crimes go unreported to the police
2. Validity of the NCVS
   - a. Overreporting due to misinterpretation of events
   - b. Underreporting due to embarrassment, fear, or forgetfulness
   - c. Inability to record the personal criminal activity of those interviewed
   - d. Sampling errors
   - e. Inadequate question format that invalidates responses

D. Evaluating primary crime data sources
1. UCR
   - a. Strengths
     - 1) Contains data on number and characteristics of people arrested
     - 2) Arrest data can provide a measure of criminal activity
     - 3) Sole source of data on homicide
     - 4) Standard upon which most criminological research is based
   - b. Weaknesses
     - 1) Omits those crimes not reported to the police
2. NCVS
   - a. Strengths
     - 1) Includes unreported crimes
     - 2) Includes important information on the personal characteristics of victims
   - b. Weaknesses
     - 1) Limited sample
     - 2) Relies on personal recollections
     - 3) Does not include data on crime patterns, including murder and drug abuse
3. Self-report surveys
   - a. Strength: can provide information on personal characteristics of offenders
   - b. Weakness: relies on honesty of criminal offenders and drug abusers, a population not generally known for accuracy and integrity
4. Overall
   - a. Crime patterns and trends often quite similar
   - b. Agreement re: personal characteristics of serious criminals
   - c. Reliable indicators of changes and fluctuations in yearly crime rates

II. Secondary Sources of Crime Data
    A. Cohort research
        1. Difficult, expensive, and time consuming to follow a cohort over time
        2. Sometimes researchers do retrospective cohort studies.
    B. Experimental research
        1. True experiments have three elements
            a. Random selection of subjects
            b. Control or comparison group
            c. An experimental condition
        2. Quasi-experimental design if it is impossible to randomly select subjects or manipulate conditions
        3. Criminological experiments
            a. Relatively rare because they are difficult and expensive to conduct
            b. Ethical and legal roadblocks to manipulating subjects' lives
            c. Require long follow-up to verify results
    C. Observational and interview research
        1. Sometimes researchers focus on a relatively few subjects.
        2. Sometimes they observe criminals firsthand to gather insight into their motives and activities.
        3. Sometimes they bring subjects into a laboratory setting to observe how they react to a predetermined condition or stimulus.
    D. Meta-analysis and systematic review
        1. Meta-analysis
            a. Gathers data from a number of previous studies
            b. Compatible information and data are extracted and pooled together
            c. When analyzed, more powerful and valid indicator of results than a single study
        2. Systematic review
            a. Collect findings from previous studies addressing a particular problem
            b. Appraise and synthesize the evidence
            c. Use collective evidence to address a particular scientific question
    E. Data mining
        1. Using computers to analyze large data sets from one or more sources
            a. Goal: identify significant and recognizable patterns, trends, and relationships not otherwise detected
            b. Used to predict future events or behaviors
    F. Crime mapping
        1. Creating graphic representations of the spatial geography of crime
            a. Simple maps indicating crime locations or concentrations
            b. Complex maps to chart trends in criminal activity

III. Crime trends
    A. Changes in crime trends over time
        1. 1830 – 1860: gradual increase in violent crime
        2. 1880 – WWI: number of reported crimes decreased
        3. WWI – 1930: Crime rates declined until 1930
        4. 1930 – 1960: crime rates increased gradually; homicide rate declined
        5. 1960s – 1981: crime rate growth had a greater rate of increase
        6. 1981 – 1984: a consistent decline in index crimes
        7. 1984 – 1991: crime rate increased

8. 1991 – 2004: declines in crime, including teenage criminality
9. Reasons for crime trends:
   a. Age
      1) Graying of America
      2) Declining birthrate
   b. Economy – strong economy helps lower crime rates
   c. Social malaise
      1) Increase in social problems related to rising crime rates
      2) Racial conflict may increase crime rates
   d. Abortion
      1) Availability of abortion related to reduced crime rates
      2) Selective abortion by women most at risk to have children
      3) Better maternal, familial, or fetal care due to having fewer children
   e. Guns
      1) Availability of guns
      2) More teens with guns
   f. Gangs
      1) Gang members more likely to possess guns
      2) Crime associated with gangs
      3) "Younger brother syndrome" – younger brothers avoid gangs after seeing what happened to older brothers.
   g. Drug use
      1) Relationship between violent crime rate and crack epidemic
      2) Decrease in crack and a decrease in violence
   h. Media
      1) Violent theme media
      2) Violence on TV correlated to aggressive behaviors
   i. Medical technology
      1) Quality of healthcare significantly reduces murder rates.
      2) Fluctuations in murder rates linked to availability of emergency medical services
   j. Justice policy
      1) Increase in the number of police on the streets
      2) Aggressive police tactics
      3) Tough laws and lengthy prison terms
   k. Crime opportunities
      1) Market conditions and the low price of pilferable items
      2) Improved home and commercial security devices
B. Trends in violent crime
   1. Decrease in the numbers of murder, rape, assault, robbery
   2. Violence in the United States has decreased 24% during the past decade.
   3. Between 1991 and 2004, murder rates dropped more than 40%.
C. Trends in property crime
   1. Drop in the property crime rate – larceny, motor vehicle theft, arson
   2. Not as dramatic as for violent crime rate
   3. Between 1995 and 2004, property crime rate declined 23% and decline and additional 2.1% between 2003 and 2004
D. Trends in victimization data (NCVS findings) – confirms UCR's view of a declining crime rates is accurate

E. Trends in self-reporting
   1. More stable that results indicated in UCR
   2. Drugs and alcohol: marked increase in the 1970s, leveled off in the 1980s, increased in mid-1990s, then declined

IV. What the future holds
   A. Fox predicts a significant increase in teen violence; not all criminologists agree.
   B. Steffensmeier and Harer predict a moderate increase in crime.
   C. The Internet and e-commerce have created new classes of crimes.

V. Crime patterns
   A. The ecology of crime
      1. Day, season, and climate
         a. Most crimes occur during the warm summer months of July and August.
         b. Murders and robberies occur frequently during December and January.
         c. Crime rates are higher on the first day of the month.
      2. Temperature
         a. Association between temperature and crime resembles an inverted U-curve.
         b. Crime rates rise with rising temperatures.
         c. Crime rates decline around 85 degrees.
      3. Regional differences
         a. Large urban areas have the highest violence rates.
         b. Exceptions to this trend are large transient or seasonal populations.
         c. Some criminologists believe regional cultural values may influence crime; others believe regional differences are explained by economic disparities.
   B. Use of firearms
      1. Play a dominant role in criminal activity
      2. Zimring and Hawkins believe that the proliferation of handguns and the high rate of lethal violence they cause separate the crime problem in the United States from the rest of the world.
      3. Kleck and Gertz maintain personal gun use may be a deterrent to crime.
   C. Social class, socioeconomic conditions, and crime
      1. Crime is a lower-class phenomenon
         a. Instrumental crimes
         b. Expressive crimes
      2. UCR data indicate higher crime rates in inner-city, high-poverty areas.
      3. Prisoners were members of the lower class, unemployed, or underemployed before incarceration.
      4. Alternative explanation – relationship between social class and crime may be a function of law enforcement practices.
         a. Police devote more resources to poor areas and apprehension rates are higher there.
         b. Police more likely to arrest and prosecute lower class citizens.
      5. Class and self-reports
         a. 1950s – no relationship between social class and youth crime
         b. Little support for the idea that crime is primarily a lower-class phenomenon
         c. Many self-report instruments include trivial offenses.
         d. If only serious offenses are considered, a significant association can be observed.

6. Class-crime controversy
   a. If crime is related to social class, then economic and social factors cause crime.
   b. Why the uncertainty? – methods to measure social class vary widely
   c. Possible that the association between class and crime is more complex than a simple linear relationship
7. Does class matter?
   a. Official crime is more prevalent among the lower class.
   b. Less serious crime is spread more evenly throughout the social structure.
   c. Lower class more likely to suffer psychological abnormalities that may promote crime – anxiety and conduct disorders.
   d. Communities lacking in economic and social opportunities produce high levels of frustration.

D. Age and crime
   1. Age is inversely related to criminality.
   2. Younger people commit crime more often than do their older peers.
   3. Relationship has been stable since 1935.
   4. Aging out of crime
      a. Crime peaks in adolescence then declines rapidly thereafter.
      b. Agnew – the peak in criminal activity can be linked to essential features of adolescence in modern, industrial societies.
         1) A reduction in supervision
         2) An increase in social and academic demands
         3) Participation in a larger, more diverse, peer-oriented world
         4) An increased desire for adult privileges
         5) A reduced ability to cope in a legitimate manner and increased incentive to solve problems in a criminal manner
      c. Aging out is a function of the natural history of the human life cycle.

E. Gender and crime
   1. All three types of crime data confirm male crime rates are much higher than those of females.
   2. In self-reports, males report criminal behavior more than females but not to the degree suggested by official data.
   3. Explaining gender differences: traits and temperament
      a. Early criminologists pointed to emotional, physical, and psychological differences to explain crime rate differences.
      b. Masculinity hypothesis
      c. Chivalry hypothesis
   4. Explaining gender differences: socialization and development
      a. Girls socialized to avoid being violent and aggressive
      b. Girls supervised more closely
      c. Research shows most girls develop moral values that strongly discourage antisocial behavior.
      d. Gender-based differences in human development that help shape behavior choices
         1) Cognitive differences
         2) Socialization differences
   5. Explaining gender differences: cognitive differences
      a. Girls superior to boys in verbal ability
      b. Girls, even at an early age, more empathic than boys

6. Explaining gender differences: feminist views
   a. Liberal feminist theory – traditionally lower crime rates for women could be explained by their "second-class" economic and social position.
   b. As women's social roles changed and their lifestyles became more like men's, it was believed that their crime rates would converge.
   c. Self-report studies seem to indicate that the pattern of female criminality is similar to that of male criminality.
7. Is convergence likely?
   a. Female arrest rates seem to be increasing at a faster pace than males.
   b. The "emancipation of women" may have had relatively little influence on female crime rates.
   c. Changes in police activity may explain differences in arrest trends.

F. Race and crime
   1. Minorities involved in a disproportionate share of criminal activity.
   2. Responsible for a disproportionate number of Part I and II arrests
   3. Possible reasons
      a. Data reflect racial differences in the crime rate.
      b. May reflect police bias in the arrest process
   4. Research – no relationship between race and self-reported delinquency
   5. Racism and discrimination
      a. Economic deprivation
      b. Legacy of racism and discrimination
      c. Black crime may be a function of the socialization process.
   6. Institutional racism
   7. Economic and social disparity
   8. Family dissolution
   9. Convergence possible – if economic and social obstacles can be removed

G. Chronic offenders/criminal careers
   1. Most offenders commit a single criminal act and discontinue antisocial activity after arrest.
   2. Small group of persistent offenders account for a majority of all criminal offenses.
   3. Wolfgang, Figlio, and Sellin
      a. "Chronic 6 percent" of total sample were arrested 5 or more times
      b. Responsible for 51.9 percent of all offenses
      c. Arrests and court experience did little to deter the chronic offender.
   4. What causes chronicity?
      a. Kids exposed to a variety of personal and social problems at an early age are the most at risk to repeat offending; "early onset"
   5. Persistence – the continuity of crime
      a. Children who are disruptive at age five or six most likely to persist in crime
      b. Apprehension and punishment have little effect.
      c. Best predictor of future behavior is past behavior.
   6. Implications of the chronic offender concept
      a. Chronic offender is the central focus of crime policy.
      b. Three strikes policies

CHAPTER SUMMARY

Criminologists study crime by using survey research, cohort research, official research, experimental research, observational and interview research, and meta-analysis and systematic reviews. Survey research includes three types: self-report surveys, victimization surveys, and cross-sectional surveys. Most experimental research in criminology is quasi-experimental as "true" experiments are difficult and expensive to conduct. There are also ethical and legal roadblocks to manipulating subjects' lives and they require long follow-up to verify results.

Criminologists measure crime trends and rates using the Uniform Crime Report (UCR), the National Crime Victimization Survey (NCVS), and self report surveys. The Federal Bureau of Investigation publishes the UCR which contains data provided by law enforcement agencies across the country. Data, once compiled, are reported as Part I and Part II crimes. Part I crimes include murder and nonnegligent manslaughter, forcible rape, robbery, aggravated assault, burglary, larceny, arson, and motor vehicle theft. Part II crimes are all other offenses not included in Part I. Crime data in the UCR are expressed as raw figures and arrests made, rates per 100,000 people, and changes in the number and rate of crime over time. The main weaknesses concerning the validity of the UCR are that not all crimes are reported, law enforcement practices distort the reporting, and methodology issues. The FBI is looking to eventually replace the UCR with the National Incident-Based Reporting System (NIBRS) that collects information on 46 specific offenses and includes more comprehensive information than the UCR.

The National Crime Victimization Survey (NCVS) is designed to overcome the problems of the UCR by including crimes not reported to the police. It includes information from a large nationally representative sample and it reports the victimization experiences of the participants. The NCVS has some weaknesses, especially underreporting and overreporting. Like the NCVS, self-report surveys help to illuminate the "dark figure of crime." Most of these studies focus on delinquency and youth crime. The main weaknesses of self-report surveys are 1) a lot of trivial offenses are included in self-reports; 2) participants may exaggerate, be confused, or forget; and 3) they may not candidly admit illegal acts. Although the data from the UCR, the NCVS, and self-report surveys are not completely in sync, the crime patterns and trends are similar

Crime rates have risen and fallen over the many years our nation has been in existence. Several factors affect crime trends, including the age distribution of the population, the economy, social malaise, abortion, the availability of guns, gangs, drug usage, the media, medical technology, justice policy, and crime opportunities. The violent crime rate has been decreasing as has the rate of property crime, although the decline in property crime has not been as dramatic as the decrease in violent crime. These trends are apparent in the UCR and are confirmed by the NCVS. Self-report surveys, however, indicate that crime rates are more stable than the UCR indicates. Crime trend projections for the future are mixed.

Crime has followed several predictable patterns over the years. Most crimes occur during the warm summer months of July and August. Murders, however, are most frequent in December and January. The association between crime and temperature is an inverted U-curve with crime rising with temperature, but beginning to decline around 85 degrees. Crime rates are also highest in urban areas and in the southern and western United States. Although crime rates are highest in inner city, high poverty areas, criminologists have never shown a strong correlation between crime and social class. One main reason may be that the methods used to measure social class vary widely and a second reason may be that the relationship between social class and crime may be more complex than a simple linear relationship.

Age is inversely related to crime; younger people commit more crime than their older peers. Aging out refers to the process by which offenders reduce the frequency of their offending behavior as they age. Aging out may be due to a reduction in supervision or it may be a function of the natural history of the life cycle.

All three types of crime data confirm that male crime rates are higher than those of females. Over the years a variety of reasons have been given for this phenomenon such as the masculinity hypothesis, the chivalry hypothesis, socialization and development, and liberal feminist theory. Self-report studies indicate that the pattern of female criminality is similar to that of male criminality. Recent data also indicate that female crime rates are rising faster than male crime rates and that females are joining gangs in record numbers.

Minorities are involved in a disproportionate share of criminal activity. However, research indicates no relationship between race and self-reported delinquency. Some of the reasons for high minority levels of criminal activity may be racism, discrimination, and institutional racism (economic disparity, social disparity, and family dissolution). If social and economic obstacles are removed, convergence of majority and minority crime rates is possible.

Most offenders commit a single crime and discontinue after arrest. Nevertheless, as Wolfgang, Figlio, and Sellin found, there is a small group responsible for the majority of all crimes. The offenders in this group are called chronic offenders or career criminals. The chronic offender has been the central focus of crime policy.

STUDENT EXERCISES

Exercise 1

Take a look at your local newspaper or any other paper that is in your university library or online. Look at ten to fifteen articles dealing with different crimes. Make notes concerning the demographic characteristics of the victims and the offenders. What did you find out? How do your findings compare with the information provided in the textbook? Give reasons for any differences you find.

Exercise 2

Go online to http://www.ojp.usdoj.gov/bjs/pub/ascii/cv03.txt and scan the article concerning criminal victimization in 2003. Write a summary of your findings.

CRIMINOLOGY WEB LINKS

http://www.fbi.gov/ucr/ucr.htm
This website is designed to provide information on the Uniform Crime Reports. Check out the website to see the wealth of information that is contained there.

http://www.ojp.usdoj.gov/bjs/cvict.htm
This website contains information concerning the National Crime Victimization Survey. Check out the variety of links to see detailed information pertaining to this crime measurement instrument.

http://www.albany.edu/sourcebook/
This website contains statistics from a wide variety of sources (more than 100). It is under the auspices of the Bureau of Justice Statistics.

http://www.ncjrs.org/pdffiles1/nij/180973.pdf
This publication from the National Institute of Justice is entitled *Research on Women and Girls In the Justice System: Plenary Papers of the 1999 Conference on Criminal Justice Research and Evaluation—Enhancing Policy and Practice Through Research,* Volume 3. It contains three articles on women and the criminal justice system.

TEST BANK

FILL-IN THE BLANKS

1. Criminologists conduct _____ when they want to measure attitudes, beliefs, values, characteristics, and behavior.

2. _____ is the process of selecting for study a limited number of subjects who are representative of entire groups sharing similar characteristics.

3. _____ research involves observing a group of people who share a like characteristic over time.

4. _____ _____ are more likely to be solved than property crimes because police devote more resources to serious acts.

5. The National Crime Victimization Survey confirms that many crimes go _____ to the police.

6. Some experts believe that the presence and quality of _____ can have a significant impact on murder rates.

7. Most reported crimes occur during the months of _____ and _____.

8. The term used to describe the resorting to theft and other illegal activities to obtain desired goods and services the person is unable to obtain legitimately is _____ _____.

9. There is general agreement that _____ is inversely related to criminality.

10. The perspective which holds that much female criminality is hidden because of the culture's generally protective and benevolent attitude toward women is called _____.

TRUE/FALSE QUESTIONS

1. T/F Taking an intact cohort of known offenders and looking back into their early life experiences by checking their educational, family, police, and hospital records is called a longitudinal cohort study.

2. T/F Experimental research is very common in criminology.

3. T/F When some element beyond police control precludes the physical arrest of an offender, the case is considered by the Uniform Crime Report to be cleared by exceptional means.

4. T/F Higher crime rates may occur as departments adopt more sophisticated computer technology and hire better-educated, better-trained employees.

5. T/F National Crime Victimization Survey data are considered a relatively unbiased, valid estimate of all victimizations for the target crimes included in the survey.

6. T/F Most self-report studies have focused on juvenile delinquency and youth crime.

7. T/F There is strong evidence that the reporting accuracy in self-report surveys is similar among racial, ethnic, and gender groups.

8. T/F Crime experts view change in the population age distribution as having the greatest influence on crime trends.

9. T/F As the level of social problems increases, crime rates decrease.

10. T/F The drop in property crime rates in recent years has been more dramatic than the decline in violent crime rates.

11. T/F Large urban areas have by far the highest violence rates.

12. T/F There is a very strong correlation between social class and crime.

13. T/F Aging out is caused by the physical inability to commit crime.

14. T/F The masculinity hypothesis argues that a few "masculine" females were responsible for the handful of crimes women commit.

15. T/F Racial differentials in crime rates may also be tied to economic disparity.

MULTIPLE CHOICE QUESTIONS

1. The Uniform Crime Report is published by the:
    a. Supreme Court
    b. Federal Bureau of Investigation
    c. Bureau of Justice Statistics
    d. Census Bureau

2. Which of the following is **not** an element of true experiments?
    a. a survey
    b. random selection of subjects
    c. a control or comparison group
    d. an experimental condition

3. Surveys that ask crime victims about their encounters with criminals are known as the:
    a. Uniform Crime Report
    b. National Crime Victimization Survey
    c. Youth Survey
    d. Self-Report Study

4. Criminological experiments are relatively rare because:
    a.   they are prohibited in criminology
    b.   criminologists do not like to conduct them
    c.   there are no funds to conduct them
    d.   there are ethical and legal roadblocks

5. Gathering data from a number of previous studies and pooling the data together is called:
    a.   systematic review
    b.   survey research
    c.   meta-analysis
    d.   multiple study research

6. Which of the following is **not** a Part I crime?
    a.   arson
    b.   robbery
    c.   forcible rape
    d.   assault

7. The Uniform Crime Report does **not** show statistics for which of the following crimes?
    a.   traffic violations
    b.   murder
    c.   arson
    d.   motor-vehicle theft

8. The Uniform Crime Report expresses data as:
    a.   raw figures only
    b.   crime rates per 100,000
    c.   crime rates per 1,000
    d.   raw figures Part II crimes only

9. Which crime is cleared at the highest rate?
    a.   robbery
    b.   larceny
    c.   murder
    d.   motor vehicle theft

10. Most self-report studies focus on:
    a.   serious crime
    b.   adult crime
    c.   prisoners
    d.   juvenile delinquency

11. Which of the following is correct concerning the three major sources of crime data?
    a.   the crime tallies are in sync
    b.   the crime patterns they report are quite similar
    c.   the crime trends they report are different
    d.   the personal characteristics of criminals they report are different

12. Murders in this country, overall, have:
    a. declined
    b. risen
    c. stabilized
    d. none of the above

13. In recent years, the property crime rate:
    a. has dropped substantially more than the violent crime rate
    b. has dropped about the same as the violent crime rate
    c. has risen more than the violent crime rate
    d. has dropped, but not as much as the violent crime rate

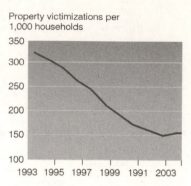

Property victimizations per
1,000 households

350

300

250

200

150

100

1993 1995 1997 1999 1991 2003

14. The studies on the ecology of crime tell us that:
    a. most crimes occur in the winter
    b. crime rates are higher on pay day
    c. rural areas have high per capita rates of crime
    d. robberies occur frequently in December and January

15. The assumption that a criminal career begins early in life and that people who are deviant at a very young age are the ones most likely to persist in crime is known as:
    a. aging out
    b. aging in
    c. early onset
    d. late onset

16. The notion that female's criminality is often masked because criminal justice authorities were reluctant to take action against a woman is known as:
    a. biological view
    b. gender difference
    c. masculinity hypothesis
    d. chivalry hypothesis

17. The view that women commit crimes have biological and psychological traits similar to men is known as:
    a. biological view
    b. gender difference
    c. masculinity hypothesis
    d. chivalry hypothesis

18. Evidence of African-Americans receiving longer prison sentences than like Caucasians is an example of:
    a. institutional racism
    b. gender bias
    c. socialization
    d. masculinity hypothesis

19. According to Wolfgang, a delinquent offender who is arrested five or more times before he/she is 18 and who stands a good chance of becoming an adult criminal is known as a:
    a. compliant citizen
    b. chronic offender
    c. seasoned official
    d. none of the above

20. The view that crime begins early in life and continues throughout the life course is known as:
    a. desistance
    b. resistance
    c. continuity of crime
    d. aging out

Arrest rate per 100,000 persons

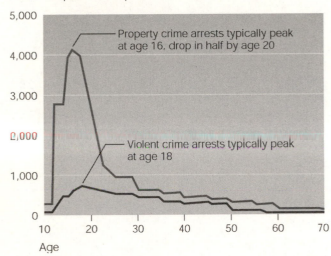

21. The process in which crime rate declines with the perpetrator's age is known as:
    a. termination
    b. resistance
    c. continuity of crime
    d. aging out

22. Which of the following explains gender differences in crime?
    a. cognitive differences
    b. socialization differences
    c. gender schema theory
    d. all of the above

23. The perspective that America has different expectations for males and females is called:
    a. masculinity hypothesis
    b. gender schema theory
    c. chivalry hypothesis
    d. liberal feminist theory

24. The perspective that the traditionally lower crime rate for women can be explained by their "second class" economic and social position is:
    a. masculinity hypothesis
    b. gender schema theory
    c. chivalry hypothesis
    d. liberal feminist theory

25. Which of the following is **NOT** a characteristic of chronic offenders?
    a. cognitive ability problems
    b. family relations problems
    c. punishment changes their behavior
    d. lower aspirations

ESSAY QUESTIONS

1. Discuss the validity of the Uniform Crime Report.

2. Describe the National Crime Victimization Survey, explaining its purpose, its usefulness in measuring crime, and its positive and negative aspects.

3. Explain the factors that influence crime trends.

4. Explain the relationship between crime and social class.

5. List and discuss the major explanations for gender differences in crime rates.

MATCHING

1. _____ Uniform Crime Report
2. _____ Index Crimes
3. _____ Part I Crimes
4. _____ Cleared Crimes
5. _____ National Incident-Based Reporting System
6. _____ U-Shaped Curve
7. _____ Expressive Crimes
8. _____ Self-Report Survey
9. _____ Aging Out
10. _____ Early Onset

A. What the association between temperature and crime resembles
B. The best-known and most widely cited source of official criminal statistics
C. The eight crimes that, because of their seriousness and frequency, the FBI reports the incidence of the annual Uniform Crime Reports
D. A new program that is attempting to provide more detailed information on individual criminal incidents by using a uniform, comprehensive program
E. Crimes where at least one person is arrested, charged, and turned over to the court for prosecution
F. The major analysis of the Uniform Crime Report
G. A research approach that requires subjects to reveal their own participation in delinquent or criminal acts
H. A term that refers to the assumption that a criminal career begins early in life and that people who are deviant at a very young age are the ones most likely to persist in crime
I. The process by which individuals reduce the frequency of their offending behavior as they age
J. Crimes committed that show rage, frustration, and anger against society

CHAPTER 2 ANSWER KEY

Fill in the Blank Answers

1. surveys
2. sampling
3. cohort
4. violent crimes
5. unreported
6. healthcare
7. July, August
8. instrumental crimes
9. age
10. chivalry hypothesis

True/False Answers

1.	F	6.	T	11.	T
2.	F	7.	F	12.	F
3.	T	8.	T	13.	F
4.	T	9.	T	14.	T
5.	T	10.	F	15.	T

Multiple Choice Answers

1.	B	11.	B	21.	D
2.	A	12.	A	22.	D
3.	B	13.	D	23.	B
4.	D	14.	D	24.	D
5.	C	15.	C	25.	C
6.	D	16.	D		
7.	A	17.	C		
8.	B	18.	A		
9.	C	19.	B		
10.	D	20.	C		

Essay Questions

1. Pages 31-33
2. Pages 35-36
3. Pages 38-44
4. Pages 47-51
5. Pages 52-54

Matching Answers

1.	B	6.	A
2.	C	7.	J
3.	F	8.	G
4.	E	9.	I
5.	D	10.	H

VICTIMS AND VICTIMIZATION

OUTLINE

Chapter 3

Victims and Victimization

LEARNING OBJECTIVES

1. Be familiar with the concept of victimization

2. Be familiar with the costs of victimization

3. Be able to discuss the problems of crime victims

4. Know the nature of victimization

5. Recognize that there are age, gender, and racial patterns in the victimization data

6. Be familiar with the term "victim precipitation"

7. Be able to discuss the association between lifestyle and victimization

8. List the routine activities associated with victimization risk

9. Be able to discuss the various victim assistance programs

KEYWORDS AND DEFINITIONS

Victimologists: Criminologists who focus on crime victims.

Victimization (by the justice system): While crime is still fresh in their minds, victims may find that the police interrogation following the crime is handled callously, with innuendos or insinuations that they are somehow at fault.

Posttraumatic stress disorder (PTSD): An emotional disturbance following exposure to stresses outside the range of normal human experience.

Obsessive-compulsive disorder: An extreme preoccupation with certain thoughts and compulsive performance of certain behaviors.

Cycle of violence: The idea that victims of crime, especially childhood abuse, are more likely to commit crimes themselves.

Elder abuse: A disturbing form of domestic violence by children and other relatives with whom elderly people live.

Chronic victimization: Households that have experienced victimization in the past are the ones most likely to experience it again in the future; most repeat victimizations occur soon after a previous crime has occurred, suggesting repeat victims share some personal characteristic that makes them a magnet for predators.

Siblicide: Sibling homicide.

Victim precipitation theory: Some people may actually initiate the confrontation that eventually leads to their injury or death.

Active precipitation: Occurs when victims act provocatively, use threats or fighting words, or even attack first.

Passive precipitation: Occurs when the victim exhibits some personal characteristic that unknowingly threatens or encourages the attacker.

Lifestyle theory: Crime is not a random occurrence but rather a function of a victim's lifestyle.

Deviant place theory: Victims do not encourage crime but are victim prone because they reside in socially disorganized high-crime areas where they have the greatest risk of coming into contact with criminal offenders, irrespective of their own behavior or lifestyle.

Routine activities theory: The volume and distribution of predatory crime are related to the interaction of the availability of suitable targets, the absence of capable guardians, and the presence of motivated offenders.

Suitable targets: A target for crime that is relatively valuable, easily transportable, and not capably guarded.

Capable guardians: Effective deterrents to crime such as the police or watchful neighbors.

Motivated offenders: The potential offenders in a population.

Date rape: Forcible sex during a courting relationship.

Victim-witness assistance programs: Government programs that help crime victims and witnesses; may include compensation, court services, and/or crisis intervention.

Victim compensation: Victim receives compensation from the state to pay for damages associated with crime.

Crisis intervention: Emergency counseling for crime victims at counseling offices, victim's home, the crime scene, or a hospital.

Restitution agreements: A condition of the offender's sentence in which he or she repays society or the victim of the crime for the trouble caused.

Target hardening: Making one's home and business crime proof through locks, bars, alarms, or other devices.

CHAPTER OUTLINE

I.   Problems of crime victims
    A.   Economic Loss
        1.   System costs
            a.   Cost of maintaining the justice system
            b.   Legal costs
            c.   Treatment costs
        2.   Individual costs
            a.   Losses in earnings and occupational attainment
            b.   Psychological and physical ills
    B.   System abuse: victimization by the justice system
    C.   Long-term stress
        1.   Among adolescents who experience abuse
        2.   Post-traumatic stress disorder of spousal abuse victims
        3.   Physical disability as a result of wounds
    D.   Fear
        1.   Victims fearful long after victimization
        2.   Often victims go through a fundamental life change
    E.   Antisocial behavior
        1.   Crime victims likely to commit crimes themselves
        2.   Cycle of violence

II.   The nature of victimization
    A.   The social ecology of victimization
        1.   Violent crimes more likely to take place in an open, public area
        2.   Neighborhood characteristics affect victimization
            a.   Central cities have higher rates of theft and violence.
            b.   Rural areas have a victimization almost half that of city dwellers.
            c.   Risk of murder of both men and women is significantly higher in the disorganized inner city.
    B.   The victim's household
        1.   Within the U.S. larger, African-American, western, and urban homes are the most vulnerable to crime.
        2.   Rural, white homes in the Northeast are the least likely victims.
        3.   Decline in household victimization rates may be due to smaller households in less populated areas.
    C.   Victim characteristics
        1.   Gender
            a.   Males are most likely to be victims.
            b.   Gender differences appear to be narrowing.
            c.   Females are victimized by someone they know.
            d.   Men are more likely to be victimized by strangers.
        2.   Age
            a.   Young people are more likely to be victimized.
            b.   Elderly are much safer than their grandchildren.
            c.   Elderly are susceptible to fraud schemes.

    3.   Social status
        a.   Poorest Americans are the most likely to be victims of violent and property crimes
        b.   This association holds true across all gender, age, and racial groups
        c.   Wealthy attract the attention of thieves
    4.   Marital status
        a.   Never-married males and females are victimized more often than married people.
        b.   Widows and widowers have the lowest victimization risk.
        c.   Association between marital status and victimization probably influenced by age, gender, and lifestyle.
    5.   Race and ethnicity
        a.   Blacks are more likely than whites to be victims of violent crime.
        b.   Income inequality influences black victimization.
        c.   Rate of black victimization has been in a steep decline.
    6.   Repeat victimization
        a.   Prior victims are the most likely to experience repeat victimization.
        b.   Characteristics that increase victimization potential
            1)   Target vulnerability
            2)   Target gratifiability
            3)   Target antagonism
        c.   May occur when the victim does not take defensive action

D.   Victims and their criminals
    1.   Most crimes are committed by a single offender.
    2.   Victims report substance abuse in about one-third of violent crime incidents.
    3.   More than half of all nonfatal personal crimes are committed by persons known to the victim.

III.   Theories of victimization
   A.   Victim precipitation theory
      1.   Some people may actually initiate the confrontation that eventually leads to their injury or death.
      2.   Two types of victim precipitation
         a.   Active – victim provokes or threatens
         b.   Passive
             1)   Victim has some personal characteristic that unknowingly threatens or encourages attacker
             2)   Belongs to a group that threatens or encourages the attacker's reputation, status, or economic well-being
   B.   Lifestyle theory
      1.   Lifestyle increases exposure to criminal offenders.
      2.   High-risk lifestyles
         a.   Drinking, taking drugs, or crime involvement
         b.   Risks continue in adulthood
      3.   Victims and criminals – criminal career may lead to victimization
   C.   Deviant place theory
      1.   Victims live in socially disorganized high-crime areas.
      2.   The more often a victim visits a dangerous place, the more likely they will be exposed to crime.

3. Deviant place – poor, densely populated, highly transient neighborhoods where commercial and residential property exist side by side

    D. Routine activities theory

        1. Volume and distribution of predatory crime are closely related to the interaction of three variables that reflect the routine activities of American lifestyle.

            a. Availability of suitable targets

            b. Presence of motivated offenders

            c. Absence of capable guardians

        2. Hot spots – congregation of motivated offenders in a particular neighborhood

        3. Moral guardianship – peer rejection and disapproval

        4. Lifestyle, opportunity, and routine activities are related

        5. Empirical support

IV. Caring for the victim

    A. The government's response

        1. Task Force on Victims of Crime – 1982

            a. Suggested a balance between victim's rights and the defendant's due process rights

            b. Protecting witnesses and victims from intimidation

            c. Requiring restitution in criminal cases

            d. Development of guidelines for fair treatment of victims and witnesses

            e. Expanding programs of victim compensation

        2. Omnibus Victim and Witness Protection Act

            a. Use of victim impact statements at sentencing in federal criminal cases

            b. Greater protection for witnesses

            c. More stringent bail laws

            d. Use of restitution in criminal cases

        3. Comprehensive Crime Control Act and the Victims of Crime Act

            a. Federal funding for state victim compensation and assistance projects

            b. Victim aid and assistance began with these acts.

    B. Victim service programs

        1. Victim compensation

            a. Victim receives compensation from the state to pay for damages from crime

            b. No two state schemes are alike

            c. Victim of Crime Act – grants money to state compensation boards from fines and penalties imposed on federal offenders

        2. Court services

            a. Help victims deal with the justice system

            b. Many programs provide transportation to and from court and counselors.

        3. Public education – help familiarize the general public with victim services

        4. Crisis intervention

        5. Victim-offender reconciliation programs

            a. Mediators facilitate face-to-face encounters between the victim and the offender.

            b. May lead to restitution agreements and possibly reconciliation

        6. Victim impact statements – statements made before the sentencing judge

    C. Victims' rights – every state now has some form of legal rights for crime victims in its code of laws.

    D. Victim advocacy

E. Self-protection
    1. Target hardening
    2. Crime prevention techniques
    3. Use of guns for self-defense
F. Community organization

CHAPTER SUMMARY

The problems of being a victim of crime are wide and varied. There are economic losses such as the cost of the justice system, treatment costs, and economic losses to the individual, including lost earnings, psychological pain, and physical pain and injury. A crime victim often finds that processing through the criminal justice system is an abusive occurrence, especially if the victim feels it was his or her fault for being victimized. Other problems a victim may experience include long-term stress, long-term fear, and antisocial behavior resulting from victimization.

Victimization is not evenly distributed throughout the country. Violent crimes usually occur in open, public areas. Central cities have higher rates of theft and violence and the disorganized inner city has the highest risk for murder of both men and women. Within the United States, larger, African-American, western, and urban homes are the most vulnerable to crime. The current decline in household victimization may be due to an increase in smaller households located in less populated areas. Males are most likely to be crime victims but gender differences appear to be narrowing. While females are victimized by someone they know, males are more likely to be the victims of strangers. Young people are more likely to be the victims of crime, as are the poor. The association between social status and crime holds true across all gender, age, and social groups. The never-married are most likely to be victimized. Blacks are more likely than whites to be victims; however, the rate of black victimization has been in steep decline. Prior victims are the most likely to be revictimized. The characteristics that increase the potential for becoming a victim are target vulnerability, target gratifiability, and target antagonism.

There are several major theories of victimization. Victim precipitation theory postulates that some people may actually initiate the confrontation that eventually leads to their injury or death. Victim precipitation may be active or passive. Lifestyle theory argues that one's lifestyle may increase exposure to victimization by one's engaging in high-risk behaviors such as drinking, taking drugs, or being involved in crime. Deviant place theory proposes that victims live in socially disorganized high-crime areas or visit dangerous places. Routine activities theory argues that the volume and distribution of predatory crime are closely related to the interaction of three major variables: 1) the availability of suitable targets, 2) the presence of motivated offenders, and 3) the absence of capable guardians.

There has been a significant improvement in caring for victims over the past two decades. The Omnibus Victim and Witness Protection Act permitted the use of victim impact statements in federal criminal cases and authorized the use of restitution. The Comprehensive Crime Control Act and the Victims of Crime Act began federal funding for state victim compensation and assistance projects. No two states have victim compensation programs that are alike, but under the Victims of Crime Act all states receive federal grants to their state compensation boards from fines and penalties imposed on federal offenders. Many victim assistance efforts are being made within court services, public education, and crisis intervention. Victim-offender reconciliation programs have also worked to achieve restitution and possible reconciliation. Every state now has some form of legal rights for crime victims in its code of laws. Individuals have also begun to engage in self-protection through the use of target hardening, crime prevention techniques, and possession of guns for self-defense.

STUDENT EXERCISES

Exercise 1

Go online to http://www.google.com and do a search using the terms "victim advocacy center." Make sure you put the three words between quotation marks. Look at several of the links in the results that deal with victim advocacy centers. Make a note of the characteristics of those advocacy centers. Summarize the results of what you found, especially noting what those victim advocacy centers have in common.

Exercise 2

Go online to http://www.ncjrs.org/pdffiles1/nij/205004.pdf and read the article, *When Violence Hits Home: How Economics and Neighborhood Play a Role* by Michael L. Benson and Greer Litton Fox. Summarize the article focusing on the relationship of socioeconomic status and neighborhood to domestic violence. How does this article's results compare to the victimization theories contained in the textbook?

CRIMINOLOGY WEB LINKS

http://www.ojp.usdoj.gov/ovc/
This is the official website of the Office for Victims of Crime sponsored by the United States Department of Justice.

http://www.cvb.state.ny.us/index.htm
This is the official website of the New York State Crime Victims Board. The material in this website concerns all aspects of victim support in the state of New York.

http://www.tdcj.state.tx.us/victim/victim-home.htm
This is the official website of the Victims Services Division of the Texas Department of Criminal Justice.

http://content.healthaffairs.org/cgi/reprint/12/4/186.pdf
This website contains an article entitled *Victim Costs of Violent Crime and Resulting Injuries* by Ted R. Miller, Mark A. Cohen, and Shelli B. Rossman. It addresses the total monetary costs of a wide variety of crimes.

http://www.ncjrs.org/pdffiles1/ojjdp/195737.pdf
This article entitled *Violent Victimization as a Risk Factor for Violent Offending Among Juveniles* by Jennifer N. Shaffer and R. Barry Ruback addresses the issue of the correlation between victimization and offending among juveniles.

TEST BANK

FILL-IN THE BLANKS

1. An emotional disturbance following exposure to stresses outside the range of normal human experience is called _____ _____ _____.

2. The abuse-crime phenomenon is referred to as the _____ _____ _____.

3. _____ _____ refers to some characteristics that increase risk of victimization because they arouse anger, jealousy, or destructive impulses in potential offenders.

4. _____ _____ _____ proposes that some people may actually initiate the confrontation that eventually leads to injury or death.

5. _____ _____ _____ states that people are victim prone because they reside in socially disorganized high-crime areas.

6. If motivated offenders congregate in a particular neighborhood, it becomes a _____ for crime and violence.

7. Peer rejection and disapproval may be a form of _____ _____ that can deter even motivated offenders from engaging in law-violating behavior.

8. Under victim compensation programs, the victim ordinarily receives compensation from the _____ to pay for damages associated with crime.

9. More than half of victim programs provide _____ _____ to victims, many of whom feel isolated, vulnerable, and in need of immediate services.

10. Making one's home and business crime proof through locks, bars, alarms, and other devices is known as _____ _____.

TRUE/FALSE QUESTIONS

1. T/F The suffering endured by crime victims ends when their attacker leaves the scene.

2. T/F the elderly, the poor, and minority group members especially fear crime.

3. T/F Victimization survey findings suggest that victimization is not random but is a function of personal and ecological factors.

4. T/F The more serious crimes, such as rape and aggravated assault, typically take place after 6:00 P.M.

5.   T/F Victimization is most likely to take place in the Northeast.

6.   T/F Females are more likely than males to be victimized.

7.   T/F Grandparents are much safer from victimization than their grandchildren.

8.   T/F Households that have experienced victimization in the past are the ones least likely to experience it in the future.

9.   T/F Married people are victimized more often than single people.

10.   T/F African-Americans are more likely than Whites to be victims of violent crime.

11.   T/F Passive precipitation occurs when victims act provocatively, use threats or fighting words, or even attack first.

12.   T/F The basis of lifestyle theory is that crime is not a random occurrence, but rather a function of the victim's lifestyle.

13.   T/F One element of lifestyle that may place people at risk for victimization is ongoing involvement in a criminal career.

14.   T/F Victim-offender reconciliation programs use the courts to facilitate face-to-face encounters between victims and their attackers.

15.   T/F Only a few jurisdictions allow victims to make an impact statement before a sentencing judge.

MULTIPLE CHOICE QUESTIONS

1.   The NCVS show that violent crimes are more likely to occur in:
      a.   dark alleys
      b.   secluded areas
      c.   open public areas
      d.   private homes

2.   Neighborhood characteristics that increase the chances of victimization are:
      a.   suburban area
      b.   rural area
      c.   high class area
      d.   central city area

3.   Which characteristic does **not** distinguish victims from non-victims?
      a.   gender
      b.   religion
      c.   age
      d.   race

4. Who is most often victimized by someone they know?
   a. whites
   b. males
   c. African-Americans
   d. females

5. To which crime are the elderly most susceptible?
   a. fraud
   b. rape
   c. assault
   d. robbery

6. A victims' physical weakness or psychological distress that renders them incapable of resisting or deterring crime and makes them an easy target is:
   a. target gratifiability
   b. target vulnerability
   c. target antagonism
   d. target opposition

7. Some victims have a quality, possession, skill, or attribute that an offender wants to obtain, use, have access to, or manipulate. This is known as:
   a. target gratifiability
   b. target vulnerability
   c. target antagonism
   d. target opposition

8. What is the term for victims acting provocatively, using threats or fighting words, or even attacking first?
   a. lifestyle precipitation
   b. deviant precipitation
   c. passive precipitation
   d. active precipitation

9. People may become crime victims because of their behaviors – such as associating with young men, going out in public places late at night or living in an urban area. This is known as:
   a. routine activities theory
   b. victim precipitation theory
   c. lifestyle theory
   d. deviant place theory

10. Victims who do not encourage crime but are victim-prone because they reside in socially disorganized high-crime areas where they have the greatest risk of coming into contact with criminal offenders are victimized due to:
    a. lifestyle theory
    b. active precipitation
    c. deviant place theory
    d. passive precipitation

11. The theory explaining the volume and distribution of predatory crime as being closely related to the interaction of three variables (suitable targets, motivated offenders, absence of capable guardians) is known as:
    a. lifestyle theory
    b. active precipitation theory
    c. routine activities theory
    d. passive precipitation theory

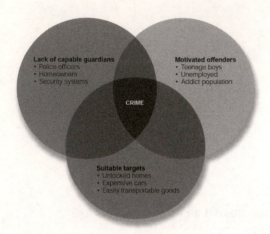

12. Which of the following is **not** a suitable target in routine activities theory?
    a. an unlocked house
    b. a house with a security system
    c. an expensive car
    d. easily transportable goods

13. Cohen and Felson argued that crime rates increased between the 1960s and 1980s because the number of adult caretakers at home during the day had decreased due to an increase in:
    a. females in the workplace
    b. the employment rate
    c. automobile ownership
    d. the number of juveniles

14. The dramatic increase in crime rates in the 1980s was due to skyrocketing drug use that created an excess of:
    a. suitable targets
    b. motivated offenders
    c. weak victims
    d. capable guardians

15. Victim compensation may be made for which of the following:
    a. medical bills
    b. loss of wages
    c. loss of future earnings
    d. all of the above

16. What is the name of the law passed in 1984 that granted money to state compensation boards derived from fines and penalties imposed on federal offenders?
    a. Victim-Offender Act
    b. Omnibus Crime Act
    c. Victim of Crime Act
    d. none of the above

17. Programs that familiarize the general public with their services to and with other agencies that assist crime victims are known as:
    a. public education programs
    b. victim-offender reconciliation programs
    c. community service programs
    d. crisis intervention programs

18. A local network of public and private social service agencies that can provide emergency and long-term assistance with transportation, medical care, shelter, food and clothing is known as:
    a. victim support
    b. crisis intervention
    c. court services
    d. victim education

19. When victims fight back, it may cause which of the following?
    a. others may help
    b. the assailant may flee
    c. the assailant may attack in a more violent manner
    d. all of the above

20. These programs use mediators to facilitate face-to-face encounters between victims and their attackers.
    a. victim-offender reconciliation program
    b. crisis intervention
    c. community service
    d. restitution circles

21. Victim service programs may provide which of the following:
    a. compensation
    b. court services
    c. public education
    d. all of the above

22. The abuse-crime phenomenon is known as:
    a. deviant place hypothesis
    b. siblicide
    c. cycle of violence
    d. parricide

23. Victim advocates can be especially helpful when victims need to interact with the:
    a. media
    b. agencies of justice
    c. police
    d. sentencing judge

24. Using locks, bars, alarms, and other devices to make one's home or business crime proof is called:
    a. self-protection
    b. target hardening
    c. crime stopping
    d. physical security

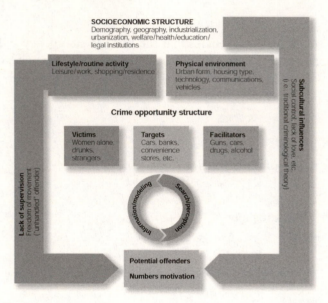

25. When communities organize against crime at the neighborhood level:
    a. effectiveness is greater in low-income, high-crime areas
    b. there is strong evidence such efforts affect the crime rate
    c. efforts might involve block watches and neighborhood patrols
    d. none of the above

ESSAY QUESTIONS

1. List and describe the major problems faced by crime victims.

2. Describe the characteristics of crime victims.

3. Explain victim precipitation theory.

4. Describe how American society is taking care of America's crime victims today.

5.   Describe the actions citizens are taking to prevent themselves from becoming victims.

MATCHING

1.   _____   Passive Precipitation
2.   _____   Capable Guardians
3.   _____   Chronic Victims
4   _____   Crisis Intervention
5.   _____   Cycle of Violence
6.   _____   Deviant Place Hypothesis
7.   _____   Lifestyle Theory
8.   _____   Target Vulnerability
9.   _____   Motivated Offenders
10.   _____   Siblicide

A.   Based on the idea that crime is not a random occurrence but rather a function of one's lifestyle
B.   Victims do not encourage crime, but are victim prone because they reside in socially disorganized high-crime areas where they have the greatest risk of coming into contact with criminal offenders
C.   Victim's physical weakness or psychological distress that renders them incapable of resisting crime and makes them a target
D.   Abuse-crime phenomenon
E.   A variable of routine activities theory. An example would be a large number of teenagers
F.   A local network of public and private social service agencies that can provide emergency and long-term assistance with transportation, medical care, shelter, food and clothing
G.   Murdering one's brother or sister
H.   Individuals who are repeatedly crime victims
I.   Victim exhibits some personal characteristic that unknowingly threatens or encourages the attacker
J.   Effective deterrents to crime such as the police or watchful neighbors

CHAPTER 3 ANSWER KEY

Fill in the Blank Answers

1. posttraumatic stress syndrome
2. cycle of violence
3. target antagonism
4. victim precipitation theory
5. deviant place theory
6. hot spot
7. moral guardianship
8. state
9. crisis intervention
10. target hardening

True/False Answers

1.	F	6.	F	11.	F
2.	T	7.	T	12.	T
3.	T	8.	F	13.	T
4.	T	9.	F	14.	F
5.	F	10.	T	15.	F

Multiple Choice Answers

1.	C	11.	C	21	.D
2.	D	12.	B	22.	C
3.	B	13.	A	23.	B
4.	D	14.	B	24.	B
5.	A	15.	D	25.	C
6.	B	16.	C		
7.	A	17.	A		
8.	D	18.	B		
9.	C	19.	D		
10.	C	20.	A		

Essay Questions

1. Pages 68-71
2. Pages 72-74
3. Page 75
4. Pages 81-86
5. Pages 85-86

Matching Answers

1.	I	6.	B
2.	J	7.	A
3.	H	8.	C
4.	F	9.	E
5.	D	10.	G

CHOICE THEORIES

OUTLINE

Chapter 4

Choice Theories

LEARNING OBJECTIVES

1.   Be familiar with the concept of rational choice

2.   Know the work of Beccaria

3.   Be familiar with the concept of offense-specific crime

4.   Be familiar with the concept of offender-specific crime

5.   Be able to discuss why violent and drug crimes are rational

6.   Know the various techniques of situational crime prevention

7.   Be able to discuss the association between punishment and crime

8.   Be familiar with the concepts of certainty, severity, and speed of punishment

9.   Know what is meant by specific deterrence

10. Be able to discuss the issues involving the use of incapacitation

11. Understand the concept of just desert

KEYWORDS AND DEFINITIONS

Rational choice: the view that crime is a function of a decision-making process in which the potential offender weighs the potential costs and benefits of an illegal action.

Marginal deterrence: the idea that if petty offenses were subject to the same punishment as more serious crimes, offenders would choose the worse crime because the resulting punishment would be the same.

Reasoning criminal: the individual who, before choosing to commit a crime, evaluates the risk of apprehension, the seriousness of the expected punishment, the potential value of the criminal enterprise, and his or her immediate need for criminal gain.

Offense-specific crime: offenders react selectively to the characteristics of particular offenses.

Offender-specific crime: before deciding to commit crime, individuals determine whether they have the prerequisites to commit a successful criminal act, including the proper skills, motives, needs, and fears.

Criminality: a personal trait of the individual as distinct from crime, which is an event.

Boosters: professional shoplifters who use complex methods to avoid detection.

Permeable neighborhood: neighborhood with a greater than usual number of access streets from traffic arteries into the neighborhood.

Edgework: the exhilarating, momentary integration of danger, risk, and skill that motivates people to try a variety of dangerous criminal and noncriminal behaviors.

Situational crime prevention: the perspective that crime prevention can be achieved by reducing opportunities people have to commit particular crimes.

Defensible space: the term that signifies that crime can be prevented or displaced through the use of residential architectural designs that reduce criminal opportunity.

Crime discouragers: those who manage crime, namely guardians (who monitor targets), handlers (who monitor offenders), and managers (who monitor places).

Diffusion: the process whereby efforts to prevent one crime unintentionally prevent another and when control efforts in one locale reduce crime in other nontarget areas.

Discouragement: the process whereby crime efforts targeting a particular locale help reduce crime in surrounding areas and populations.

Crime displacement: the phenomenon in which a program that seems successful because it helps lower crime rates at specific locations or neighborhoods may simply be redistributing offenders to alternative targets; crime is not prevented but deflected or displaced.

Extinction: the phenomena in which crime reduction programs may produce a short-term positive effect, but benefits dissipate as criminals adjust to new conditions.

General deterrence: the concept that crime rates are influenced and controlled by the threat of criminal punishment.

Deterrence theory: the view that if the probability of arrest, conviction, and sanctioning could be increased, crime rates should decline.

Crackdowns: sudden changes in police activity designed to increase the communicated threat or actual certainty of punishment.

Informal sanctions: occur when significant others direct their disapproval, stigma, anger, and indignation toward an offender.

Specific deterrence: the perspective that criminal sanctions should be so powerful that known criminals will never repeat their criminal acts.

Incapacitation effect: placing offenders behind bars during their prime crime years should lessen their lifetime opportunity to commit crime.

Selective incapacitation: if a small number of people account for a relatively large percentage of the nation's crime, then an effort to incarcerate these few troublemakers might have significant payoff.

Just desert: punishment is needed to preserve the social equity disturbed by crime.

CHAPTER OUTLINE

I. The development of rational choice theory
    A. The classical theory of crime
        1. Roots are in the classical school of criminology
        2. Purpose of law – to produce and support the total happiness of the community it serves
        3. Punishment is harmful, so it is justified only to prevent greater evil than it creates.
        4. Four objectives of punishment
            a. To prevent all criminal offenses
            b. When it cannot prevent crime, to convince the offender to commit a less serious crime
            c. To ensure that a criminal uses no more force than is necessary
            d. To prevent crime as cheaply as possible
    B. Choice theory emerges
        1. Resurgence of classical approach in the 1970s
        2. James Q. Wilson's *Thinking About Crime*
            a. Must deter would-be offenders
            b. Must incarcerate known criminals
        3. Impact on crime control
            a. Mandatory prison sentences for drug offenders
            b. Get tough attitude
            c. Rise in prison population

II. The concepts of rational choice
    A. Offense- and offender-specific crimes
        1. Offense-specific crime – offenders react selectively to the characteristics of particular offenses.
        2. Offender-specific crime – offenders make a decision based on whether they have the prerequisites to commit a successful criminal act.
        3. Crime – an event
        4. Criminality – a personal trait
    B. Structuring criminality - personal factors condition people to choose crime
        1. Economic opportunity
            a. Offenders are likely to desist if they believe criminal earnings will be low and that attractive and legal opportunities exist to generate income.
        2. Learning and experience
            a. Learn limitations of power
            b. Know when to take chances or be cautious
        3. Knowledge of criminal techniques – to avoid detection
    C. Structuring crime
        1. Choosing the type of crime

    a. Some are specialists.

    b. Others are generalists.

    c. Sometimes crime is based on the immediacy of the need for funds.

   2. Choosing the time and place of crime

    a. Burglars like 9 – 11 A.M. and mid-afternoon.

    b. Thieves avoid freestanding buildings.

    c. Criminals rarely travel long distances.

    d. Aware of police capabilities

   3. Choosing the target of crime

    a. Shy away from those who are armed

    b. Avoid targets if police are in the area

III. Is Crime Rational?

  A. Is theft rational?

   1. Seemingly unplanned theft-related crimes may be the product of careful risk assessment

   2. Boosters use complex methods to avoid detection.

   3. Burglars use skill and knowledge when choosing targets.

   4. Burglars prefer permeable neighborhoods.

  B. Is drug use rational?

   1. Onset of drug use is controlled by rational decision-making.

   2. Heavy drug users and dealers show signs of rationality and cunning.

  C. Is violence rational?

   1. Street robbers choose vulnerable victims.

   2. Robbers pick time and day to commit crimes carefully.

   3. Those who carry guns and are ready to use them typically do so for rational reasons.

   4. Serial murderers pick targets with care.

   5. Rapist use rationality in choice of victims – avoid victims who might recognize them later, travel at least three miles from home to commit crime.

   6. Want to avoid detection and obtain a victim with little effort

  E. Attraction of crime

   1. Brings rewards, excitement, prestige

   2. Edgework

   3. Crime is a means to pleasure and solution to vexing personal problems.

IV. Eliminating crime

  A. Situational crime prevention

   1. Originated in 1970s

   2. Began with the concept of defensible space

   3. Application of defensible space to nonresidential areas such as schools and factories

   4. Clarke's *Situational Crime Prevention*

    a. Create an environment to reduce overall crime rate

    b. Limit access to tempting targets

   5. Targeting specific crimes – situational crime prevention can also be used to reduce or eliminate a specific crime

    a. Increase effort needed to commit crime

     1) Target hardening

     2) Develop new security products

> 3) Reduce opportunities for crime
>
> b. Reduce rewards for committing crime – target reduction strategies
>
> c. Increase risks of committing crime
>
>> 1) Efforts of crime discouragers
>>
>> 2) Research show crime discouragers can have an impact on crime rates
>>
>> 3) Use of mechanical devices
>
> d. Induce guilt or shame for committing crime
>
> 6. Situational crime prevention: costs and benefits
>
>> a. Benefits
>>
>>> 1) Diffusion
>>>
>>> 2) Discouragement
>>
>> b. Problems
>>
>>> 1) Crime displacement
>>>
>>> 2) Extinction

B. General deterrence

1. Inverse relationship between crime rates and the severity, certainty, and speed of legal sanctions

2. Certainty of punishment

    a. As certainty of punishment rises, offenders will desist from crime because risks outweigh rewards.

    b. Certainty is seen as the *tipping point* when the likelihood of getting caught reaches a critical level.

    c. Crime persists because we have not reached the tipping point.

    d. Most criminal believe

      1) There is only a small chance of arrest for crime.

      2) Police are often reluctant to arrest even when they are aware of a crime.

      3) Even if arrested, there is a good chance of lenient punishment.

    e. Research shows experienced criminals are the ones most likely to fear the deterrent power of the law.

3. Does increasing police activity deter crime?

    a. Past – little evidence that adding officers could produce a deterrent effect

    b. Current research shows increased police levels produce substantial reductions in crime over time.

    c. Crackdowns

4. Severity of punishment and deterrence

    a. Severity of punishment is inversely proportional to the level of crime rates.

    b. Little consensus that the severity of criminal sanctions alone can reduce criminal activities.

    c. Not proven that just increasing punishment can reduce crime

5. Capital punishment – remains topic of debate

6. Informal sanctions

    a. Informal sanctions may have a greater crime-reducing impact than the fear of formal legal punishment.

    b. Social control is influenced by the way the people perceive negative reactions from interpersonal acquaintances.

7. Shame and humiliation

    a. Those who fear being rejected by family and peers are reluctant to engage in deviant behavior.

    b. Anticrime campaigns have been designed to play on this fear of shame.

      c.   Women are more likely to fear shame and embarrassment than men.

      d.   Effect of informal sanctions may vary according to the cohesiveness of community.

  8.   Critique of general deterrence

      a.   Rationality – questioned

      b.   Need – underclass not deterred by fear of punishment

      c.   Greed – some may be immune to the deterrent effects

      d.   Severity and speed – legal system is not very effective

C. Specific deterrence

  1.   General deterrence focuses on future or potential criminals.

  2.   Specific deterrence focuses on offenders not repeating criminal acts.

  3.   Does not seem to work because most criminals are not deterred by punishment

  4.   Punishment may bring defiance rather than deterrence.

D. Incapacitation

  1.   Placing offenders in prison during their prime crime years should lessen lifetime opportunity to commit crime.

  2.   Many criminologists believe incapacitation does not produce drops in crime rates.

  3.   Can incapacitation reduce crime? – research is inconclusive

  4.   The logic behind incarceration

      a.   Those in prison cannot commit crime.

      b.   Impact may be less than expected

      c.   Prison experience may escalate frequency of crime once released

      d.   Most crimes are committed by young teens and young adult offenders who do not go to prison for a single felony conviction.

  5.   Incapacitation is expensive.

  6.   Produces an ever expanding population

  7.   Selective incapacitation

      a.   Incarceration of chronic offenders

      b.   Some criminologists disagree because

          1)   Most three time losers are aging out.

          2)   Current sentences are already severe.

          3)   Pushes prison costs up

          4)   Racial disparity in sentencing

          5)   Violent offenders will resist the third arrest so police will be in danger.

      c.   Prison already contains the high-frequency criminals.

      d.   More low-rate criminals will be confined.

V. Public policy implications of choice theory

  A. Research on choice theory produced mixed results.

  B. Just desert

    1.   Punishment is needed to preserve the social equity disturbed by crime.

      a.   Those that violate others' rights deserve to be punished

      b.   Punishment prevents more misery than it inflicts

    2.   Supports the rights of the accused

    3.   People deserve what they get for past deeds.

CHAPTER SUMMARY

The roots of rational choice theory are contained in the classical school of criminology. According to classical theory, the purpose of the law is to produce and support the total happiness of the community it serves. Punishment is designed to prevent crime and if punishment cannot prevent crime then punishment is to convince the offender to commit a less serious crime.

According to rational choice theory, crime is an event and criminality is a personal trait. Several personal factors condition people to choose crime. Among these are economic opportunity, learning and experience, and knowledge of criminal techniques. Rational choice theorists propose that offenders choose the type of crime to commit, choose the time and place of the crime, and choose the target of crime.

When criminologists study criminal behavior, they find that there is a great deal of rational decision-making in criminal behavior. Boosters use complex methods to avoid detection of their shoplifting and burglars prefer permeable neighborhoods. Heavy drug users and dealers show signs of rationality and cunning. Street robbers choose vulnerable targets, while serial murderers pick targets with care. Serial rapists look for targets that will require them to expend little effort.

Situational crime prevention originated with the concept of defensible space in an effort to raise the risks associated with crime and to reduce the rewards offenders achieve from committing crime. From situational crime prevention emerged the prevention technique of target hardening and the development of new security products designed to reduce opportunities for crime. The benefits of situational crime prevention are diffusion and discouragement, while the problems are displacement and extinction.

General deterrence argues that there is an inverse relationship between crime rates and the severity, certainty, and speed of legal sanctions. General deterrence focuses on future criminals. Specific deterrence proposes that punishment will deter offenders from repeating criminal acts. Incapacitation focuses on placing offenders in prison during their prime crime years in order to reduce their lifetime opportunity to commit crime. Research on general deterrence, specific deterrence, and incapacitation is mixed.

STUDENT EXERCISES

Exercise 1

Go online to http://www.ncjrs.org/pdffiles/cptedpkg.pdf and read the article, *Crime Prevention through Environmental Design in Parking Facilities* by Mary S. Smith. Summarize the major findings of the study concerning how to prevent crimes in parking lots.

Exercise 2

Go online and conduct a search for the words "crime displacement." Take a look at the links you retrieved and summarize your findings concerning crime displacement.

CRIMINOLOGY WEB LINKS

http://www.popcenter.org/default.htm
This is the official website of the Center for Problem-Oriented Policing of the United States Department of Justice.

http://www.crimereduction.gov.uk/
This is the official website of the government of the United Kingdom. The material in this website concerns crime reduction techniques advocated by the UK government.

http://www.communitypolicing.org/publications/comlinks/cl16/cl16_kroek.htm
This is an article written for *Community Links*, a publication of the Community Policing Consortium, by the Chief of Police of Portland, Oregon about crime prevention through environmental design.

http://www.ncjrs.org/pdffiles/crimepre.pdf
This is a publication of the National Institute of Justice called *Crime Prevention Through Environmental Design and Community Policing* by Dan Fleissner and Fred Heinzelmann.

http://www.aei.org/news/newsID.18871,filter./news_detail.asp
This is an interesting article by John DiIulio, a conservative criminologist, on why deterrence is not working in the United States. DiIulio's article summarizes much of the philosophy of those criminologists who subscribe to choice theories.

TEST BANK

FILL-IN THE BLANKS

1. Rational choice theory has its roots in the _____ school of criminology.

2. Beccaria believed that crime and punishment must be _____; if not, people would be encouraged to commit more serious offenses.

3. Beccaria stated that criminals _____ to commit crime and that crime can be controlled by judicious punishment.

4. The _____ _____ evaluates the risk of apprehension, the seriousness of the expected punishment, the potential value of the criminal enterprise, and his or her immediate need for criminal gain.

5. _____ is an event; _____ is a personal trait.

6. Professional shoplifters who use complex methods to avoid detection are called _____.

7. _____ _____ refers to the use of residential architectural designs that reduce criminal opportunity.

8. Crime control efforts targeting a particular locale helping to reduce crime in the surrounding areas and populations are referred to as _____.

9. The idea that the certainty of punishment will only have a deterrent effect if the likelihood of getting caught reaches a critical level is known as the _____ _____.

10. Imprisoning the small number of people who account for a relatively large percentage of the nation's crime in order to produce a significant payoff is called _____ _____.

TRUE/FALSE QUESTIONS

1. T/F Specific deterrence refers to the concept that if petty offenses were subject to the same punishment as more serious crimes, offenders would choose the worse crime.

2. T/F Jeremy Bentham helped popularize Beccaria's views in his writings on utilitarianism.

3. T/F The reasoning criminal evaluates the risk of apprehension.

4. T/F An offender-specific crime means that offenders will react selectively to the characteristics of particular offenses.

5. T/F Perceptions of economic opportunity influence the decision to commit crime.

6. T/F There is little evidence of rationality in the choosing of the type of crime to commit.

7. T/F As an indicator that serial rapists show rationality, they travel an average of three miles from their homes to commit their crimes in order to avoid victims who might recognize them.

8. T/F For many people, crime is attractive.

9. T/F Controlling truancy can be an element of a strategy under situational crime prevention.

10. T/F Research indicates that crime discouragers do not have much of an impact on crime.

11. T/F Research shows that experienced criminals are the ones most likely to fear the deterrent power of the law.

12. T/F The fear of informal sanctions may have a greater crime-reducing impact than the fear of formal legal punishment.

13. T/F Women fear shame and embarrassment more than men.

14. T/F Habitual offender laws that provide long or life sentences for repeat offenders reduce crime substantially.

15. T/F Desert theory is not at all concerned with the rights of the accused.

MULTIPLE CHOICE QUESTIONS

1. A prohibition against cruel and unusual punishment was incorporated into which Amendment to the United States Constitution?
   a. Fourth
   b. Fifth
   c. Sixth
   d. Eighth

2. The concept that if petty offenses were subject to the same punishment as more serious crimes, offenders would choose the worse crime because the punishments would be about the same is called:
   a. general deterrence
   b. specific deterrence
   c. marginal deterrence
   d. deterrence theory

3. Beccaria's writings have been credited as the basis for the elimination of:
   a. probation
   b. torture
   c. capital punishment
   d. due process

4. Which theory states that law-violating behavior occurs when an offender decides to break the law after considering both personal factors and situational factors?
   a. rational choice theory
   b. situational crime prevention
   c. classical theory
   d. deterrence theory

5. Which personal factor is one considered by someone in the decision to commit crime?
   a. economic opportunity
   b. learning and experience
   c. knowledge of criminal techniques
   d. all of the above

6. Burglars prefer to commit crimes in permeable neighborhoods because:
   a. street lighting is sparse
   b. they offer more potential escape routes
   c. population levels are lower
   d. police patrol is lighter

7. Street robbers choose victims who have all of the following characteristics **except**:
   a. are vulnerable
   b. are short
   c. have low coercive power
   d. do not pose any threat

8. Robbers prefer to rob businesses that deal primarily in:
   a. credit cards
   b. checks
   c. cash
   d. convenience items

9. The rationality of a rapist is demonstrated in their desire to:
   a. find a weak victim
   b. rape an acquaintance
   c. find a victim of their own race
   d. avoid detection

10. Reducing the opportunities people have to commit crimes is known as:
    a. deterrence theory
    b. situational crime prevention
    c. defensible space
    d. environmental design

11. What are designed to reduce the value of crime to the potential criminal?
    a. target reduction strategies
    b. environmental design strategies
    c. crime discouragers
    d. diffusion strategies

12. Those who monitor targets are called:
    a. discouragers
    b. guardians
    c. handlers
    d. managers

13. Those who monitor places are called:
    a. discouragers
    b. guardians
    c. handlers
    d. managers

14. The reduction in stolen cars by using the Lojack® system resulted in a decline in the sale of stolen auto parts. This is known as:
    a. crime displacement
    b. diffusion
    c. discouragement
    d. extinction

15. The effect produced by video cameras reducing shoplifting and also reducing property vandalism is known as:
    a. crime displacement
    b. diffusion
    c. discouragement
    d. extinction

16. The phenomenon in which crime reduction programs may produce a short-term positive effect, but benefits dissipate as criminals adjust to new conditions is known as:
    a. crime displacement
    b. diffusion
    c. discouragement
    d. extinction

17. The concept that crime rates are influenced and controlled by the threat of punishment is known as:
    a. general deterrence
    b. specific deterrence
    c. deterrence theory
    d. crime prevention

18. The concept that if the probability of arrest, conviction, and sanctioning could be increased, crime rates would decline is called:
    a. general deterrence
    b. specific deterrence
    c. deterrence theory
    d. crime prevention

19. The concept of tipping point is associated with:
    a. severity of punishment
    b. certainty of punishment
    c. swiftness of punishment
    d. none of the above

20. The concept that the shorter the span of opportunity, the fewer offenses offenders can commit during their lives is called:
    a. general deterrence
    b. incapacitation effect
    c. selective incapacitation
    d. just desert

21. What is the concept that describes an effort to incapacitate the few troublemakers who account for the most crime?
    a. general deterrence
    b. incapacitation effect
    c. selective incapacitation
    d. just desert

22. The utilitarian view that punishment is needed to preserve the social equity disturbed by crime is called:
    a. general deterrence
    b. incapacitation effect
    c. selective incapacitation
    d. just desert

23. Beccaria believed that to deter people from committing more serious offenses, crime and punishment must be:
    a. proportional
    b. severe
    c. certain
    d. swift

24. The _____ model suggests that retribution justifies punishment because people deserve what they get for past deeds.
    a. deterrence
    b. just desert
    c. choice intervention
    d. incapacitation

25. Why is it that arrest only minimally deters domestic abusers?
    a. because domestic abusers are committing an expressive crime
    b. because domestic abusers suffer from psychological impairments
    c. because the initial deterrent effect of arrest decays over time
    d. because formal arrest does not stigmatize domestic offenders

ESSAY QUESTIONS

1. Explain the concept of rational choice.

2. Explain the differences between offense-specific crime and offender-specific crime.

3.   Describe the various techniques of situational crime prevention.

4.   Explain the difference between general deterrence and specific deterrence.

5.   Discuss the issues involving the use of incapacitation.

MATCHING

1. _____ Crackdowns
2. _____ Crime
3. _____ Jeremy Bentham
4. _____ Offender-Specific Crime
5. _____ Offense-Specific Crime
6. _____ Permeable Neighborhood
7. _____ Diffusion
8. _____ Discouragement
9. _____ Specific Deterrence
10. _____ Incapacitation Effect

A. Offenders react selectively to the characteristics of particular offenses
B. Efforts to prevent one crime unintentionally prevent another
C. Criminal sanctions should be so powerful that known criminals will never repeat their criminal acts
D. Sudden changes in police activity designed to increase the communicated threat or actual certainty of punishment
E. The shorter the opportunity, the fewer offenses an offender can commit during his or her life, so crime is reduced
F. Utilitarianism
G. Criminals are not automatons who engage in random acts of antisocial behavior
H. Crime efforts in one locale help reduce crime in surrounding areas and populations
I. Event
J. Greater than normal number of access streets from traffic arteries into the neighborhood

CHAPTER 4 ANSWER KEY

Fill in the Blank Answers

1. classical
2. proportional
3. choose
4. reasoning criminal
5. crime; criminality
6. boosters
7. defensible space
8. discouragement
9. tipping point
10. selective incapacitation

True/False Answers

1.	F	6.	F	11.	T
2.	T	7.	T	12.	T
3.	T	8.	T	13.	T
4.	F	9.	T	14.	F
5.	T	10.	F	15.	F

Multiple Choice Answers

1.	D	11.	A	21.	C
2.	C	12.	B	22.	D
3.	A	13.	D	23.	A
4.	D	14.	C	24.	B
5.	B	15.	B	25.	C
6.	B	16.	D		
7.	B	17.	A		
8.	C	18.	C		
9.	D	19.	B		
10.	B	20.	B		

Essay Questions

1. Pages 96-97
2. Pages 98-99
3. Pages 105-110
4. Pages 110-117
5. Pages 118-120

Matching Answers

1.	D	6.	J	
2.	I	7.	B	
3.	F	8.	H	
4.	G	9.	C	
5.	A	10.	E	

TRAIT THEORIES

OUTLINE

Chapter 5

Trait Theories

LEARNING OBJECTIVES

1.   Be familiar with the concept of sociobiology

2.   Know what is meant by the term equipotentiality

3.   Be able to discuss the relationship between diet and crime

4.   Be familiar with the association between hormones and crime

5.   Be able to discuss why violent offenders may suffer from neurological problems

6.   Know the factors that make up the ADHD syndrome

7.   Be able to discuss the role genetics plays in violent behavior

8.   Be familiar with the concepts of evolutionary theory

9.   Be able to discuss the psychodynamics of criminality

10. Understand the association between media and crime

11. Discuss the role of personality and intelligence in antisocial behaviors

KEYWORDS AND DEFINITIONS

Inheritance school: traced the activities of several generations of families believed to have an especially large number of criminal members.

Somatotype: a system developed for categorizing people on the basis of their body build.

Biophobia: the view that no serious consideration should be given to biological factors when attempting to understand human nature.

Reciprocal altruism: even when they come to the aid of others, people are motivated by the belief that their actions will be reciprocated and that their gene survival capability will be enhanced.

Trait theory: if biological (genetic) makeup controls human behavior, it follows that it should also be responsible for determining whether a person chooses law-violating or conventional behavior.

Equipotentiality: view that all individuals are equal at birth and are thereafter influenced by their environment.

Wernicke-Korsakoff disease: a deadly neurological disorder to which alcoholics are susceptible because they often suffer from thiamine deficiency due to their poor diets.

Hypoglycemia: occurs when glucose in the blood falls below levels necessary for normal and efficient brain functioning.

Androgens: male sex hormones that produce aggressive behavior.

Testosterone: the most abundant androgen and principal male steroid hormone that controls secondary sex characteristics such as facial hair and voice timbre.

Neocortex: the part of the brain that controls sympathetic feelings toward others.

Premenstrual syndrome (PMS): the onset of the menstrual cycle triggers excessive amounts of the female sex hormones that affect antisocial, aggressive behavior.

Cerebral allergies: allergies cause an excessive reaction in the brain.

Neuroallergies: allergies that affect the nervous system.

Neurophysiology: the study of brain activity.

Electroencephalograph (EEG): records the electrical impulses given off by the brain.

Attention deficit hyperactivity disorder (ADHD): a condition in which a child shows a developmentally inappropriate lack of attention, impulsivity, and hyperactivity.

Conduct disorder (CD): behaviors such as fighting that are early signs that the child is among the most at risk for persistent antisocial behaviors continuing into adulthood.

Chemical restraints or chemical straitjackets: antipsychotic drugs such as Haldol, Stelazine, Prolixin, and Risperdal that help control levels of neurotransmitters (such as serotonin/dopamine).

Arousal theory: for a variety of genetic and environmental reasons, some people's brains function differently in response to environmental stimuli.

Contagion effect: it is possible that what appears to be a genetic effect picked up by the twin research is actually the effect of sibling influence on criminality.

Defective intelligence: Charles Goring uncovered a significant relationship between crime and traits as feeblemindedness, epilepsy, insanity, and defective social instinct, which he called defective intelligence.

Psychoanalytic or psychodynamic perspective: focus is on early childhood experience and its effect on personality.

Behaviorism: stresses social learning and behavior modeling as the keys to criminality.

Cognitive theory: analyzes human perception and how it affects behavior.

Id: the primitive part of an individual's mental makeup present at birth; it represents unconscious biological drives for sex, food, and other life-sustaining necessities.

Pleasure principle: the id requires instant gratification without concern for the rights of others.

Ego: that part of the personality that compensates for the demands of the id by helping the individual guide his or her actions to remain within the boundaries of social convention.

Reality principle: ego takes into account what is practical and conventional by societal standards.

Superego: develops as a result of incorporating within the personality the moral standards and values of parents, community, and significant others. It is the moral aspect of an individual's personality; it passes judgments on behavior.

Conscience: tells what is right and wrong.

Ego ideal: part of superego; directs the individual into morally acceptable and responsible behaviors that may not be pleasurable.

Eros: the instinct to preserve and create life.

Thanatos: the death instinct, which is expressed as aggression.

Oral stage: named by Freud, it is the first year of life in which a child attains pleasure by sucking and biting.

Anal stage: the second and third years of life in which the focus of sexual attention is on the elimination of bodily wastes.

Phallic stage: occurs during the third year when children focus their attention on their genitals.

Oedipus complex: a stage of development when males begin to have sexual feelings for their mothers.

Electra complex: a stage of development when females begin to have sexual feelings for their fathers.

Latency: begins at age 6; during this period, feelings of sexuality are repressed until the genital stage begins at puberty.

Fixated: an adult who exhibits behavior traits characteristic of those encountered during infantile sexual development.

Inferiority complex: coined by Alfred Adler, it describes people who have feelings of inferiority and compensate for them with a drive for superiority.

Identity crisis: a period of serious personal questioning people undertake in an effort to determine their own values and sense of direction.

Latent delinquency: a predisposition that psychologically prepares youths for antisocial acts.

Bipolar disorder: a condition in which a person's moods alternate between periods of wild elation and deep depression.

Psychosis: includes severe mental disorders, such as depression, bipolar disorder (manic depression), and schizophrenia.

Disorders: the condition in which a person exhibits illogical and incoherent thought processes and a lack of insight into their behavior.

Schizophrenia: the conditions in which a person may hear nonexistent voices, hallucinate, and make inappropriate behavioral responses.

Paranoid schizophrenic: suffers complex behavior delusions involving wrongdoing or persecution; they think everyone is out to get them.

Social learning: the branch of behavior theory that proposes that people are not actually born with the ability to act violently but that they learn to be aggressive through their life experiences.

Behavior modeling: process of learning behavior (notably aggression) by observing others; the models may be parents, criminals in the neighborhood, or characters on television or in the movies.

Moral development: concerned with the way people morally represent and reason about the world.

Humanistic psychology: stresses self-awareness and "getting in touch with feelings."

Information processing: focuses on the way people process, store, encode, retrieve, and manipulate information to make decisions and solve problems.

Personality: the reasonably stable patterns of behavior, including thoughts and emotions that distinguish one person from another.

Minnesota Multiphasic Personality Inventory (MMPI): the test that has subscales designed to measure many different personality traits, including psychopathic deviation (Pd scale), schizophrenia (Sc), and hypomania (Ma).

California Personality Inventory (CPI): has been used to distinguish deviants from nondeviant groups.

Multidimensional Personality Questionnaire (MPQ): allows researchers to assess such personality traits as control, aggression, alienation, and well-being.

Nature theory: argues that intelligence is largely determined genetically, that ancestry determines IQ, and that low intelligence, as demonstrated by low IQ, is linked to criminal behavior.

Nurture theory: states that intelligence must be viewed as partly biological but primarily sociological.

Wechsler Adult Intelligence Scale: one of the standard IQ tests.

Primary prevention programs: programs that seek to treat personal problems before they manifest themselves as crime.

Secondary prevention programs: provide treatment such as psychological counseling to youths and adults after they have violated the law.

Tertiary prevention programs: prevention programs that are required by a probation order, part of a diversionary sentence, or associated with aftercare following a prison sentence.

CHAPTER OUTLINE

I. Foundations of trait theory
    A. General
        1. Lombroso and biological theory
        2. Inheritance school
        3. Body types
            a. Mesomorphs
            b. Endomorphs
            c. Ectomporphs
    B. Impact of sociobiology
        1. Biophobia
        2. Sociobiology stresses that biological and genetic conditioning affect how social behaviors are learned and perceived.
        3. Gene is the ultimate unit of life that controls all human destiny.
        4. Since biology controls human behavior, it is responsible for a person's choice to violate the law.
    C. Modern trait theories
        1. Trait theories are not overly concerned with the legal definitions of crime.
        2. Trait theorists focus on human behavior and drives.
        3. Traits do not produce criminality.
        4. Crime involves both personal traits and environmental factors.
        5. Equipotentiality
        6. Chronic offenders suffer some biological/psychological condition or trait that renders them incapable of resisting social pressures and problems.
        7. Two major subdivisions of trait theories
            a. One that stresses psychological functioning
            b. One that stresses biological functioning

II. Biosocial trait theories
    A. Biochemical conditions and crime
        1. Chemical and mineral influences
            a. Minimal levels of minerals and chemicals are needed for normal brain functioning.
            b. Oversupply or undersupply of certain chemicals and minerals can lead to depression, mania, cognitive, and other problems.
            c. What people eat and take into their bodies may influence their behavior.

        d.   Vitamin deficiency or dependency can manifest many physical, mental, and behavioral problems.

2. Diet and crime
   a. Excessive amounts of harmful substances such as food dyes and artificial colors/flavors seem to provoke hostile, impulsive, and antisocial behaviors.
   b. Recent research supports the link.

3. Sugar and crime
   a. High sugar content in diets is linked to violence and aggression.
   b. Other research does not support the link.

4. Glucose metabolism/hypoglycemia
   a. Abnormality in the brain's metabolizing glucose has been linked to antisocial behaviors.
   b. Hypoglycemia is linked to outbursts of antisocial behavior and violence.

5. Hormonal influences
   a. Wilson argues that hormones, enzymes, and neurotransmitters may be the key to understanding human behavior.
   b. Androgens
   c. Testosterone

6. How hormones may influence behavior
   a. Hormones cause areas of the brain to become less sensitive to environmental stimuli.
   b. Hormones influence the neocortex.
   c. Physical effects of excessive hormones promote violence.

7. Premenstrual syndrome (PMS)
   a. Menstrual cycle triggers excessive amounts of female hormones that affect antisocial, aggressive behavior.
   b. Fishbein concludes that there is an association between female aggression and menstruation.

8. Allergies
   a. Cerebral allergies cause excessive reaction in the brain.
   b. Neuroallergies affect the nervous system.
   c. Cerebral allergies and neuroallergies have been linked to hyperactivity in children.

9. Environmental contaminants are found in the environment.

10. Lead levels
    a. Research studies suggest that lead ingestion is linked to aggressive behaviors at both a macro- and micro-level.
    b. Areas of the U.S. with high lead levels had the highest levels of homicide.
    c. High lead ingestion is related to lower IQ.

B. Neurophysiological conditions and crime
   1. General
      a. Some researchers believe that neurological and physical abnormalities are acquired as early as the fetal or prenatal stage or through birth delivery trauma.
      b. Research indicates that this relationship can be detected quite early.
   2. Neurological impairments and crime
      a. Neurological tests have been found to distinguish criminal offenders from noncriminal control groups.
      b. Chronic violent offenders have far higher levels of brain dysfunction than the general population.

3. Minimal brain dysfunction
   a. Linked to serious antisocial acts
   b. Criminals have been characterized as having dysfunction of the dominant hemisphere of the brain.
4. Attention deficit hyperactivity disorder (ADHD)
   a. Most common reason children are referred to mental health clinics
   b. ADHD is linked to the onset and sustenance of a delinquent career.
   c. Many ADHD suffer from conduct disorder and engage in aggressive and antisocial behavior in early childhood.
   d. Relationship between chronic delinquency and attention disorders may be mediated by school performance.
   e. Early school-based intervention programs may be of special benefit to ADHD children.
5. Tumors, lesions, injury, and disease
   a. Brain tumors and lesions have been linked to a wide variety of psychological problems.
   b. People with tumors are prone to depression, irritability, temper outbursts, and even homicide attacks.
6. Brain chemistry
   a. Abnormal levels of neurotransmitters are associated with aggression.
   b. Individuals with low monamine oxidase (MAO) engage in behaviors linked with violence and property crime.
   c. Violence prone people are commonly treated with antipsychotic drugs.
C. Arousal theory
   1. Obtaining thrills is a crime motivator.
   2. Crime can satisfy personal needs for thrills and excitement.
D. Genetics and crime
   1. Parental deviance
      a. If criminal tendencies are inherited, then children of criminal parents should be more likely to be criminal than children of non-criminal parents.
      b. Schoolyard aggression or bullying may be both inter- and intragenerational.
      c. Quality of family life may be a key in determining children's behavior.
      d. Parental conflict and authoritarian parenting were related to early childhood conduct problems in two successive generations.
   2. Sibling similarities
      a. Research shows if one sibling engages in antisocial behavior, so do the other siblings.
      b. Effect is greatest among same sex siblings.
      c. Effect can be explained by genetics, but also by other factors such as environment.
   3. Twin behavior
      a. Monozygotic (MZ) twins share the same genetic makeup.
      b. Dizygotic (DZ) twins share 50% of their genetic combinations.
      c. Research shows a greater probability of shared criminal behavior in MZ twins than in DZ twins.
      d. Research shows similarities between twins are due to genes, not environment.
   4. Evaluating genetic research
      a. Not all criminologists support the idea that crime is genetically predetermined.
      b. Opponents point to inadequate research designs and weak methodologies.
      c. Also point to contagion effect

5. Adoption studies
    a. Avoids the pitfalls of twin studies
    b. Relationship exists between biological parents' behavior and the behavior of children even when contact has been nonexistent.
    c. Gene-crime relationship controversial
        1) Implies propensity to crime cannot be altered
        2) Raises moral dilemmas
E. Evolutionary theory
    1. Violence and evolution – violent offenses driven by evolutionary and reproductive factors
    2. Gender and evolution
        a. Aggressive males have had the highest impact on the gene pool.
        b. Descendants of aggressive males now account for the disproportionate amount of male aggression and violence.
    3. Theories of evolutionary criminology
        a. Rushton's theory of race and evolution
            1) Evolutionary changes are responsible for present-day crime rate differences between the races.
            2) Harshly received and condemned
        b. R/K selection theory
            1) R-people are cunning and deceptive
            2) K-people are cooperative and sensitive
        c. Cheater theory
            1) Subpopulation of men with genes that incline them toward low parental involvement
            2) Prey on young, less intelligent women who have children at very early ages
            3) Producing an ever expanding supply of cheaters who are antisocial and sexually aggressive
F. Evaluation of the biosocial branch of trait theory
    1. Critics find the theories racist and dysfunctional.
    2. Cannot explain geographic social and temporal patterns in crime rates
    3. Biggest complaint is the lack of empirical testing
    4. Biosocial theorists maintain only that some people carry the potential for violence and antisocial behavior.
    5. They argue that the environment triggers antisocial responses.
    6. Biosocial theorists have the view that behavior is the product of biology and environment.

III. Psychological trait theories
A. Psychodynamic perspective – developed by Freud
    1. Elements of psychodynamic theory
        a. Id – pleasure principle
        b. Ego – reality principle
        c. Superego – conscience and ego ideal
    2. Psychosexual stages of human development
        a. Oral stage
        b. Anal stage
        c. Phallic stage
            1) Oedipus complex

          2)   Electra complex

    3.   The psychodynamics of antisocial behavior

        a.   Inferiority complex

        b.   Identity crisis

        c.   Latent delinquency

        d.   Psychodynamic model depicts an aggressive, frustrated, person dominated by early childhood events.

        e.   Crime is a manifestation of oppression and the inability to develop proper psychological defenses.

    4.   Mood disorders and crime

        a.   Disruptive behavior disorder

            1)   Oppositional defiant disorder

            2)   Conduct disorder

        b.   Causes – biosocial and psychological factors

    5.   Crime and mental illness

        a.   Psychosis – includes several mental disorders

        b.   Depression often found in serious, violent offenders.

        c.   Diagnosed mentally ill appear in court at a rate disproportionate to their presence in the population

    6.   Is the link valid?

        a.   Questions exist about whether there is a mental illness link to crime and violence.

        b.   Link between crime and mental illness may be spurious.

B.   Behavioral theories

    1.   Human actions are developed through learning experiences.

    2.   People alter their behavior according to reactions they receive from others.

    3.   Behavior

        a.   Supported by rewards

        b.   Extinguished by negative reactions or punishments

C.   Social learning theory

    1.   Bandura – people learn to be aggressive through their life experiences.

    2.   Experiences include

        a.   Observing others act aggressively to achieve some goal

        b.   Watching people rewarded for violent acts

    3.   Social learning and violence

        a.   Violence learned through behavior modeling

        b.   Modeled after three sources

            1)   Family interaction

            2)   Environmental experiences

            3)   Mass media

        c.   Four factors contribute to violent/aggressive behavior

            1)   Event that heightens arousal

            2)   Aggressive skills

            3)   Expected incomes

            4)   Consistency of behavior with values

D.   Cognitive theory

    1.   Moral and intellectual development theory

        a.   Most important for criminological theory

        b.   Piaget – people's reasoning develops in an orderly process.

        c.   Kohlberg – applied moral development to issues in criminology.

        d.   Decision not to commit crimes may be influenced by one's stage of moral development.

   2.   Information processing
      a.   People who use information properly are best able to avoid antisocial behavior.
      b.   Crime-prone people may have cognitive deficits.

   3.   Shaping perceptions
      a.   Hostile children may have learned improper scripts by observing how others react to events.
      b.   May have had early and prolonged exposure to violence

E.   Personality and crime
   1.   Personality reflects a characteristic way of adapting to life's demands and problems.
   2.   Criminal personality traits
      a.   Impulsivity
      b.   Hostility
      c.   Aggressiveness
   3.   Antisocial personality/psychopathy/sociopathy
      a.   Disturbed personality that makes them incapable of developing enduring relationships.
      b.   Came from dysfunctional homes
      c.   Uncertain of causes
   4.   Research on personality
      a.   Wide variety of personality tests
      b.   Crime control efforts might be better focused on helping families raise children.

F.   Intelligence and crime
   1.   Nature theory
      a.   Intelligence determined genetically
      b.   Low intelligence linked to crime
   2.   Nurture theory
      a.   IQ is partly biological but primarily sociological.
      b.   Low IQs result from an environment that also encourages delinquent and criminal behavior.
   3.   Rediscovering IQ and criminality
      a.   Hirschi and Hindelang – IQ is more important than race and socioeconomic class in predicting crime and delinquency.
      b.   Their research has been supported by other research.
   4.   Cross-national studies – supported by research in other countries
   5.   IQ and crime reconsidered
      a.   Recent studies find IQ has negligible effect on crime.
      b.   Herrnstein and Murray conclude there is a link.

IV. Public policy implications of trait theory
   A.   Primary prevention programs treat personal problems before they manifest themselves as crime.
   B.   Secondary prevention programs provide support after crime has occurred.
   C.   Tertiary prevention programs may be a requirement of a probation order, part of a diversionary sentence, or associated with aftercare following a prison sentence.

CHAPTER SUMMARY

The foundations of trait theory are found in Cesare Lombroso's work and biological theory. Many criminologists reacted harshly to the crime-biology link; this reaction was called biophobia. Sociobiology developed later stressing that biological and genetic conditioning affect how social behaviors are learned and perceived. Sociobiologists argued that the gene is the ultimate unit of life that controls human destiny. Under this argument, since biology controls human behavior, it is responsible for a person's choice to violate the law.

Modern trait theories are not overly concerned with the legal definitions of crime. Trait theorists focus on human behavior and drives and argue that traits do not produce criminality. Rather, crime involves both personal traits and environmental factors. Chronic offenders suffer some biological/psychological condition or trait that renders them incapable of resisting social pressures and problems.

There are two major subdivisions of trait theories, one that stresses biological functioning and one that stresses psychological functioning. Biosocial trait theories look at the relationship between a wide variety of variables and crime. Among those variables are biochemical conditions, neurophysiological conditions, arousal, genetics, and evolution. Biochemical conditions include chemicals, diet, hormones, allergies, and environmental contaminants. Neurophysiological conditions include impairments, minimal brain dysfunction, ADHD, tumors, and brain chemistry. Arousal deals with the thrills some offenders obtain from crime, so the motivation for crime becomes the obtaining of thrills. Research on the relationship between genetics and crime has focused on the criminal behavior of offenders and their parents, the criminal behavior of twins (identical and fraternal), and adoption studies. Evolutionary theory addresses the idea that violent offenses are driven by evolutionary and reproductive factors.

Psychological trait theories include a wide range of theories. Among them are the psychodynamic perspective developed by Sigmund Freud, behavioral theories, social learning theory, cognitive theory, personality and crime, and intelligence and crime.

Trait theories have two major implications for public policy on crime prevention. First, primary prevention programs are those crime prevention programs that focus on the treatment of personal problems before they manifest as crime. The second policy implication involves secondary prevention programs that provide treatment and support after crime has occurred.

STUDENT EXERCISES

Exercise 1

Go online to http://www.google.com and search the internet using the words "diet and crime." Peruse the various links that you receive and make a short summary of your search results. How does the search results compare with the material presented in the textbook?

Exercise 2

Go online to http://www.vathek.com/ijpsm/pdf/jpsm.4.4.344.pdf and read the article, *The Relationship of Attention Deficit Hyperactivity Disorder to Crime and Delinquency: a Meta-Analysis* by Travis C. Pratt, Francis T. Cullen, Kristie R. Blevins, Leah Daigle and James D. Unnever. Summarize the major findings of the study concerning the relationship between ADHD and crime.

CRIMINOLOGY WEB LINKS

http://www.ncjrs.org/pdffiles1/ojjdp/fs200120.pdf
This is a fact sheet from the Office of Juvenile Justice and Delinquency Prevention concerning ADHD and delinquency. It pertains to a study from the National Institute of Health.

http://www.psychology.iastate.edu/faculty/caa/abstracts/1995-1999/95ADD.pdf
This is an article entitled *Hot Temperatures, Hostile Affect, Hostile Cognition, and Arousal: Tests of a General Model of Affective Aggression* by Craig A. Anderson, William E. Deuser, and Kristina M. Deneve.

http://www.psychology.iastate.edu/faculty/caa/abstracts/2000-2004/03CA.pdf
This is an article entitled *Theory in the Study of Media Violence: The General Aggression Model* by Nicholas L. Carnagey and Craig A. Anderson.

http://cms.psychologytoday.com/articles/pto-20030514-000001.html
This an article from *Psychology Today* on crime and nutrition.

http://www.schizophrenia.com/poverty.htm
This is the official website of schizophrenia.com and contains information pertaining to the relationship between schizophrenia and crime.

TEST BANK

FILL-IN THE BLANKS

1. The _____ school held that criminals possessed distinct physiques that made them susceptible to particular types of delinquent behavior.

2. The concept that all humans are born with equal potential to learn and achieve is called _____.

3. Diets high in sugar and carbohydrates have been linked to _____ and _____.

4. Many people with attention deficit hyperactivity disorder (ADHD) also suffer from _____ _____ and continually engage in aggressive and antisocial behavior in early childhood.

5. _____ _____ have identical genetic make up and are significantly close in personal characteristics, such as intelligence.

6. _____ _____ suggests that a subpopulation of men has evolved with genes that incline them toward extremely low parental involvement.

7. _____ _____ analyzes human perception and how it affects behavior.

8. In _____ _____, moods alternate between periods of wild elation and deep depression.

9. _____ _____ states that intelligence must be viewed as partly biological but primarily sociological.

10. _____ can be defined as the reasonably stable patterns of behavior, including thoughts and emotions that distinguish one person from another.

TRUE/FALSE QUESTIONS

1. T/F The inheritance school traced the activities of several generations of families believed to have an especially large number of criminal members.

2. T/F Some trait theorists believe biochemical conditions, including both those that are genetically predetermined and those acquired through diet and the environment, control and influence antisocial behavior.

3. T/F Some recent research efforts have failed to find a link between sugar consumption and violence.

4.   T/F An association between hormonal activity and antisocial behavior is suggested because rates of both factors peak in adulthood.

5.   T/F Neuroallergies cause an excessive reaction in the brain, whereas cerebral allergies affect the nervous system.

6.   T/F Neurophysiology is the study of brain activity.

7.   T/F Immediate gratifications from criminality are called the seductions of crime and help satisfy personal needs for thrills and excitement.

8.   T/F Although there is a significant correspondence in MZ twin behavior in many activities, crime is not one of them.

9.   T/F Sibling influence on criminality is referred to as the contagion effect.

10. T/F According to evolutionary theory, crime rate differences between the genders may be a matter of socialization.

11. T/F The biosocial view is that behavior is a product of interacting biological and environmental events.

12. T/F The major premise of behavior theory is that people alter their behavior according to the reactions it receives from others.

13. T/F The ego follows the pleasure principle.

14. T/F The superego is divided into two parts: conscience and ego ideal.

15. T/F Humanistic psychology stresses self-awareness and "getting in touch with feelings."

MULTIPLE CHOICE QUESTIONS

1.   According to the somatotype school, the person with well-developed muscles and an athletic appearance is a(n):
     a.   mesomorph
     b.   ectomorph
     c.   endomorph
     d.   mezzomorph

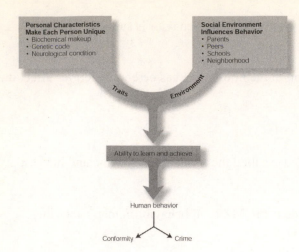

2. Biosocial theorists believe that ___, ___, and ___ conditions work in concert to produce human behavior.
   a. physical, environmental, economic
   b. physical, economic, social
   c. physical, environmental, social
   d. economic, environmental, social

3. The concept that not all humans are born with equal potential to learn and achieve is known as:
   a. trait theory
   b. equpotentiality
   c. reciprocal altruism
   d. sociobiology

4. Unusual or excessive reactions of the body to foreign substances are called:
   a. allergies
   b. environmental contamination
   c. neuroresponses
   d. biological contamination

5. Allergies that cause an excessive reaction in the brain are:
   a. neuroallergies
   b. physioallergies
   c. cerebral allergies
   d. cortex allergies

6. Dangerous amounts of copper, cadmium, mercury and inorganic gases found in the ecosystem are known as:
   a. environmental contaminants
   b. neuro-contaminants
   c. elemental contaminants
   d. metal contaminants

7. The study of brain activity is called:
   a. arousal theory
   b. neurophysiology
   c. minimal brain dysfunction
   d. genetics

8. An abruptly appearing maladaptive behavior that interrupts an individual's lifestyle and life flow is called:
    a. minimal brain dysfunction (MBD)
    b. attention deficit hyperactive disorder (ADHD)
    c. conduct disorder (CD)
    d. antisocial personality (ASP)

9. Which theory holds that all organisms can be located along a continuum based upon their reproductive drives?
    a. R/K selection theory
    b. arousal theory
    c. cheater theory
    d. evolutionary theory

10. Which theory suggests that a subpopulation of men has evolved with genes that incline them toward extremely low parental involvement?
    a. R/K selection theory
    b. arousal theory
    c. cheater theory
    d. evolutionary theory

11. According to Goring, traits such as feeblemindedness, epilepsy, insanity and defective social instinct are referred to as:
    a. defective intelligence
    b. minimal brain dysfunction
    c. criminal mind
    d. paranoid schizophrenic

12. Which perspective analyzes human perception and how it affects behavior?
    a. psychosexual theory
    b. psychodynamic perspective
    c. behaviorism
    d. cognitive theory

13. Instant gratification without concern for the rights of others is called the:
    a. reality principle
    b. conscience
    c. superego
    d. pleasure principle

14. The concept that takes into account what is practical and conventional by societal standards is called:
    a. reality principle
    b. conscience
    c. superego
    d. pleasure principle

15. The part of the superego that tells us what is right or wrong is called:
    a. conscience
    b. reality principle
    c. id
    d. ego ideal

16. The most basic human drive present at birth is the instinct to preserve and create life, this drive is called:
    a. thantos
    b. eros
    c. oedipus
    d. latency

17. During the phallic stage, girls begin to have sexual feelings for their fathers, this concept is called:
    a. identity crisis
    b. fixation
    c. Oedipus complex
    d. Electra complex

18. Seeking immediate gratification, considering the satisfying of personal needs as more important than relating to others, and satisfying urges without considering right or wrong is a mental state known as:
    a. superiority complex
    b. identity crisis
    c. latent delinquency
    d. bipolar disorder

19. When an individual's moods alternate between periods of wild elation and deep depression, it is referred to as:
    a. disruptive behavior disorder (DBD)
    b. bipolar disorder
    c. conduct disorder (CD)
    d. attention deficit hyperactivity disorder (ADHD)

20. Disruptive behavior disorder (DBD) can take on two distinct forms. The milder condition of uncooperative, defiant, and hostile behavior toward authority figures that seriously interferes with a youngster's day-to-day functioning is called:
    a. oppositional defiant disorder (ODD)
    b. conduct disorder (CD)
    c. psychosis
    d. schizophrenia

21. The branch of behavior theory that states people are not actually born with the ability to act violently but that they learn to be aggressive through their life experiences is:
    a. moral development branch
    b. social learning theory
    c. humanistic psychology
    d. information theory

22. According to social learning theorists, violence is something learned through a process called:
    a. behavior modeling
    b. environmental processes
    c. disinhibition
    d. information processing

23. What branch of cognitive theory stresses self-awareness and "getting in touch with feelings?"
    a. nurture theory
    b. nature theory
    c. humanist theory
    d. moral development theory

24. Reasonably stable patterns of behavior, including thoughts and emotions that distinguish one person from another is:
    a. normal
    b. personality
    c. adolescence
    d. adulthood

25. Which theory argues that intelligence is largely determined genetically, that ancestry determines IQ, and that low intelligence, as demonstrated by low IQ, is linked to criminal behavior?
    a. humanist theory
    b. nature theory
    c. latency theory
    d. nurture theory

ESSAY QUESTIONS

1. Discuss the relationship between diet and crime.

2.   Discuss the association between hormones and crime.

3.   Describe the role genetics plays in crime.

4.   Discuss the psychodynamics of criminality.

5. Discuss the effects of television and film violence on behavior.

MATCHING

1. _____ Hypoglycemia
2. _____ Attention Deficit Hyperactive Disorder (ADHD)
3. _____ Arousal Theory
4. _____ Fixated
5. _____ Oedipus Complex
6. _____ Identity Crisis
7. _____ Albert Bandura
8. _____ Lawrence Kohlberg
9. _____ Antisocial Personality
10. _____ The Bell Curve

A. A period of serious personal questioning people undertake in an effort to determine their own values and sense of direction
B. IQ-crime link
C. Social learning theory
D. Disturbed character structure
E. Lack of attention, impulsivity, and hyperactivity
F. Person exhibits behavior traits characteristic of those encountered during infantile sexual development
G. Applied the concept of moral development to crime
H. Below normal levels of glucose in the blood
I. Some peoples' brains function differently in response to environmental stimuli
J. Males have sexual feelings for their mothers

CHAPTER 5 ANSWER KEY

Fill in the Blank Answers

1. somatotype
2. equipotentiality
3. violence; aggression
4. conduct disorder
5. monozygotic (or identical) twins
6. cheater theory
7. cognitive theory
8. bipolar disorder
9. nurture theory
10. personality

True/False Answers

1.	T	6.	T	11.	T
2.	T	7.	T	12.	T
3.	T	8.	F	13.	F
4.	F	9.	T	14.	T
5.	F	10.	F	15.	T

Multiple Choice Answers

1.	A	11.	A	21.	B
2.	C	12.	D	22.	A
3.	B	13.	D	23.	C
4.	A	14.	A	24.	B
5.	C	15.	A	25.	D
6.	A	16.	B		
7.	B	17.	D		
8.	A	18.	C		
9.	A	19.	B		
10.	C	20.	A		

Essay Questions

1. Pages 135-138
2. Pages 138-139
3. Pages 143-147
4. Pages 149-152
5. Pages 152-156

Matching Answers

1.	H	6.	A
2.	E	7.	C
3.	I	8.	G
4.	F	9.	D
5.	J	10.	B

SOCIAL STRUCTURE THEORIES

OUTLINE

Chapter 6

Social Structure Theories

LEARNING OBJECTIVES

1.   Be familiar with the concept of social structure

2.   Have knowledge of the socioeconomic structure of American society

3.   Be able to discuss the concept of social disorganization

4.   Be familiar with the works of Shaw and McKay

5.   Know the various elements of ecological theory

6.   Be able to discuss the association between collective efficacy and crime

7.   Know what is meant by the term anomie

8.   Be familiar with the concept of strain

9.   Understand the concept of cultural deviance

KEYWORDS AND DEFINITIONS

Stratified society: grouping according to social strata or levels. American society is considered stratified on the basis of economic class and wealth.

Culture of poverty: the view that people in the lower class of society form a separate culture with its own values and norms that are in conflict with conventional society; the culture is self-maintaining and ongoing.

At risk: children and adults who lack the education and skills needed to be effectively in demand in modern society.

Underclass: the lowest social stratum in any country, whose members lack the education and skills needed to function successfully in modern society.

Truly disadvantaged: Wilson's term for the lowest level of the underclass; urban, inner-city, socially isolated people who occupy the bottom rung of the social ladder and are the victims of discrimination.

Social structure theory: the view that disadvantaged economic class position is a primary cause of crime.

Social disorganization theory: branch of social structure theory that focuses on the breakdown of institutions such as the family, school, and employment in inner-city neighborhoods.

Strain theory: branch of social structure theory that sees crime as a function of the conflict between people's goals and the means available to obtain them.

Strain: the emotional turmoil and conflict caused when people believe they cannot achieve their desires and goals through legitimate means.

Cultural deviance theory: branch of social structure theory that sees strain and social disorganization together resulting in a unique lower-class culture that conflicts with conventional social norms.

Subcultures: groups that maintain a unique set of values and beliefs that are in conflict with conventional social norms.

Cultural transmission: the concept that conduct norms are passed down from one generation to the next so that they become stable within the boundaries of a culture. Cultural transmission guarantees that group lifestyle and behavior are stable and predictable.

Transitional neighborhoods: an area undergoing a shift in population and structure, usually from middle class residential to lower-class mixed use; poverty-ridden neighborhoods that suffer high rates of population turnover and are incapable of inducing residents to remain and defend the neighborhoods against criminal groups.

Social ecologists: those who believe environmental forces have a direct influence on human behavior.

Incivilities: rude and uncivil behavior; behavior that indicates little caring for the feelings of others.

Siege mentality: the idea that the outside world is considered the enemy out to destroy the neighborhood.

Gentrification: a residential renewal stage in which obsolete housing is replaced and upgraded; areas undergoing such change seem to experience an increase in their crime rates.

Collective efficacy: mutual trust, a willingness to intervene in the supervision of children, and the maintenance of public order.

Strain theorists: criminologists who view crime as a direct result of lower-class frustration and anger.

Relative deprivation: a collective sense of social injustice directly related to income inequality tends to develop in communities or nations in which the poor and wealthy live in close proximity to each other.

Anomie: a condition produced by normlessness – the individual has few guides to what is socially acceptable. According to Merton, anomie is a condition that occurs when personal goals cannot be achieved by available means. In Agnew's revision, anomie can occur when positive or valued stimuli are removed or negative or painful ones applied.

Mechanical solidarity: characteristic of a preindustrial society that is held together by traditions, shared values, and unquestioned beliefs.

Organic solidarity: in postindustrial social systems, which are highly developed and dependent upon the division of labor, people are connected by their interdependent needs for one another's services and production.

Theory of anomie: two elements of culture interact to produce potentially anomic conditions: culturally defined goals and socially approved means for obtaining them.

Institutional anomie theory: the view that anomie pervades U.S. culture because the drive for material wealth dominates and undermines social and community values.

American Dream: the goal of accumulating material goods and wealth through individual competition; the process of being socialized to purse material success and to believe it is achievable.

General strain theory (GST): the view that multiple sources of strain interact with an individual's emotional traits and responses to produce criminality.

Negative affective states: the anger, frustration, and adverse emotions that emerge in the wake of negative and destructive social relationships.

Conduct norms: the concept that the lower class develops a unique culture in response to strain.

Culture conflict: occurs when the rules expressed in the criminal law clash with the demands of group conduct norms.

Focal concerns: the unique value system that defines lower-class culture.

Status frustration: a form of culture conflict that lower-class youths experience because social conditions make them incapable of achieving success legitimately.

Middle-class measuring rods: the standards set by authority figures such as teachers, employers, or supervisors.

Corner boy: the most common response to middle-class rejection; he is not a chronic delinquent but may be a truant who engages in petty or status offenses, such as precocious sex and recreational drug abuse.

College boy: embraces the cultural and social values of the middle class; rather than scorning middle-class measuring rods, he actively strives to be successful by those standards. This type of youth is embarking on an almost hopeless path, since he is ill-equipped academically, socially, and linguistically to achieve the rewards of middle-class life.

Delinquent boy: adopts a set of norms and principles in direct opposition to middle-class values; he engages in short-run hedonism, living for today and letting "tomorrow take care of itself."

Reaction formation: frustrated by their inability to succeed, these boys resort to overly intense responses that seem disproportionate to the stimuli that trigger them.

Differential opportunity: people in all strata of society share the same success goals but that those in the lower class have limited means of achieving them; those who conclude that there is little hope for advancement by legitimate means may join with like-minded peers to form a gang.

CHAPTER OUTLINE

I.   Socioeconomic structure and crime
  A.   General
     1.   People in the U.S. live in a stratified society.
     2.   Created by the unequal distribution of wealth, power, and prestige
     3.   Lower class members have inadequate housing and health care, disrupted family lives, underemployment, and despair.
  B.   Child poverty
     1.   Poverty during early childhood may have a more sever impact on poverty during adolescence and adulthood.
     2.   Poor children more likely to suffer health problems, educational underachievement, and behavior impairments.
     3.   25% of children under the age of six live in poverty – 6% of white children described as extremely poor, 50% of black children live in extreme poverty
  C.   The underclass
     1.   Culture of poverty is passed from one generation to the next.
     2.   Underclass is cut off from society.
     3.   Lack of educational success and lack of success in the workplace lead to crime and drug use.
  D.   Minority group poverty
     1.   Burdens of underclass are most often felt by minorities.
     2.   Rates of poverty vary by race and ethnicity: 10% of whites live in poverty, 20% of African Americans and Latinos live in poverty.
     3.   Up to half of all minority males are under the control of the criminal justice system.
     4.   Interracial crime rate differences can be explained by differences in standard of living.

II.   Social structure theories
  A.   General
     1.   Crime rates are highest in neighborhoods characterized by poverty and social disorder.
     2.   Social and economic forces operating in deteriorated lower-class areas are the key determinants of criminal behavior patterns.
     3.   Middle and upper-classes also engage in crime but their crimes are lower in frequency, seriousness, and danger to the general public.
     4.   Social forces that cause crime begin to affect people while they are relatively young and continue to influence them throughout their lives.
  B.   Three branches of social structure theories

1. Social disorganization theories
    a. Conditions within the urban environment affect crime rates.
2. Strain theories
    a. Crime is a function of the conflict between the goals people have and their means to legally obtain them.
3. Cultural deviance theories
    a. Combines elements of strain and social disorganization

III. Social disorganization theories
    A. Foundations of social disorganization theory
        1. Heavily influenced by the work of Burgess and Park
        2. Studied Chicago, a city fairly typical of the transition taking place in many other urban areas
        3. City was deteriorating
        4. Transitional neighborhoods
            a. Suffered high population turnovers
            b. Low rents attracted groups with different racial and ethnic backgrounds.
            c. Immigrants congregated in these transitional neighborhoods.
            d. These neighborhoods had dissolution of the neighborhood culture and organization caused by:
                1) Successive changes in the population composition
                2) Disintegration of traditional cultures
                3) Diffusion of divergent cultural standards
                4) Gradual industrialization
        5. Concentric zones
            a. Shaw and McKay identified the areas in Chicago that had excessive crime rates.
            b. These were the transitional inner-city zones.
            c. Zones farthest from the city center had the lowest crime rates.
            d. This pattern was stable over a period of 65 years.
            e. Even though crime rates changed, the highest crime rates were always in Zones I and II.
            f. The areas with the highest crime rates retained high crime rates even when the ethnic composition changed.
        6. The legacy of Shaw and McKay
            a. Social disorganization concepts have remained prominent for more than 75 years.
            b. Their most important finding – crime rates correspond to neighborhood structure – still holds.
            c. Crime is the result of destructive ecological conditions in lower-class neighborhoods.
            d. Crime is a normal response to adverse social conditions.
    B. The social ecology school
        1. Community deterioration
            a. Crime rates are associated with deterioration, disorder, poverty, alienation, disassociation, and fear of crime.
            b. Slum areas have the highest violence rates and gun crime.
        2. Poverty concentration
            a. Poverty becomes consolidated in deteriorated areas.
            b. Businesses are disinclined to locate in poverty areas.

c. People living in areas of poverty concentration experience significant income and wealth disparities, nonexistent employment opportunities, inferior housing, and unequal access to healthcare.

3. Chronic unemployment
   a. Relationship between unemployment and crime is unsettled
   b. Unemployment destabilizes households.
   c. Limited employment opportunities reduce the stabilizing influence of parents and other adults.

4. Community fear
   a. Those in disorganized neighborhoods suffer social and physical incivilities – rowdy youth, trash, litter, graffiti, drunks, etc.
   b. Fear is contagious.
   c. Fear is based on experience.
   d. Fear is associated with other community-level factors.
      1) Race and fear
      2) Gangs and fear
      3) Mistrust and fear

5. Community change
   a. Change, not stability, is the hallmark of inner-city areas.
   b. As areas decline, those residents who are able flee to more stable areas.

6. Cycles of community change
   a. Building residential dwellings
   b. Period of decline
   c. Changing racial and ethnic makeup, population thinning
   d. Renewal stage - gentrification

7. Change and decline
   a. Neighborhoods most at risk for crime rate increases contain large numbers of single-parent families.
   b. Changing lifestyles (declining economic status, increasing population, and racial shifts) are associated with increased neighborhood crime rates.

8. Collective efficacy – three forms
   a. Informed social control
   b. Institutional social control
   c. Public social control

9. The effect of collective efficacy
   a. In areas with high collective efficacy, children are less likely to become involved with deviant peers and to engage in problem behaviors.
   b. In areas where social institutions and processes are working adequately, residents are willing to intervene to help control incivility.
   c. In areas with high levels of social control and collective efficacy, crime rates have been show to decrease – no matter what the economic situation.

IV. Strain theories
   A. General
      1. People share similar values and goals.
      2. The ability to achieve these personals goals is stratified by socioeconomic class.
      3. Those shut out from achieving goals experience strain.
      4. Strain is related to criminal motivation.
      5. Generalized feelings of relative deprivation are precursors to high crime rates.
   B. The concept of anomie

     1.   Greek *a nomos*, "without norms"

     2.   Rules of behavior (norms) have broken down or become inoperative during periods of rapid social change or social crisis.

     3.   Anomie is most likely to occur in a society moving from mechanical to organic solidarity.

     4.   Anomie undermines the social control function.

C.   Merton's Theory of anomie

     1.   Merton applied Durkheim's ideas to criminology in his theory of anomie.

     2.   Two elements of culture interact to produce potentially anomic conditions.

         a.   Culturally defined goals

         b.   Socially approved means for obtaining goals

     3.   Legitimate means are stratified across class and status lines.

     4.   Those with little education and few economic resources find they are denied the ability to acquire wealth.

     5.   Social adaptations

         a.   Conformity

         b.   Innovation

         c.   Ritualism

         d.   Retreatism

         e.   Rebellion

     6.   Evaluation of anomie theory

         a.   Merton's view is one of the most enduring and influential sociological theories of crime.

         b.   Theory explains high-crime areas and predominance of crime among the lower-class.

         c.   Why people choose certain types of crime is not explained.

         d.   Anomie theory assumes we all share the same goals and values.

     7.   Anomie reconsidered

         a.   Strain fell out of favor

         b.   Resurgence of interest in strain and anomie

         c.   Newer versions of Merton's concepts

D.   Macro level: Institutional anomie theory

     1.   Messner and Rosenfeld

     2.   Antisocial behavior is a function of cultural and institutional influences in U.S. society.

     3.   American Dream – success goal is pervasive in American culture.

         a.   As a goal – accumulating material goods and wealth via open individual competition

         b.   As a process – being socialized to pursue material successes and believing prosperity is an achievable goal

     4.   Impact of anomie

         a.   Institutions that might control exaggerated emphasis on financial success have been rendered powerless or obsolete.

            1)   Noneconomic functions and roles have been devalued.

            2)   Noneconomic roles became subordinate to and must accommodate economic roles.

            3)   Economic language, standards, and norms penetrate into the noneconomic realms.

         b.   High crime rates are explained by the interrelationship between culture and institutions.

5. Supporting research
   a. Dominance of economic concerns weakens the informal social control exerted by family, church, and school.
   b. Expectation may be greater for whites than African Americans.
   c. May be a blueprint for crime reduction strategies
E. Micro level: General strain theory
   1. Robert Agnew identified micro-level or individual influences of strain.
   2. Multiple sources of stress
      a. Criminality is the direct result of negative affective states: anger, frustration, and adverse emotions that emerge in the wake of negative and destructive social relationships.
   4. Elements of general strain theory
      a. Failure to achieve positively valued goals
      b. Disjunction of expectations and achievements
      c. Removal of positively valued stimuli
      d. Presentation of negative stimuli
   5. The greater the intensity and frequency of strain experiences, the greater their impact and the greater the likelihood of crime.
F. Sources of strain
   1. Social sources of strain
      a. Membership in a peer group
   2. Community sources of strain
      a. Deprived communities or mixed-areas that result in relative deprivation.
G. Coping with strain
   1. Coping ability may be a function of both individual traits and personal experiences over the life course.
   2. Some defenses are cognitive.
   3. Strain and criminal careers
      a. Some people have traits that make them particularly sensitive to strain over the course of their lives.
      b. Crime peaks in late adolescence because this is a period of social stress caused by the weakening of parental supervision and the development of relationships with peer groups.
H. Evaluating general strain theory
   1. Clarifies the concept of strain
   2. Directs future research agendas
   3. Empirical support for general strain theory
   4. Evidence that the presence of negative stimuli provokes strain.
   5. Gender issues
      a. One of the biggest question marks about general strain theory
      b. Females experience as much or more strain, but their crime rate is much lower.
V. Cultural deviance theories
   A. General
      1. Combines the effects of social disorganization and strain
   B. Conduct norms
      1. Lower class develops a unique culture
      2. Group maintains their own set of conduct norms that govern day-to-day living conditions within subcultures.

3. Culture conflict – rules expressed in criminal law clash with the demands of group conduct norms.

C. Focal Concerns – Walter Miller
  1. Unique value system that defines lower-class culture
    a. Trouble
    b. Toughness
    c. Smartness
    d. Excitement
    e. Fate
    f. Autonomy

D. Theory of delinquent subcultures – Albert Cohen's *Delinquent Boys* (1955)
  1. Behavior of lower-class youths is a protest against the norms and values of middle-class culture.
  2. Status frustration – a form of culture conflict
  3. Delinquent gang a separate subculture
  4. Delinquent subculture results from socialization practices found in ghettos and slums.
  5. Middle-class measuring rods
    a. Inability to impress authority figures
    b. Failure to meet the standards of the middle-class measuring rod is the primary cause of delinquency.
  6. Formation of deviant subcultures
    a. Corner boy
    b. College boy
    c. Delinquent boy
      1) Adopts a set of norms and principles in direct opposition to the middle-class
      2) Resorts to a process of reaction formation-overly intense responses disproportionate to the stimuli that trigger them

E. Theory of differential opportunity – Cloward and Ohlin
  1. Differential opportunities
    a. All people share the same success goals, but the lower class has limited means of achieving them.
    b. Those that cannot advance by legitimate means join with like-minded peers to form a gang.
    c. Opportunity for successful conventional and criminal careers is limited
      1) Stable areas have professional criminals.
      2) Unstable areas do not have criminal opportunities.
    d. Opportunities for success, both illegal and legal, are closed for the "truly disadvantaged" youth.
    e. Because of differential opportunity kids are likely to join one of three gangs.
      1) Criminal gangs
      2) Conflict gangs
      3) Retreatist gangs

F. Evaluating social structure theories
  1. They have influenced both criminological theory and crime prevention strategies.
  2. Core concepts of social structure theory seem to be valid.
  3. Each branch seems to support and amplify others.
  4. Critics charge

     a.   Cannot be sure lower class culture promotes crime
     b.   Residence in an urban area alone does not cause violations of the law.
     c.   Most members of the lower-class are not criminals.
     d.   Lower-class crime rates may be an artifact of bias in the criminal justice system.
     e.   It is questionable whether a distinct lower-class culture actually exists.

VI. Public policy implications of social structure theory
    A.   Provide inner-city dwellers with opportunities to share the rewards of conventional society
    B.   Improve community structure in high crime areas to reduce crime
    C.   War on Poverty used concepts from differential opportunity
    D.   Weed and Seed programs

CHAPTER SUMMARY

Social structure theories propose that being in the disadvantaged economic class is the primary cause of crime and, as a result, lower-class crime is often violent and committed by gang members or marginally employed young adults. Social structure theorists argue that people living in equivalent circumstances behave in similar, predictable ways. The three branches of social structure theories are social disorganization theories, strain theories, and cultural deviance theories.

Social disorganization theories were heavily influenced by the work of Burgess and Park. Shaw and McKay studied Chicago, a city fairly typical of the transition taking place in many other urban areas. Shaw and McKay found what they called transitional neighborhoods, the neighborhoods that had excessive crime rates. At the opposite end, those zones farthest from the city center had the lowest crime rates. This pattern was stable over a period of 65 years; even though crime rates changed, the highest crime rates were always in Zones I and II. The areas with the highest crime rates retained high crime rates even when the ethnic composition changed.

Emile Durkheim coined the term "anomie," the condition in which the rules of behavior (norms) have broken down or become inoperative during periods of rapid social change or social crisis. Durkheim noted that anomie undermines the social control function. Robert Merton modified the concept of anomie for modern U.S. society. According to Merton, two elements of culture interact to produce potentially anomic conditions: culturally defined goals and socially approved means to obtain them. He noted that legitimate means of achieving success are stratified across class and status lines, so those with little education and few economic resources find they are denied the ability to acquire wealth. It is this inability to succeed that leads to crime.

Messner and Rosenfeld developed institutional anomie theory that states antisocial behavior is a function of cultural and institutional influences. They described the American Dream as a goal (the accumulation of material goods and wealth by competition) and as a process (being socialized to pursue material successes and believing prosperity is an achievable goal). American institutions that might control exaggerated emphasis on financial success have been rendered powerless or obsolete because noneconomic functions and roles have been devalued, noneconomic roles became subordinate to and must accommodate economic roles, and economic language, standards, and norms penetrate into the noneconomic realms.

Robert Agnew developed general strain theory that identifies micro-level or individual influences of strain. According to the theory, crime arises from failure to achieve positively valued goals, a disjunction of expectations and achievements, the removal of positively valued stimuli, or the presentation of negative stimuli. The greater the intensity and frequency of strain experiences, the greater their impact and the greater the likelihood of crime.

Cohen developed the theory of delinquent subcultures that states the behavior of lower-class youth is a protest against the norms and values of middle-class culture. The delinquent gang is a separate subculture that results from socialization practices of ghettos and slums. Cohen identified middle-class measuring rods that arise from the inability to impress authority figures and the failure to meet the standards of the middle-class as the primary cause of delinquency. As a result, three possible types of subcultural gang roles develop: corner boy, college boy, or delinquent boy. The delinquent boy adopts a set of norms and principles in direct opposition to the middle-class and resorts to a process of reaction formation.

Cloward and Ohlin's theory of differential opportunity states that all people share the same success goals, but the lower class has limited means of achieving them. Those who cannot advance by legitimate means join with like-minded peers to form a gang. Opportunities for success, both illegal and legal, are closed for the "truly disadvantaged" youth. These young people join one of three gangs: criminal gangs, conflict gangs, or retreatist gangs.

Public policy implications of social structure theory center on providing inner-city dwellers with opportunities to share in the rewards of conventional society. Approaches of this nature include financial assistance via welfare, improving the community structure in high-crime, inner city areas, employment assistance programs and other "War on Poverty" efforts, in addition to Weed and Seed crime reduction strategies.

STUDENT EXERCISES

Exercise 1

Go online to http://www.aei.org/publications/pubID.14891/pub_detail.asp and read the article, "The Underclass Revisited" by Charles Murray. This article provides you with a conservative view of the issue of the underclass. After reading the article, write a one to two page essay that contrasts Murray's view with that contained in the textbook.

Exercise 2

Take a ride in your city or a nearby city. Make sure you drive from the center of the city out to the boundaries of the city. Make notes about what each neighborhood looks like as far as types of buildings, environment, what the land is used for, and types of residences. How do the neighborhoods change as one moves out from the center of town and how dramatic are the changes? Do the changes in your city support the social structure theories?

CRIMINOLOGY WEB LINKS

http://www.iejs.com/Criminology/anomie_and_strain_theory.htm
This website provides a summary of anomie from the viewpoint of both Durkheim and Merton. It also provides background information on the two authors.

http://www.ncjrs.org/pdffiles1/nij/186049.pdf
This website contains an article on the relationship between urban disorder and crime from two of America's leading criminologists.

http://www.crimereduction.gov.uk/
This website shows how the United Kingdom is using social structure theories as the foundations for its crime prevention programs.

http://faculty.ncwc.edu/toconnor/301/301lect08.htm
This website provides and excellent summary of the Chicago School, social disorganization theory, gang theory, and other references to social structure theory.

http://www.news.wisc.edu/6148.html
This website provides an excellent example of using social structure theory to drive policy decisions. The article provides a review of the results of a study on providing early intervention to at risk children in the Chicago area.

TEST BANK

FILL-IN THE BLANKS

1. _____ _____ are created by the unequal distribution of wealth, power, and prestige.

2. Poverty during _____ _____ may have a more severe impact on behavior than poverty during adolescence and adulthood.

3. Social structure theory views disadvantaged _____ class position as a primary cause of crime.

4. Subcultural values are handed down from one generation to the next in a process called _____ _____.

5. Various sources of crime data show that crime rates are highest in neighborhoods characterized by _____ and _____ _____.

6. _____ _____ is mutual trust, a willingness to intervene in the supervision of children, and the maintenance of public order.

7. _____ _____ is a characteristic of a preindustrial society, which is held together by traditions, shared values, and unquestioned beliefs.

8. According to the _____ _____ view, lower-class people might feel both deprived and embittered when they compare their life circumstances to those of the more affluent.

9. Agnew suggests that criminality is the direct result of _____ _____ _____ – the anger, frustration, and adverse emotions that emerge in the wake of negative and destructive social relationships.

10. _____ _____ comprise the unique value system that defines lower class culture.

TRUE/FALSE QUESTIONS

1. T/F Findings suggest that poverty during early childhood may have a more severe impact than poverty during adolescence and adulthood.

2. T/F The underclass lacks an education and the skills necessary to be effectively in demand in modern society.

3. T/F The rates of child poverty in the United States vary by race and ethnicity, but not significantly.

4. T/F William Julius Wilson provided a description of the plight of the lowest levels of the underclass, which he labeled the truly disadvantaged.

5. T/F Although members of the middle and upper classes also engage in crime, social structure theorists view middle-class, or white-collar, crime as being of relatively lower frequency, seriousness, and danger to the general public.

6. T/F Transitional neighborhoods are those that have low crime rates.

7. T/F Aggregate crime rates and aggregate unemployment rates seem strongly related.

8. T/F Siege mentality refers to the rich considering the poor as their enemy out to destroy the neighborhood.

9. T/F Public social control is not an element of collective efficacy.

10. T/F Social altruism has been found to be inversely related to crime rates both in the United States and abroad.

11. T/F Merton used a modified version of the concept of anomie to fit social, economic, and cultural conditions found in modern U.S. society.

12. T/F Retreatists reject the goals and accept the means of society.

13. T/F Because social conditions make them incapable of achieving success legitimately, lower-class youths experience a form of culture conflict that Cohen labels status frustration.

14. T/F Differential opportunity states that people in all strata of society share the same success goals but that those in the lower class do not take advantage of the opportunities given to them.

15. T/F Retreatist gang members are double failures, unable to gain success through legitimate means and unwilling to do so through illegal ones.

MULTIPLE CHOICE QUESTIONS

1. What is produced by the crushing lifestyle of slum areas and passed from one generation to the next?
   a. underclass
   b. at-risk adults
   c. culture of poverty
   d. ritualism

2. The lowest levels of the underclass are called:
   a. truly disadvantaged
   b. at-risk
   c. truly impoverished
   d. transitional residents

3. Subcultural values are handed down from one generation to the next in a process called:
   a. cultural mutation
   b. cultural transmission
   c. subcultural transmission
   d. subcultural mutation

4. Poverty-ridden areas that suffer high rates of population turnover and are incapable of inducing residents to remain and defend the area against criminal groups are called:
   a. at-risk neighborhoods
   b. transitional neighborhoods
   c. concentric zones
   d. anomic areas

5. In some neighborhoods, neighbors are willing to practice informal social control through:
   a. staying indoors
   b. identifying criminals
   c. being auxiliary police
   d. surveillance

6. Substitution of an alternative set of goals and means for conventional ones is called:
   a. innovation
   b. ritualism
   c. rebellion
   d. retreatism

7. Agnew suggests that criminality is the direct result of:
   a. negative affective states
   b. poverty
   c. underclass
   d. incivility

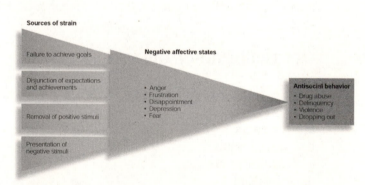

8. The elements of general strain theory include all of the following **except**:
   a. introduction into a life of poverty
   b. failure to achieve positively valued goals
   c. disjunction of expectations and achievements
   d. removal of positively valued stimuli

9. According to general strain theory, why is it that some people who experience strain do **not** fall into a life of crime and eventually resort to criminality?
    a. they do not really experience strain.
    b. they have coping skills.
    c. people help them out.
    d. they live in good communities.

10. One of the biggest question marks about GST is its ability to adequately explain what concerning the crime rate?
    a. age differences
    b. racial differences
    c. economic status differences
    d. gender differences

11. What occurs when the rules expressed in the criminal law clash with the demands of group conduct norms?
    a. focal concerns
    b. strain
    c. culture conflict
    d. concentration effect

12. Who wrote *Culture Conflict and Crime*, a theoretical attempt to link cultural adaptation to criminality?
    a. Cloward
    b. Miller
    c. Sellin
    d. Ohlin

13. Which of the following is one of Miller's lower class focal concerns?
    a. trouble
    b. toughness
    c. smartness
    d. achievement

14. Being independent of authority figures, such as the police, teachers, and parents is an example of:
    a. trouble
    b. autonomy
    c. toughness
    d. smartness

15. The author of the classic book, *Delinquent Boys*, was:
    a. Freud
    b. Martin
    c. Sutherland
    d. Cohen

16. A truant who engages in petty or status offenses is a:
    a. corner boy
    b. college boy
    c. delinquent boy
    d. conflict boy

17. One who embraces the cultural and social values of the middle class is:
    a. a corner boy
    b. a college boy
    c. a delinquent boy
    d. a conflict boy

18. One who adopts a set on norms and principles in direct opposition to middle-class values is:
    a. a corner boy
    b. a college boy
    c. a delinquent boy
    d. a conflict boy

19. Overly intense responses that seem disproportionate to the stimuli that trigger them are called:
    a. reaction formations
    b. conduct norms
    c. cultural deviance
    d. focal concerns

20. Whose names do we associate with concentric zones and the concept of transitional neighborhoods?
    a. Durkheim and Miller
    b. Merton and Miller
    c. Cloward and Ohlin
    d. Shaw and McKay

21. The concept that people in all strata of society share the same success goals but those in the lower class have limited means of achieving them is known as:
    a. differential opportunity
    b. differential association
    c. differential reinforcement
    d. differential timing

22. Those who are double failures and unable to gain success through legitimate means and unwilling to do so through illegal ones are likely to join which of the following gangs?
    a. criminal
    b. conflict
    c. retreatist
    d. corner boy gang

23. Gangs that exist in stable slum areas in which close connections among adolescent, young adults and adult offenders create environments for successful enterprises are known as:
    a. criminal gangs
    b. conflict gangs
    c. retreatist gangs
    d. corner boy gangs

24. Gangs that develop in communities unable to provide either legitimate or illegitimate opportunities are known as:
    a. criminal gangs
    b. conflict gangs
    c. retreatist gangs
    d. corner boy gangs

25. The foremost structural theory based crime reduction strategy today is known as:
    a. War on Poverty
    b. Operation Weed and Seed
    c. VISTA (the urban Peace Corps)
    d. Head Start

ESSAY QUESTIONS

1. Describe three major issues concerning poverty in America.

2.   Discuss the concept of social disorganization.

3.   Describe the association between collective efficacy and crime.

4.   Discuss the term anomie, including the points of view of both Durkheim and Merton.

5. Discuss the concept of cultural deviance.

MATCHING

1. Siege Mentality
2. Stratified Society
3. Concentration Effect
4. Incivilities
5. Collective Efficacy
6. Institutional social control
7. Anomie
8. American Dream
9. Status Frustration
10. Reaction Formation

A. Mutual trust, a willingness to intervene in the supervision of children, and the maintenance of public order
B. Outside world is considered the enemy out to destroy the neighborhood
C. Rowdy youth, trash and litter, graffiti, abandoned storefronts, burned-out buildings, littered lots, strangers
D. Accumulating material goods and wealth via open individual competition
E. Created by the unequal distribution of wealth, power, and prestige
F. Overly intense responses that seem disproportionate to the stimuli that trigger them
G. Lower-class youths experience a form of culture conflict because social conditions make them incapable of achieving success legitimately
H. Rules of behavior have broken down or become inoperative
I. working- and middle-class families flee inner-city poverty areas in which elements of the most disadvantaged population are consolidated in urban ghettos
J. Social institutions such as schools and churches

CHAPTER 6 ANSWER KEY

Fill in the Blank Answers

1. social strata
2. early childhood
3. economic
4. cultural transmission
5. poverty and social disorder
6. collective efficacy
7. mechanical solidarity
8. relative deprivation
9. negative affective states
10. focal concerns

True/False Answers

1.	T	6.	F	11.	T
2.	T	7.	F	12.	F
3.	F	8.	F	13.	T
4.	T	9.	F	14.	F
5.	T	10.	T	15.	T

Multiple Choice Answers

1.	C	11.	C	21.	D
2.	A	12.	C	22.	C
3.	B	13.	D	23.	A
4.	B	14.	B	24.	B
5.	D	15.	D	25.	B
6.	C	16.	A		
7.	A	17.	B		
8.	A	18.	C		
9.	B	19.	A		
10.	D	20.	D		

Essay Questions

1. Pages 176-179
2. Pages 180-184
3. Pages 188-190
4. Pages 191-193
5. Pages 198-203

Matching Answers

1.	B	6.	J
2.	E	7.	H
3.	I	8.	D
4.	C	9.	G
5.	A	10.	F

SOCIAL PROCESS THEORIES

OUTLINE

Chapter 7

Social Process Theories

LEARNING OBJECTIVES

1. Be familiar with the concept of socialization

2. Discuss the effect of schools, family, and friends on crime

3. Be able to discuss the differences of learning, control, and reaction

4. Be familiar with the concept of differential association

5. Be able to discuss what is meant by a definition toward criminality

6. Understand the concept of neutralization

7. Be able to discuss the relationship between self-concept and crime

8. Know the elements of the social bond

9. Describe the labeling process and how it leads to criminal careers

10. Be familiar with the concepts of primary and secondary deviance

11. Show how the process of labeling leads to criminal careers

KEYWORDS AND DEFINITIONS

Social process theory: the view that if relationships are positive and supportive, people can succeed within the rules of society; if these relationships are dysfunctional and destructive, conventional success may be impossible, and criminal solutions may become a feasible alternative.

Social learning theory: the view that human behavior is modeled through observation of human social interactions, either directly from observing those who are close and from intimate contact, or indirectly through the media. Interactions that are rewarded are copied, while those that are punished are avoided.

Social control theory: maintains that everyone has the potential to become a criminal but that most people are controlled by their bonds to society.

Social reaction theory: the view that people become criminals when significant members of society label them as such, and they accept those labels as a personal identity; also known as labeling theory.

Labeling theory: theory that views society as creating deviance through a system of social control agencies that designate certain individuals as deviants. The stigmatized individual is made to feel unwanted in the normal social order. Eventually, the individual begins to believe that the label is accurate, assumes it as a personal identity, and enters into a deviant or criminal career.

Differential association theory: criminality stemmed neither from individual traits nor from socioeconomic position; instead, he believed it to be a function of a learning process that could affect any individual in any culture.

Differential reinforcement theory: attempts to explain crime as a type of learned behavior; first proposed by Ronald Akers in collaboration with Robert Burgess in 1966, it is a version of the social learning view that employs both differential association concepts along with elements of psychological learning theory.

Direct conditioning: behavior is reinforced by being either rewarded or punished while interacting with others; also called differential reinforcement.

Differential reinforcement: Behavior is reinforced by being either rewarded or punished while interacting with others; also called direct conditioning.

Negative reinforcement: when behavior is punished.

Neutralization theory: views the process of becoming a criminal as a learning experience in which potential delinquents and criminals master techniques that enable them to counterbalance or neutralize conventional values and drift back and forth between illegitimate and conventional behavior.

Subterranean values: morally tinged influences that have become entrenched in the culture but are publicly condemned.

Drift: refers to the movement from one extreme of behavior to another, resulting in behavior that is sometimes unconventional, free, or deviant and at other times constrained and sober.

Self-control: a strong moral sense, which renders people incapable of hurting others and violating social norms.

Commitment to conformity: conformity is adhered to because there is a real, present, and logical reason to obey the rules of society.

Containment theory: the idea that a strong self-image insulates a youth from the pressures and pulls of crimogenic influences in the environment.

Normative groups: groups, such as the high school in-crowd, which conform to the social rules of society.

Social bond: the ties that bind people to society; according to Hirschi, elements of social bonds include attachment, commitment, involvement, and belief.

Symbolic interaction theory: holds that people communicate via symbols – gestures, signs, words, or images – that stand for or represent something else.

Stigma: an enduring label that taints a person's identity and changes him or her in the eyes of others.

Differential social control: the process of labeling may produce a re-evaluation of the self, which reflects actual or perceived appraisals made by others.

Reflective role taking: when youths believe that others view them as antisocial or troublemakers, they take on attitudes and roles that reflect this assumption; they expect to become suspects and then to be rejected.

Retrospective reading: people begin to react to the label description and what it signifies instead of reacting to the actual behavior of the person who bears it.

Dramatization of evil: as the negative feedback of law enforcement agencies, parents, friends, teachers, and other figures amplifies the force of the original label, stigmatized offenders may begin to re-evaluate their own identities. The person becomes the thing he or she is described as being.

Primary deviance: norm violations or crimes that have very little influence on the actor and can be quickly forgotten.

Secondary deviance: occurs when a deviant event comes to the attention of significant others or social control agents who apply a negative label.

Contextual discrimination: refers to judges' practices in some jurisdictions of imposing harsher sentences on African Americans only in some instances, such as when they victimize whites and not other African Americans.

Diversion programs: designed to remove both juvenile and adult offenders from the normal channels of the criminal justice process by placing them in programs designed for rehabilitation.

CHAPTER OUTLINE

I.   Socialization and crime
   A.   Family relations
      1.   Children from households characterized by conflict and tension are susceptible to the crime-promoting forces in the environment.
      2.   Living in a disadvantaged neighborhood places terrific strain on family functioning.
      3.   Relationship between family structure and crime is critical when the high rates of divorce and single parents are considered.
      4.   Family conflict and discord are more important determinants of behavior than family structure.
      5.   Children living with a stepparent exhibit
         a.   As many problems as youth in single-parent families
         b.   Considerably more problems than those who are living with both biological parents

B. Child abuse and crime
   1. There is a suspected link between child abuse, neglect, sexual abuse, and crime.
   2. The effect of the family on delinquency has also been observed in other cultures.

C. Educational experience
   1. Educational process and adolescent achievement in school have been linked to criminality.
   2. Schools contribute to criminality in that when they label problem youths they set them apart from conventional society.
   3. Many school dropouts, especially those who have been expelled, face a significant chance of entering a criminal career.
   4. Schools can also be the scene of crime and violence.
   5. School level and size have a significant impact on the likelihood of experiencing theft and violence.
   6. Presence of weapons and violence

D. Peer relations
   1. General
      a. Peer influence may be a universal norm.
      b. Peer relations are a vital aspect of maturation.
      c. Adolescents feel a persistent pressure to conform to group values.
      d. When peer pressure is exerted from positive relationships, peers guide one another and help friends cope with aggressive impulses.
      e. When the peer group is not among friends who are positive influences, adolescent criminal activity can begin to be initiated as a group process.
   2. Peer rejection/peer acceptance
      a. Peers may abandon or snub those who are unpopular, out of control, or unruly.
      b. Peer rejection may help increase and sustain antisocial behaviors.
      c. Having prosocial friends who are committed to conventional success may help shield kids from crime.
   3. Peers and criminality
      a. Paths to the onset and continuation of criminality
         1) Delinquent friends cause law-abiding youth to "get in trouble."
         2) Antisocial youths seek out and join up with like-minded friends.
         3) Antisocial friends help youths maintain delinquent careers and obstruct the aging-out process.
         4) Troubled kids choose delinquent peers out of necessity rather than desire.
      b. Criminal peers may exert tremendous influence on behavior, attitudes, and beliefs.
      c. Some children join more than one deviant group.
         1) Leadership role in one
         2) Follower in another

E. Institutional involvement and belief
   1. Those who regularly attend religious services should also eschew crime and other antisocial behaviors.
   2. Association between religious attendance and belief and delinquent behavior patterns is negligible and insignificant.
   3. Participation seems to be a more significant inhibitor of crime than merely having religious beliefs and values.

F. The effects of socialization on crime
    1. Socialization, not the social structure, determines life chances.
    2. The more social problems encountered during the socialization process, the greater the likelihood that youths will encounter difficulties and obstacles.

II. Social learning theory
    A. Differential association theory
        1. General
            a. Contained in Edwin H. Sutherland's Principles of Criminology
            b. One of the most enduring explanations of criminal behavior
            c. Crime is a function of a learning process that could affect any individual in any culture.
        2. Principles of differential association
            a. Criminal behavior is learned.
            b. Learning is a by-product of interaction.
            c. Learning occurs within intimate groups.
            d. Criminal techniques are learned.
            e. Perceptions of legal code influence motives and drives.
            f. A person becomes a criminal when he or she perceives more favorable than unfavorable consequences to violating the law.
            g. Differential associations may vary in frequency, duration, priority, and intensity.
            h. The process of learning criminal behavior by association with criminal and anticriminal patterns involves all of the mechanisms involved in any other learning process.
            i. Criminal behavior is an expression of general needs and values, but it is not excused by those general needs and values because noncriminal behavior is also an expression of those same needs and values.
        3. Testing differential association theory
            a. Relatively sparse research
            b. Difficult to conceptualize the principles of the theory
            c. Notable research efforts have shown a correlation between three variables
                1) Having deviant friends
                2) Holding deviant attitudes
                3) Committing deviant acts
            d. Relevant in trying to explain
                1) Onset of substance abuse
                2) Career in the drug trade
        4. Analysis of differential association theory
            a. Some oppose the idea that criminals are people "properly" socialized into a deviant subculture.
            b. Fails to explain why one youth who is exposed to delinquent definitions eventually succumbs to them, while another does not.
            c. Important place in the study of criminal behavior
    B. Differential reinforcement theory
        1. Akers and Burgess
        2. Employs both differential association concepts and elements of psychological learning theory
        3. Same processes used in learning both deviant and conventional behavior
        4. Several learning processes shape behavior.
            a. Direct conditioning or differential reinforcement

          b.   Negative reinforcement
5.   People evaluate their behavior through interactions with significant others and groups in their lives.
6.   Principal influence on behavior comes from those who
        a.   Control reinforcement and punishment
        b.   Expose them to behavioral models and normative definitions
7.   Testing differential reinforcement
        a.   Strong association between drug and alcohol abuse and social learning variables.
        b.   Learning-deviant behavior link is not static.

C.   Neutralization theory
1.   Sykes and Matza
2.   Delinquents learn to counterbalance or neutralize conventional values so they can drift back and forth between legitimate and illegitimate behavior.
3.   Subterranean values
4.   Drift – moving from legal to illegal behavior
5.   Bases of the theory
        a.   Criminals voice guilt over illegal acts.
        b.   Offenders respect and admire honest, law-abiding people.
        c.   Criminals draw a line between whom they can victimize and whom they cannot.
        d.   Criminals are not immune to the demands of conformity.
6.   Techniques of neutralization
        a.   Denial of responsibility
        b.   Denial of injury
        c.   Denial of victim
        d.   Condemning the condemners
        e.   Appeal to higher loyalties
7.   Testing neutralization theory
        a.   Results have been inconclusive
        b.   Weight of evidence is that
               1)   Most delinquents disapprove of violence.
               2)   Neutralizations enable youth to engage in delinquency.
        c.   Major contribution to crime and delinquency literature

D.   Are learning theories valid?
1.   Explain the onset of criminal behavior
2.   Subject to criticism
3.   Who was the first teacher?
4.   Fail to explain spontaneous and wanton acts of violence
5.   Maintain an important place in the study of crime and delinquency

III. Social control theory
    A.   Self-concept and crime
        1.   Early control theories speculated that low self-control was a product of weak self-concept and poor self-esteem.
        2.   Reckless' containment theory argued that strong self-image insulates one from the pressures and pulls of criminogenic influences in society.
        3.   Kaplan argued that
            a.   Youths with poor self-concepts are the ones most likely to engage in delinquent behavior.
            b.   Successful participation in criminality actually helps raise their self-esteem.

B. Hirschi's social bond theory (also called social control theory)
   1. Onset of criminality is linked to the weakening of the bonds to society.
   2. All individuals are potential law violators.
   3. Without these social ties or bonds, a person is free to commit criminal acts.
   4. Elements of social bond
      a. Attachment
      b. Commitment
      c. Involvement
      d. Belief
   5. Testing social bond theory
      a. Hirschi found considerable evidence to support social bond theory.
      b. Corroborated by numerous research studies that show delinquents detached from society.
      c. Cross-national surveys have also supported the general findings of Hirschi's theory.
   6. Opposing views
      a. Research efforts do show that delinquents maintain relationships with deviant peers and are influenced by members of their deviant peer group.
      b. Not all elements of the bond are equal.
      c. Rather than deter delinquency, attachment to deviant peers may support and nurture antisocial behavior.
      d. Some question as to whether the theory can explain all modes of criminality
      e. Social bonds seem to change over time.
      f. Agnew claims that Hirschi miscalculated the direction of the relationship between criminality and a weakened social bond.

IV. Social reaction theory
   A. General
      1. Roots are found in symbolic interaction theory.
      2. People communicate via symbols that stand for or represent something else.
      3. Both positive and negative labels involve subjective interpretation of behavior.
      4. If a devalued status is conferred by a significant other, the negative label may cause permanent harm.
      5. Depending on the visibility of the label and the manner and severity with which it is applied, a person may have an increasing commitment to a deviant career.
   B. Crime and labeling theory
      1. Crime and deviance are defined
         a. By the social audience's reaction to people and their behavior and the subsequent effects of that reaction
         b. Not by the moral content of the illegal act itself
      2. Social reaction theory argues that such crimes as murder, rape, and assault are only bad or evil because people label them as such.
      3. People who create rules are moral entrepreneurs.
      4. Crime is a subjective concept whose definition is totally dependent on the viewing audience.
   C. Differential enforcement
      1. An important principle of social reaction theory is that the law is differentially applied.
      2. Social reaction theorists also argue that the content of the law reflects power relationships in society.

3. The law
   a. Favors the powerful members of society who direct its content
   b. Penalizes people whose actions represent a threat to those in control

D. Becoming labeled
  1. Social reaction theory is not especially concerned with why people originally engage in acts that result in their being labeled.
  2. Not all labeled people have chosen to engage in label-producing activities.

E. Consequences of labeling
  1. Social reaction theorists are most concerned with two effects of labeling.
    a. The creation of stigma
    b. The effect on self-image
  2. Public condemnation an important part of the label-producing process.
  3. Differential social control
    a. Process of labeling may produce a re-evaluation of the self, which reflects actual or perceived appraisals made by others.
    b. When they believe that others view them as antisocial or troublemakers
      1) They take on attitudes and roles that reflect this assumption
      2) They expect to become suspects and then to be rejected
  4. Joining deviant cliques
    a. Those labeled as deviant, they may join up with similarly outcast delinquent peers who facilitate their behavior.
    b. Antisocial behavior becomes habitual and automatic
    c. May acquire motives to deviate from social norms
  5. Retrospective reading
    a. Labels tend to redefine the whole person.
    b. People begin to react to the label description and what it signifies instead of reacting to the actual behavior of the person who bears it.
    c. Past of the labeled person is reviewed and re-evaluated to fit his or her current status.
    d. We can now understand what prompted his current behavior.
    e. The label must be accurate.
  6. Dramatization of evil
    a. Labels become the basis of personal identity.
    b. Stigmatized offenders may begin to re-evaluate their own identities.
    c. The person becomes what he is described as.
    d. This process is called the dramatization of evil.

F. Primary and secondary deviance
  1. Primary deviance – norm violations or crimes that have very little influence on the actor and can be quickly forgotten
  2. Secondary
    a. Deviant event comes to the attention of significant others or social control agents who apply a negative label
    b. Involves resocialization into a deviant role
    c. Produces a deviance amplification effect

G. Research on social reaction theory
  1. Who gets labeled?

          a.   The poor and powerless people are victimized by the law and justice system

          b.   Reviews indicate that race bias adversely influences decision making in many critical areas of the justice system.

          c.   Little definitive evidence exists that the justice system is inherently unfair and biased.

     2.   Effects of labeling

          a.   Empirical evidence exists that indicates negative labels actually have a dramatic influence on self-image and subsequent behavior.

          b.   Family interaction can influence the labeling process.

     3.   Labeling and criminal careers

          a.   Empirical evidence supports the fact that labeling plays an important role in persistent offending.

          b.   Official intervention actually increases the probability that a labeled person will get involved in subsequent involvement in antisocial behavior.

  H.   Is labeling theory valid?

     1.   Its inability to specify the conditions that must exist before an act or individual is labeled deviant.

     2.   Fails to explain differences in crime rates

     3.   Ignores the onset of deviant behavior

     4.   Tittle claims that many criminal careers occur without labeling.

     5.   Labeling reexamined

          a.   Important contributions to the study of criminality

             1)   The labeling perspective identifies the role played by social control agents in the process of crime causation.

             2)   Labeling theory recognizes that criminality is not a disease or pathological behavior.

             3)   Shows that the concepts of primary and secondary deviance must be interpreted and treated differently

          b.   Focus on interaction as well as the situations surrounding the crime

V.   Evaluating social process theories

  A.   Social process theories suggest that criminal behavior is part of the socialization process.

  B.   Theories do not always account for the patterns and fluctuations in the crime rate.

VI. Public policy implications of social process theory

  A.   Social process theories have had a major influence on policymaking since the 1950s.

  B.   Learning theories have greatly influenced the way criminal offenders are dealt with and treated.

  C.   Control theories have also influenced criminal justice and other public policy.

  D.   Labeling theorists caution against too much intervention.

  E.   The influence of labeling theory can be viewed in the development of diversion and restitution programs.

  F.   Despite their good intentions, stigma-reducing programs have not met with great success.

CHAPTER SUMMARY

This chapter deals with the association between socialization and crime. Social process theories argue that socialization, not the social structure, determines life chances. The more social problems encountered during the socialization process, the greater the likelihood that youths will encounter difficulties and obstacles. The relationship between family structure and crime is critical when the high rates of divorce and single parents are considered, but family conflict and discord are more important determinants of behavior than are family structure. The effect of the family on delinquency has also been observed in other cultures. Educational process and adolescent achievement in school have been linked to criminality. Schools contribute to criminality in that when they label problem youths they set them apart from conventional society. Many school dropouts, especially those who have been expelled, face a significant chance of entering a criminal career. Peer influence may be a universal norm. Peer relations are a vital aspect of maturation and adolescents feel a persistent pressure to conform to group values. Those who regularly attend religious services should also eschew crime and other antisocial behaviors. The association between religious attendance and belief and delinquent behavior patterns is negligible and insignificant; participation seems to be a more significant inhibitor of crime than merely having religious beliefs and values.

Differential association theory, contained in Edwin H. Sutherland's Principles of Criminology, is one of the most enduring explanations of criminal behavior. The principles of differential association include 1) criminal behavior is learned; 2) learning is a by-product of interaction; 3) learning occurs within intimate groups; 4) criminal techniques are learned; 5) perceptions of legal code influence motives and drives; 6) a person becomes a criminal when he or she perceives more favorable than unfavorable consequences to violating the law; 7) differential associations may vary in frequency, duration, priority, and intensity; 8) The process of learning criminal behavior by association with criminal and anticriminal patterns involves all of the mechanisms involved in any other learning process; and 9) criminal behavior is an expression of general needs and values, but it is not excused by those general needs and values because noncriminal behavior is also an expression of those same needs and values. Differential reinforcement theory by Akers and Burgess employs both differential association concepts and elements of psychological learning theory. The same processes used in learning both deviant and conventional behavior. Several learning processes shape behavior, including direct conditioning or differential reinforcement and negative reinforcement.

Sykes and Matza's neutralization theory argues that delinquents learn to counterbalance or neutralize conventional values so they can drift back and forth between legitimate and illegitimate behavior. The techniques of neutralization include the denial of responsibility, the denial of injury, the denial of a victim, the condemning of the condemners, and an appeal to higher loyalties. Early control theories speculated that low self-control was a product of weak self-concept and poor self-esteem. The major social control theory is Hirschi's social bond theory (also called social control theory) which states that the onset of criminality is linked to the weakening of the bonds to society. Hirschi argues that all individuals are potential law violators and without these social ties or bonds a person is free to commit criminal acts. The four elements of the bond are attachment, commitment, involvement, and belief.

The roots of social reaction theory are found in symbolic interaction theory that postulates people communicate via symbols that stand for or represent something else. One of the most prominent social reaction theories is labeling theory. Under this approach, crime and deviance are defined by the social audience's reaction to people and their behavior and the subsequent effects of that reaction, not by the moral content of the illegal act itself. Crime, therefore, is a subjective concept with a definition that is totally dependent on the viewing audience. An important principle of social reaction theory is that the law is differentially applied because the law favors the powerful members of society who direct its content and penalizes people whose actions represent a threat to those in control.

Social reaction theory (labeling theory) is not especially concerned with why people originally engage in acts that result in their being labeled; they are most concerned with two effects of labeling: the creation of stigma and the effect on self-image. One key component of labeling theory is retrospective reading. Labels tend to redefine the whole person and people begin to react to the label description and what it signifies instead of reacting to the actual behavior of the person who bears it. The past of the labeled person is reviewed and re-evaluated to fit his or her current status. Society can now understand what prompted his or her current behavior. Labels become the basis of personal identity and stigmatized offenders may begin to re-evaluate their own identities. The person becomes as described in a process called the dramatization of evil. Two other major concepts of social reaction theory are primary and secondary deviance. Primary deviance means norm violations or crimes that have very little influence on the actor and can be quickly forgotten. Secondary deviance refers to the deviant event that comes to the attention of significant others or social control agents who apply a negative label. Secondary deviance involves resocialization into a deviant role and produces a deviance amplification effect.

STUDENT EXERCISES

Exercise 1

Go online to http://www.ncjrs.org/pdffiles1/ojjdp/173423.pdf and read the article, "Families and Schools Together: Building Relationships" by Lynn McDonald and Heather E. Frey. After reading the article, write a one to two page essay that compares and contrasts McDonald and Frey's view with that of Hirschi's social bond theory.

Exercise 2

Rather than explain the causes of crime, social control theories explain why most people do not commit crime. Hirschi's social bond theory explains this through the four bonds of attachment, commitment, involvement, and belief. Think back to your younger years and make a listing for each of those bonds describing your life and what happened with respect to each of the bonds as your life progressed. For example, under involvement – I played high school baseball; under attachment – I strongly identified with my family. How does your list compare with those of your classmates?

CRIMINOLOGY WEB LINKS

http://www.allaboutkids.umn.edu/WingfortheWeb/42189%20AmSch_Libbey.pdf
The article by Heather P. Libbey at this website provides an interesting look at the relationship between attachment to school and the impact on students' lives.

http://www.pineforge.com/isw4/overviews/pdfs/Svensson.pdf
The article by Robert Svensson at this website provides the results of an investigation into gender differences in adolescent drug use in terms of parental monitoring and peer deviance.

http://www.findarticles.com/p/articles/mi_m0825/is_4_61/ai_61522787
This website contains the article, "Hirschi's Social Control Theory: A Sociological Perspective on Drug Abuse Among Persons with Disabilities" by Reginald J. Alston, Debra Harley, and Karen Lenhoff. The authors examine social control theory as an explanation for drug abuse among the disabled.

http://www.shsu.edu/~piic/summer2002/Hanser.htm
This article provides an excellent discussion of the labeling theory paradigm as an explanation for the complex developments that lead from an inmate's first rape victimization to the eventual acceptance of a new label.

http://www.findarticles.com/p/articles/mi_m2248/is_n125_v32/ai_19417313
This article looks at social control theory, labeling theory, and the delivery of services for drug abuse to adolescents under the supervision of the juvenile justice system. This article will provide you with an understanding of how two theories can explain the same phenomenon.

TEST BANK

FILL-IN THE BLANKS

1. For some time, family relationships have been considered a major determinant of _____.

2. The educational process and adolescent achievement in school have been linked to _____.

3. _____ rejection helps lock already aggressive kids into a cycle of persistent violence that is likely to continue into early adulthood.

4. _____ seems to be a more significant inhibitor of crime than merely having religious beliefs and values.

5. _____ _____ occurs when behavior is reinforced by being either rewarded or punished while interacting with others.

6. _____ _____ are morally tinged influences that have become entrenched in the culture but are publicly condemned.

7. _____ refers to the movement from one extreme of behavior to another, resulting in behavior that is sometimes unconventional, free, or deviant and at other times constrained and sober.

8. _____ _____ argues that a strong self-image insulates a youth from the pressures and pulls of crimogenic influences in the environment.

9. _____ _____ _____ states that people communicate via symbols – gestures, signs, words, or images – that stand for or represent something else.

10. _____ _____ is a process in which the past of the labeled person is reviewed and re-evaluated to fit his or her current status.

TRUE/FALSE QUESTIONS

1. T/F Many criminologists agree that a person's place in the social structure alone can control or predict the onset of criminality.

2. T/F The relationship between family structure and crime is critical when the high rates of divorce and single parents are considered.

3. T/F Schools contribute to criminality because when they label problem youths they set them apart from conventional society.

4. T/F School level and size have little impact on the likelihood of experiencing theft and violence.

5. T/F As children move through the life course, antisocial friends help youths maintain delinquent careers and obstruct the aging-out process.

6. T/F Social learning theory assumes people are born good and learn to be bad.

7. T/F According to differential association theory, criminal behavior is an expression of general needs and values and is excused by those general needs and values.

8. T/F Negative reinforcement occurs when behavior is punished.

9. T/F Sykes and Matza suggest that people develop a distinct set of justifications for their law-violating behavior.

10. T/F Self-control is manifested through a strong moral sense, which renders people incapable of hurting others and violating social norms.

11. T/F Hirschi's version of social control theory has not been corroborated by other research studies.

12. T/F People interpret symbolic gestures from others and incorporate them in their self-image.

13. T/F Social reaction theory is especially concerned with why people originally engage in acts that result in their being labeled.

14. T/F Secondary deviance involves resocialization into a deviant role.

15. T/F In an in-depth analysis of research on the crime-producing effects of labels, criminologist Charles Tittle found little evidence that stigma produces crime.

MULTIPLE CHOICE QUESTIONS

1. The social process theories include all of the following **except**:
   a. social learning theory
   b. social control theory
   c. labeling theory
   d. theory of anomie

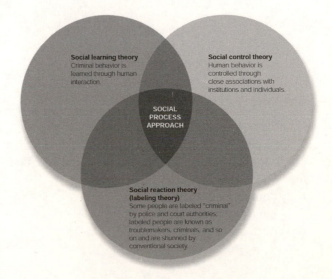

2. Which is not one of Sutherland's principles of differential association?
   a.   Criminal behavior is learned.
   b.   Learning criminal behavior is different from other learning.
   c.   Learning is a by-product of interaction.
   d.   Criminal techniques are learned.

3. Punishing behavior is referred to as:
   a.   differential reinforcement
   b.   direct conditioning
   c.   negative reinforcement
   d.   differential conditioning

4. Morally tinged influences that have become entrenched in the culture but are publicly condemned are called:
   a.   techniques
   b.   drift
   c.   neutralizations
   d.   subterranean values

5. The movement from one extreme of behavior to another, resulting in behavior that is sometimes unconventional, free, or deviant and at other times constrained and sober is called:
   a.   drift
   b.   schizophrenia
   c.   neutralization
   d.   denial

6. Which of the following is **not** one of Sykes and Matza's techniques of neutralization?
   a.   denial of victim
   b.   denial of responsibility
   c.   denial of crime
   d.   condemning the condemners

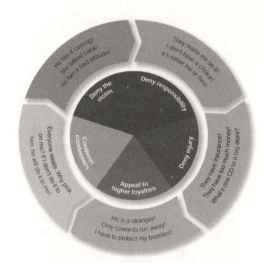

7. The theory that argued that a strong self-image insulates a youth from the pressures and pulls of crimogenic influences in the environment is called:
   a.   social bond theory
   b.   containment theory
   c.   neutralization theory
   d.   normative theory

8. A person's sensitivity to and interest in others is known as:
   a. involvement
   b. attachment
   c. commitment
   d. belief

9. According to Hirschi, which social institution is the most important attachment an individual should have?
   a. parents
   b. schools
   c. peers
   d. police

10. Time, energy, and effort expended in conventional lines of action such as getting an education and saving money for the future is known as:
    a. attachment
    b. belief
    c. involvement
    d. commitment

11. When people who live in the same social setting often share values, sensitivity to the rights of others and admiration for the legal code, it is known as:
    a. attachment
    b. involvement
    c. belief
    d. commitment

12. Labeling theory is also known as:
    a. social control theory
    b. social learning theory
    c. social reaction theory
    d. neutralization theory

13. The important principle of social reaction theory that the law is applied in a manner benefiting those who hold economic and social power and penalizing the powerless is called:
    a. differential association
    b. differential enforcement
    c. retrospective interpretation
    d. deviance amplification

14. What is **not** one of the concerns of labeling theory?
    a. why people are labeled
    b. why people originally engage in criminal acts
    c. the effects of labeling
    d. how the label is applied

15. What is an enduring label that taints a person's identity and changes him or her in the eyes of others called?
    a. primary deviance
    b. reflective role taking
    c. differential social control
    d. stigma

16. The process of labeling produces a re-evaluation of the self, which reflects actual or perceived appraisals made by others. This re-evaluation is called:
    a. reflective role taking
    b. stigma
    c. differential social control
    d. secondary deviance

17. When youths believe that others view them as antisocial or troublemakers they take on attitudes and roles that reflect this assumption; they expect to become suspects and then to be rejected. This process is called:
    a. reflective role taking
    b. stigma
    c. differential social control
    d. secondary deviance

18. The process in which the past of the labeled person is reviewed and re-evaluated to fit his or her current status is called:
    a. deviance amplification
    b. dramatization of evil
    c. reflective role taking
    d. retrospective reading

19. As the negative feedback of law enforcement agencies, parents, friends, teachers, and other figures amplifies the force of the original label, stigmatized offenders may begin to re-evaluate their own identities in a process called:
    a. deviance amplification
    b. dramatization of evil
    c. reflective role taking
    d. retrospective reading

20. Norm violations or crimes that have very little influence on the actor and can be quickly forgotten are called:
    a. contextual discrimination
    b. deviance amplification
    c. primary deviance
    d. secondary deviance

21. The concept of _____ occurs when a deviant event comes to the attention of significant others or social control agents who apply a negative label.
    a. contextual discrimination
    b. deviance amplification
    c. primary deviance
    d. secondary deviance

22. The term that refers to judges' practices in some jurisdictions of imposing harsher sentences on African Americans only in some instances, such as when they victimize whites and not other African Americans, is called:
    a. contextual discrimination
    b. deviance amplification
    c. primary deviance
    d. secondary deviance

23. A person who has been arrested and therefore labeled multiple times over the course of his or her offending career is called a:
    a. labeled person
    b. chronic offender
    c. deviant
    d. career offender

24. What is designed to remove both juvenile and adult offenders from the normal channels of the criminal justice process by placing them in programs designed for rehabilitation?
    a. restitution
    b. diversion programs
    c. probation
    d. parole

25. When an offender is asked to either pay back the victim of the crime for any loss incurred, or to do some useful work in the community in lieu of receiving a court-ordered sentence, it is known as:
    a. restitution
    b. diversion
    c. probation
    d. parole

ESSAY QUESTIONS

1. Discuss socialization and the effect of schools, family, and friends on crime.

2. Discuss how criminal behavior is a function of a learning process according to differential association theory.

3. List the techniques of neutralization and describe the concept of neutralization.

4.   Describe the elements of the social bond as contained in social bond theory.

5.   Describe the labeling process and how it leads to criminal careers.

MATCHING

1. Self-Control
2. Commitment to Conformity
3. Normative Groups
4. Symbolic Interaction Theory
5. Travis Hirschi
6. Primary Deviance
7. Drift
8. Stigma
9. Sykes and Matza
10. Secondary Deviance

A. Social bond theory
B. Norm violations or crimes that have very little influence on the actor
C. A strong moral sense
D. Created by an enduring label that taints a person's identity and changes him or her in the eyes of others
E. Techniques of neutralization
F. There is a real, present, and logical reason to obey the rules of society
G. Occurs when a deviant event comes to the attention of significant others or social control agents who apply a negative label
H. People communicate via gestures, signs, words, or images that represent something else
I. The movement from one extreme of behavior to another, resulting in behavior that is sometimes unconventional, free, or deviant and at other times constrained and sober
J. The high school "in-crowd"

CHAPTER 7 ANSWER KEY

Fill in the Blank Answers

1. behavior
2. criminality
3. peer
4. participation
5. differential reinforcement (or direct conditioning)
6. subterranean values
7. drift
8. containment theory
9. symbolic interaction theory
10. retrospective reading

True/False Answers

1.	F	6.	T	11.	F
2.	T	7.	F	12.	T
3.	T	8.	T	13.	F
4.	F	9.	T	14.	T
5.	T	10.	T	15.	T

Multiple Choice Answers

1.	D	11.	D	21.	D
2.	B	12.	A	22.	A
3.	C	13.	B	23.	B
4.	D	14.	B	24.	B
5.	A	15.	D	25.	A
6.	C	16.	C		
7.	B	17.	A		
8.	B	18.	D		
9.	A	19.	B		
10.	D	20.	C		

Essay Questions

1. Pages 214-221
2. Pages 222-225
3. Pages 226-228
4. Pages 229-232
5. Pages 232-238

Matching Answers

1.	C	6.	B
2.	F	7.	I
3.	J	8.	D
4.	H	9.	E
5.	A	10.	G

SOCIAL CONFLICT THEORIES

Critical Criminology and Restorative Justice

OUTLINE

- Marxist Thought
- Developing a Conflict-Based Theory of Crime
- Social Conflict Theory
- Critical Criminology
- Contemporary Forms of Critical Theory
- Race, Culture, Gender, and Criminology: Capitalism and Patriarchy
- Public Policy Implications of Social Conflict Theory: Restorative Justice
- Comparative Criminology: Practicing Restorative Justice Abroad

Chapter 8

Social Conflict Theories:
Critical Criminology and Restorative Justice

LEARNING OBJECTIVES

1. Be familiar with the concept of social conflict and how it shapes behavior

2. Be able to discuss elements of conflict in the justice system

3. Be familiar with the idea of critical criminology

4. Be able to discuss the difference between structural and instrumental Marxism

5. Know the various techniques of critical research

6. Be able to discuss the term left realism

7. Understand the concept of patriarchy

8. Know what is meant by feminist criminology

9. Be able to discuss peacemaking

10. Understand the concept of restorative justice

KEYWORDS AND DEFINITIONS

Marxist criminologists: conflict theorists who stress the role that the capitalist economic system has on crime rates.

Radical criminologists: criminologists who view crime as a product of the capitalist system.

Social conflict theory: criminological theories that allege that criminal behavior is a function of social conflict, a reaction to the unfair distribution of wealth and power in society.

Communist manifesto: Marx focused his attention on the economic conditions perpetuated by the capitalist system. He stated that its development had turned workers into a dehumanized mass who lived an existence that was at the mercy of their capitalist employers.

Productive forces: include such things as technology, energy sources, and material resources.

Productive relations: the relationships that exist among the people producing goods and services.

Capitalist bourgeoisie: the owners of the means of production.

Lumpen proletariat: at the bottom, the fringe members who produce nothing and live, parasitically, off the work of others.

Surplus value: the laboring class produces goods that exceed wages in value.

Dialectic method: based on the analysis developed by the philosopher Georg Hegel (1770–1831). Hegel argued that for every idea, or thesis, there exists an opposing argument, or antithesis. Since neither position can ever be truly accepted, the result is a merger of the two ideas, a synthesis. Marx adapted this analytic method for his study of class struggle.

Thesis: in the philosophy of Hegel, an original idea or thought.

Antithesis: an opposing argument to a thesis.

Synthesis: since neither a thesis nor an antithesis can ever be truly accepted, the result is a merger of the two ideas.

Imperatively coordinated associations: these associations comprise two groups: those who possess authority and use it for social domination and those who lack authority and are dominated.

Social reality of crime: criminal definitions (law) represent the interests of those who hold power in society. Where there is conflict between social groups—for example, the wealthy and the poor—those who hold power will be the ones to create the laws that benefit themselves and hold rivals in check.

Power: refers to the ability of persons and groups to determine and control the behavior of others and to shape public opinion to meet their personal interests.

Marginalization: displacement of workers, pushing them outside the economic and social mainstream.

Critical criminologists: view crime as a function of the capitalist mode of production and not the social conflict which might occur in any society regardless of its economic system.

Critical criminology: capitalism produces haves and have-nots, each engaging in a particular branch of criminality. The mode of production shapes social life. Because economic competitiveness is the essence of capitalism, conflict increases and eventually destabilizes social institutions and the individuals within them.

Globalization: the process of creating transnational markets, politics, and legal systems in an effort to form and sustain a global economy.

Instrumental critical theory: criminal law and the criminal justice system act solely as instruments for controlling the poor, have-not members of society.

Demystify: to unmask the true purpose of law and justice.

Structural critical theory: the relationship between law and capitalism is unidirectional, not always working for the rich and against the poor.

Left realism: a branch of conflict theory that holds that crime is a "real" social problem experienced by the lower classes and that lower-class concerns about crime must be addressed by radical scholars.

Preemptive deterrence: an approach in which community organization efforts eliminate or reduce crime before police involvement becomes necessary.

Critical feminist: view gender inequality as stemming from the unequal power of men and women in a capitalist society, which leads to the exploitation of women by fathers and husbands. Under this system, women are considered a commodity worth possessing, like land or money.

Patriarchy: a system in which men dominate public, social, economic, and political affairs.

Paternalistic families: fathers assume the traditional role of breadwinners, while mothers tend to have menial jobs or remain at home to supervise domestic matters. Within the paternalistic home, mothers are expected to control the behavior of their daughters while granting greater freedom to sons.

Role exit behaviors: without legitimate behavioral outlets, girls who are unhappy or dissatisfied with their status are forced to seek out risky behaviors, including such desperate measures as running away and contemplating suicide.

Egalitarian families: those in which the husband and wife share similar positions of power at home and in the workplace—daughters gain a kind of freedom that reflects reduced parental control.

Power–control theory: encourages a new approach to the study of criminality, one that includes gender differences, class position, and the structure of the family.

Postmodernists: have embraced semiotics as a method of understanding all human relations, including criminal behavior.

Deconstructionists: those who follow the deconstructionist approach that focuses on the use of language by those in power to define crime based on their own values and biases; also called postmodernist thinking.

Semiotics: the use of language elements as signs or symbols beyond their literal meaning.

Peacemaking: the main purpose of criminology is to promote a peaceful, just society.

Restorative justice: using humanistic, nonpunitive strategies to right wrongs and restore social harmony.

Reintegrative shaming: disapproval is extended to the offenders' evil deeds, while at the same time they are cast as respected people who can be reaccepted by society.

Sentencing circle: In some Native American communities, people accused of breaking the law will meet with community members, victims (if any), village elders, and agents of the justice system in a sentencing circle. Members of the circle express their feelings about the act that was committed and raise questions or concerns.

CHAPTER OUTLINE

I.   Marxist thought
    A.   Productive forces and productive relations
        1.   Marx issued the communist manifesto in 1848.
        2.   Marx identified the economic structures in society that control all human relations.
        3.   Production has two components
            a.   Productive forces
            b.   Productive relations
        4.   Social classes
            a.   Class does not refer to an attribute or characteristic of a person or a group.
            b.   It denotes position in relation to others.
            c.   Capitalist bourgeoisie
            d.   Proletariat
            e.   Lumpen proletariat
    B.   Surplus value
        1.   The theory of surplus value
        2.   Marx believed the ebb and flow of the capitalist business cycle contained the seeds of its own destruction.
        3.   He used the dialectic method.
            a.   Thesis
            b.   Antithesis
            c.   Synthesis
            d.   In the end, the capitalist system will destroy itself
    C.   Marx on crime
        1.   Did not write a great deal on crime but mentioned it
        2.   Saw a connection between criminality and the inequities found in the capitalist system
        3.   Engels portrayed crime as a function of social demoralization.
        4.   Workers, demoralized by capitalist society, are caught up in a process that leads to crime and violence.
        5.   Working people committed crime because their choice is a slow death by starvation or a speedy one at the hands of the law.

II. Developing a conflict-based theory of crime
    A.   The contribution of Willem Bonger
        1.   Famous for his Marxist socialist concepts of crime causation
        2.   Crime lies within the boundaries of normal human behavior.
        3.   Society is divided into haves and have-nots because of capitalism not ability.
        4.   Criminal law punishes only the acts that do not injure the interests of the dominant ruling class.
        5.   Attempts to control law violations through force are a sign of a weak society.
        6.   Both the proletariat and bourgeoisie are crime-prone.
        7.   Only the proletariat are officially recognized as criminals.
            a.   The legal system discriminates against the poor by defending the actions of the wealthy.
            b.   The proletariat is deprived of the materials that are monopolized by the bourgeoisie.
        8.   Upper-class individuals will commit crime if
            a.   They sense a good opportunity to make a financial gain

           b.   Their lack of moral sense enables them to violate social rules
     9.   Bonger believed that redistribution of property according to one's needs would be the demise of crime.
- B.   The contribution of Ralf Dahrendorf
  1. Modern society is organized into imperatively coordinated associations
     a. Those that possess authority and use it for social domination
     b. Those that lack authority and are dominated
  2. Proposed a unified conflict theory human behavior
     a. Every society is at every point subject to processes of change as social change is everywhere.
     b. Every society displays at every point dissent and conflict as social conflict is everywhere.
     c. Every element in a society contributes to its disintegration and change.
     d. Every society is based on the coercion of some of its members by others.
- C.   The contribution of George Vold
  1. Conflict theory was actually adapted to criminology by George Vold.
  2. Crime can also be explained by social conflict.
  3. Criminal acts are a consequence of direct contact between forces struggling to control society.
  4. Does not explain all types of crime – limited to those involving intergroup clashes

III. Social conflict theory
- A.   Social Conflict Research
  1. Comparing the crime rates of members of powerless groups with those of members of the elite classes
  2. Criminologists routinely have found evidence that measures of social inequality are highly associated with crime rates.
  3. Economic marginalization produces an inevitable upswing in the murder rate.
  4. Racial profiling
  5. Criminal courts are more likely to dole out harsh punishments to the powerless and disenfranchised.

IV. Critical criminology
- A.   Fundamentals of critical criminology
  1. Critical criminologists view crime as
     a. A function of the capitalist mode of production
     b. Not the social conflict which might occur in any society regardless of its economic system
  2. Capitalism produces haves and have-nots.
  3. Each engages in a particular branch of criminality.
  4. The mode of production shapes social life.
  5. In a capitalist society, those with economic and political power control
     a. The definition of crime
     b. The manner in which the criminal justice system enforces the law
  6. The only crimes available to the poor, or proletariat, are the severely sanctioned "street crimes."
  7. The rich are insulated from street crimes because they live in areas far removed from crime.
  8. Globalization
     a. Has replaced imperialism and colonization as a new form of economic domination and oppression

      b.   Many critical criminologists blame globalization for the recent upswing in international crime rates.

B.   Instrumental versus structural theory
    1.   Instrumental view
        a.   Criminal law and the criminal justice system act solely as instruments for controlling the poor, have-not members of society.
        b.   Capitalist justice
            1)   Serves the powerful and rich
            2)   Enables them to impose their morality and standards of behavior on the entire society
        c.   Those who wield economic power define illegal or criminal behavior.
        d.   They impose the law on those who might threaten the status quo or interfere with their quest for ever-increasing profits.
        e.   The poor
            1)   May or may not commit more crimes than the rich
            2)   Certainly are arrested and punished more often
        f.   The poor are driven to crime out of frustration because affluence is well publicized but unattainable.
        g.   Goal of instrumental theorists – demystify law and justice
    2.   Structural view
        a.   The relationship between law and capitalism
            1)   Is unidirectional
            2)   Is not always working for the rich and against the poor
        b.   Law
            1)   Is not the exclusive domain of the rich
            2)   Is used to maintain the long-term interests of the capitalist system
            3)   Controls members of any class who threaten its existence
            4)   Is designed to keep the capitalist system operating efficiently
        c.   Anyone, capitalist or proletarian who rocks the boat is targeted for sanctioning.

C.   Research on critical criminology
    1.   Critical criminologists rarely use standard social science methodologies to test their views.
    2.   Many believe the traditional approach of measuring research subjects is antihuman and insensitive.
    3.   There have been some important efforts to test its assumptions quantitatively.
    4.   Critical research tends to be
        a.   Historical and analytical
        b.   Not quantitative and empirical
    5.   Crime, the individual, and the state
        a.   Two common themes emerge
            1)   Crime and its control are a function of capitalism.
            2)   The justice system is biased against the working class and favors upper-class interests.
        b.   Research efforts have yielded evidence linking operations of the justice system to class bias.
        c.   This type of research
            1)   Does not set out to prove statistically that capitalism causes crime
            2)   Shows that capitalism creates an environment where crime is inevitable

d.   Must rethink the criminal justice system
6.   Historical analysis – goals
    a.   To show how changes in criminal law correspond to the development of the capitalist economy
    b.   To investigate the development of modern police agencies
D.   Critique of critical criminology
  1.   Some charge that its contribution has been "hot air, heat, but no real light."
  2.   Some argue that critical theory rehashes the old tradition of helping the underdog.
  3.   Others suggest that critical theory fails to show attempts at self-regulation by the capitalist system.
  4.   Some argue critical criminologists refuse to address the problems and conflicts that exist in socialist countries.

V.   Contemporary forms of critical theory
A.   Left realism
  1.   Connected to the writings of British scholars John Lea and Jock Young
  2.   Reject the utopian views of "idealistic" critical criminologists who portray street criminals as revolutionaries
  3.   Their approach is that street criminals prey on the poor and disenfranchised.
  4.   The poor are doubly abused.
    a.   First by the capitalist system
    b.   Then by members of their own class
  5.   Approach closely resembles the relative deprivation approach
  6.   Crime protection
    a.   They argue that crime victims in all classes need and deserve protection.
    b.   Crime control reflects community needs.
    c.   Advocate preemptive deterrence
    d.   Something must be done to control crime under the existing capitalist system.
    e.   Left realism has been criticized by radical thinkers as legitimizing the existing power structure.
B.   Critical feminist theory
  1.   Views gender inequality as stemming from the unequal power of men and women in a capitalist society.
  2.   The origin of gender differences can be traced to
    a.   The development of private property
    b.   Male domination of the laws of inheritance
  3.   This led to male control over property and power
  4.   Capitalism lends itself to male supremacy.
  5.   Capitalist societies are built around patriarchy.
  6.   Patriarchy and crime
    a.   Criminal behavior patterns linked to the gender conflict are created by the economic and social struggles common in postindustrial societies.
    b.   Women are denied access to male-dominated street crimes.
    c.   Powerlessness increases the targeting of women in violent acts.
    d.   Feminists argue that men achieve masculinity at the expense of women.
    e.   Men need to defend themselves from being contaminated with femininity.
    f.   Female victimization should decline as women's place in society is elevated.
  7.   Exploitation and criminality
    a.   Sexual victimization of females is a function of male socialization.

b.   Exploitation triggers the onset of female delinquent and deviant behavior.
8.   How the justice system penalizes women
a.   The justice system and its patriarchal hierarchy contribute to the onset of female delinquency.
b.   The juvenile justice system has viewed most female delinquents as sexually precocious girls who have to be brought under control.

C.   Power–control theory
1.   Hagan's view is that crime and delinquency rates are a function of two factors.
a.   Class position (power)
b.   Family functions (control)
2.   Parents reproduce the power relationships they hold in the workplace.
3.   A position of dominance at work is equated with control in the household.
4.   Parents' work experiences and class position influence the criminality of children.
5.   Paternalistic families
a.   Fathers assume the traditional role as breadwinners.
b.   Mothers tend to have menial jobs or serve as homemakers.
c.   Mothers are expected to control the behavior of their daughters.
d.   Grant greater freedom to sons
e.   Unhappy or dissatisfied girls seek out risky role exit behaviors.
6.   Egalitarian families
a.   Husbands and wives share similar positions of power at home and at work.
b.   Daughters gain a kind of freedom that reflects reduced parental control.
c.   Daughters law-violating behavior mirrors their brothers' behavior.
d.   These relationships occur in female-headed households with absent fathers.
7.   Evaluating power-control
a.   It encourages a new approach to the study of criminality.
b.   It looks at gender differences, class position, and the structure of the family.
c.   Not all research is as supportive

D.   Postmodern theory
1.   Embrace semiotics as a method of understanding all human relations, including criminal behavior
2.   Analyze communication and language in legal codes to determine whether they contain language and content that institutionalize racism or sexism
3.   Postmodernists rely on semiotics to conduct their research efforts.
4.   Postmodernists assert that there are different languages and ways of knowing.
5.   Those in power can use their own language to define crime and law.

E.   Peacemaking theory
1.   The main purpose of criminology is to promote a peaceful, just society.
2.   View the efforts of the state to punish and control as crime-encouraging rather than crime-discouraging
3.   Advocate such policies as mediation and conflict resolution

VI. Public policy implications of social conflict theory: restorative justice
A.   Reintegrative shaming
1.   Shame is a powerful tool of informal social control.
2.   Braithwaite divides the concept of shame into two distinct types.
a.   The most common form of shaming typically involves stigmatization.
1)   Stigma is doomed to failure.
2)   Those who suffer humiliation at the hands of the justice system "reject their rejecters" by joining a deviant subculture of like-minded people.

          b.   The second is reintegrative shaming.
              1)   Disapproval is extended to the offenders' evil deeds.
              2)   Offenders begin to understand and recognize their wrongdoing and shame themselves.
      3.   To be reintegrative, shaming must be brief and controlled and then followed by ceremonies of
          a.   Forgiveness
          b.   Apology
          c.   Repentance
      4.   To prevent crime, society must encourage reintegrative shaming.

B.   The concept of restorative justice
      1.   Often hard to define because it encompasses a variety of programs and practices
      2.   Its core value can be put into one word: respect.
      3.   Respect insists that we balance concern for all parties.
      4.   What is needed instead is a justice policy that
          a.   Repairs the harm caused by crime
          b.   Includes all parties who have suffered from that harm, including
               1)   Victim
               2)   Community
               3)   Offender
      5.   Offenders must accept
          a.   Accountability for their actions
          b.   Responsibility for the harm their actions caused

C.   The process of restoration
      1.   Most conflicts are better settled in the community than in a court.
      2.   Restoration programs typically involve all the parties caught in the complex web of a criminal act in a mutual healing process.
      3.   Elements of the program
          a.   Offender is asked to recognize that he or she caused injury to personal and social relations; acceptance of responsibility
          b.   A commitment to both material restitution and symbolic reparation
          c.   Determination of community support and assistance for both victim and offender
      4.   Restoration programs
      5.   Balanced and restorative justice
          a.   Restorative justice should be centered on the principle of balance.
          b.   Should give equal weight to
               1)   Holding offenders accountable to victims
               2)   Providing competency development for offenders in the system so they can pursue legitimate endeavors after release
               3)   Ensuring community safety

D.   The challenge of restorative justice
      1.   While restorative justice holds great promise, there are also some concerns.
      2.   Fairness cannot be sacrificed for the sake of restoration
      3.   Must be wary of the cultural and social differences that can be found throughout our heterogeneous society
      4.   The greatest challenge to restorative justice is the difficult task of balancing the needs of offenders with those of their victims.
      5.   Criminologists are now conducting numerous projects to find the most effective means of returning the ownership of justice to the people and the community.

CHAPTER SUMMARY

In 1848, Karl Marx issued the communist manifesto identifying the economic structures in society that control all human relations. According to Marx, class does not refer to an attribute or characteristic of a person or a group; rather, it denotes position in relation to others. One of his key concepts is that of surplus value, the laboring class produces goods that exceed wages in value. Marx did not write on crime, but he mentioned it, seeing a connection between criminality and the inequities found in the capitalist system. Engels portrayed crime as a function of social demoralization in which workers, demoralized by capitalist society, are caught up in a process that leads to crime and violence.

Conflict-based theories of crime are founded in the works of Bonger, Dahrendorf, and Vold. Bonger argues that criminal law punishes only the acts that do not injure the interests of the dominant ruling class. The legal system discriminates against the poor by defending the actions of the wealthy. The contribution of Ralf Dahrendorf is based on his idea that modern society is organized into imperatively coordinated associations: 1) those that possess authority and use it for social domination and 2) those that lack authority and are dominated. Vold stated that crime can be explained by social conflict because criminal acts are a consequence of direct contact between forces struggling to control society.

Critical criminologists view crime as a function of the capitalist mode of production and not the social conflict which might occur in any society regardless of its economic system. Capitalism produces haves and have-nots and each engages in a particular branch of criminality. In a capitalist society, those with economic and political power control the definition of crime and the manner in which the criminal justice system enforces the law. Critical criminology has two components: instrumental theory and structural theory. In the instrumental view, criminal law and the criminal justice system act solely as instruments for controlling the poor, have-not members of society and those who wield economic power define illegal or criminal behavior. The goal of instrumental theorists is to demystify law and justice. The structural view argues that the relationship between law and capitalism is unidirectional and is not always working for the rich and against the poor. The law is not the exclusive domain of the rich, but it is used to maintain the long-term interests of the capitalist system.

Contemporary forms of critical theory include left realism that rejects the utopian views of "idealistic" critical criminologists who portray street criminals as revolutionaries. Their approach is that street criminals prey on the poor and disenfranchised, so the poor are doubly abused: first by the capitalist system and then by members of their own class. This approach closely resembles relative deprivation.

Critical feminist theory views gender inequality as stemming from the unequal power of men and women in a capitalist society. Capitalist societies are built around patriarchy. The justice system and its patriarchal hierarchy contribute to the onset of female delinquency. The juvenile justice system has viewed most female delinquents as sexually precocious girls who have to be brought under control. Power–control theory states that crime and delinquency rates are a function of two factors: class position (power) and family functions (control). Parents' work experiences and class position influence the criminality of children. In paternalistic families, mothers are expected to control the behavior of their daughters and grant greater freedom to sons. Unhappy or dissatisfied girls seek out risky role exit behaviors. On the other hand, egalitarian families are ones in which husbands and wives share similar positions of power at home and at work. Daughters gain a type of freedom that reflects reduced parental control, so the law-violating behavior of daughters mirrors their brothers' behavior.

Postmodern theory analyzes communication and language in legal codes to determine whether they contain language and content that institutionalize racism or sexism. Peacemaking theory promotes a peaceful, just society. Advocates support such policies as mediation and conflict resolution. Reintegrative shaming theory argues that shame is a powerful tool of informal social control. In reintegrative shaming, disapproval is extended to the offenders' evil deeds and offenders begin to understand and recognize their wrongdoing and shame themselves. The concept of restorative justice is often hard to define because it encompasses a variety of programs and practices such as victim offender restoration programs and sentencing circles. The core value of restorative approaches can be put into one word – respect. Respect insists that we balance concern for all parties – victim, community, and offender. Most conflicts are better settled in the community than in a court.

STUDENT EXERCISES

Exercise 1

Go online to http://www.doc.state.mn.us/aboutdoc/restorativejustice/default.htm and evaluate in one or two pages, the restorative justice program that the Minnesota Department of Corrections is using. In your answer address the following questions: does this program serve the interests of the offender? The interests of the victim? The interests of the community? Justify your answers.

Exercise 2

Go to http://www.critcrim.org/redfeather/journal-pomocrim/vol-1-intro/001overview.html and read the article that provides an excellent overview of the postmodernist school of criminology. Then prepare a one to two page paper that provides five major key points contained in the article.

CRIMINOLOGY WEB LINKS

http://www.critcrim.org/
This is the official website of the American Society of Criminology - Division on Critical Criminology and the Academy of Criminal Justice Sciences - Section on Critical Criminology.

http://www.arasite.org/critcrim.html
The website provides a wealth of information about critical criminology. Make sure you check out the various links contained in the homepage.

http://barjproject.org/index.htm
This website contains information on the Community Justice Institute of Florida Atlantic University. It contains links to a substantial number of websites on balanced and restorative justice.

http://www.findarticles.com/p/articles/mi_m2294/is_n5-6_v28/ai_14154682
This article looks at sexual assault and stranger aggression on a Canadian university campus. The

main purpose of the paper is to present exploratory Canadian incidence data collected from a sample of eastern Ontario female university students.

http://www.malcolmread.co.uk/JockYoung/
This website contains a number of articles on left realism written by Professor Jock Young.

TEST BANK

FILL-IN THE BLANKS

1. According to Marxist theory, the people who do the actual labor in society are called the
   _____.

2. In his analysis, Marx used the _____ _____, based on the
   analysis developed by the philosopher Georg Hegel.

3. Bonger believed crime lies within the boundaries of _____ human behavior.

4. According to Travis Pratt and Christopher Lowenkamp, with economic _____,
   people turn to violent crime for survival.

5. According to instrumental critical theory, criminal law and the criminal justice system act solely
   as instruments for controlling the _____.

6. _____ deterrence is an approach in which community organization efforts
   eliminate or reduce crime before police involvement becomes necessary.

7. _____ is a system in which men dominate public, social, economic, and
   political affairs.

8. In _____ families, husband and wife share similar positions of power at home
   and in the workplace.

9. Shame is a powerful tool of _____ social control.

10. According to restorative justice, crime is an offense against human _____.

TRUE/FALSE QUESTIONS

1. T/F Marx wrote a great deal on the subject of crime.

2. T/F Bonger believed society is divided into groups, on the basis of people's innate ability.

3. T/F According to Quinney, criminal definitions (laws) represent the interests of all those in
   society.

4. T/F Critical criminologists view crime as a function of the capitalist mode of production
   and not the social conflict which might occur in any society regardless of its economic system.

5. T/F An important goal of instrumental theorists is to demystify law and justice.

6. T/F Left realists state that the poor are doubly abused, first by the capitalist system and then by
   members of their own class.

7.   T/F Within the paternalistic home, mothers are expected to control the behavior of their sons while granting greater freedom to daughters.

8.   T/F The second priority of restorative justice is to restore the community, to the degree that it is possible to do.

9.   T/F In reintegrative shaming disapproval is extended to the offenders' evil deeds, while at the same time the offenders are cast as respected people who can be reaccepted by society.

10. T/F At the core of all the varying branches of critical criminology is the fact that social structure causes crime.

11. T/F The strength of feminist theory is that it explains how gender differences in the crime rate are a function of capitalist competition and the exploitation of women.

12. T/F The strength of the critical criminology is that it accounts for the associations between economic structure and crime rates.

13. T/F Peacemakers view the efforts of the state to punish and control as promoting a peaceful, just society.

14. T/F Semiotics refers to the use of language elements as signs or symbols beyond their literal meaning.

15. T/F Role exit behaviors include such desperate measures as running away and contemplating suicide.

MULTIPLE CHOICE QUESTIONS

1.   An approach in which community organization efforts eliminate or reduce crime before police involvement becomes necessary is termed:
     a.   preemptive deterrence
     b.   relative deprivation
     c.   left realism
     d.   specific deterrence

2.   Youth who feel that they are not part of society and have nothing to lose by committing crime are known as being:
     a.   successful
     b.   college-bound
     c.   stigmatized
     d.   marginalized

3.   The theory that experiencing poverty in the midst of plenty creates discontent is known as:
     a.   preemptive deterrence
     b.   relative deprivation
     c.   marginalization
     d.   left realism

4. A system where men's work is valued and women's work is devalued is known as:
    a. patriarchal
    b. matriarchal
    c. feminism
    d. status-quo

5. This concept is part of patriarchy, whereby men control women both economically and biologically, and explains why females in a capitalist society commit fewer crimes than males:
    a. relative deprivation
    b. matriarchy
    c. elite deviance
    d. double marginality

6. White-collar and economic crimes are known as:
    a. patriarchy
    b. capitalism
    c. elite deviance
    d. double marginality

7. Men who struggle to dominate women in order to prove their manliness are:
    a. doing patriarchy
    b. exploited
    c. doing gender
    d. egalitarian

8. Which group indicts the justice system and its patriarchal hierarchy as contributing to the onset of female delinquency?
    a. critical feminists
    b. radical feminists
    c. Marxist feminists
    d. left feminists

9. Women began to be exploited because they provided what type of labor in their homes?
    a. free skilled
    b. free child care
    c. free unskilled
    d. free reproductive

10. Which of the following factors have been intertwined in an effort to sustain the subordination of women?
    a. capitalism and patriarchy
    b. patriarchy and industrialization
    c. capitalism and industrialization
    d. patriarchy and egalitarianism

11. Marx's Communist Manifesto focused on the _____conditions perpetuated by the capitalist system.
    a. market
    b. social
    c. political
    d. economic

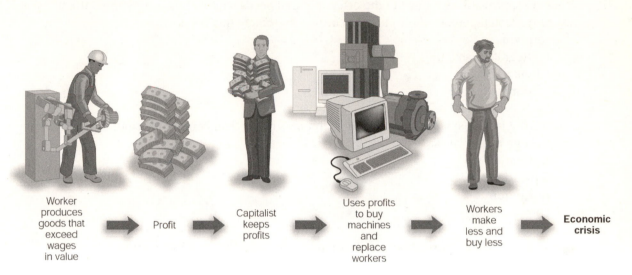

Worker produces goods that exceed wages in value ➡ Profit ➡ Capitalist keeps profits ➡ Uses profits to buy machines and replace workers ➡ Workers make less and buy less ➡ **Economic crisis**

12. Using language as signs or symbols beyond their literal meaning is:
    a. semiotics
    b. phonics
    c. symphonics
    d. acoustics

13. Which theory views the efforts of the state to punish and control as crime-encouraging rather crime-discouraging?
    a. postmodern theory
    b. peacemaking criminology
    c. left realism
    d. feminist theory

14. Restorative justice relies on what type of strategies for crime prevention and control?
    a. punitive
    b. retribution
    c. non-punitive
    d. pretrial detention

15. Which of the following is a powerful tool of informal social control?
    a. shame
    b. restitution
    c. diversion
    d. probation

16. The most common form of shaming involves:
    a.   prison
    b.   restitution
    c.   stigmatization
    d.   compensation

17. When disapproval is extended to the offenders' evil deeds while, at the same time, offenders are cast as respected people who can be reaccepted by society this is known as:
    a.   forgiving
    b.   reintegrative shaming
    c.   stigmatizing
    d.   pardoning

18. Turning the justice system into a "healing" process rather than being a distributor of retribution and revenge is known as:
    a.   restoration
    b.   reparation
    c.   restitution
    d.   compensation

19. Balanced restorative justice centers on offender accountability, competency development, and:
    a.   community oversight
    b.   police oversight
    c.   police protection
    d.   community protection

20. The core value of restorative justice is:
    a.   honesty
    b.   respect
    c.   truth
    d.   restoration

21. The second priority of restorative justice is:
    a.   to assist victims
    b.   to improve human relationships
    c.   to restore the community
    d.   to restore the offender

22. What theory claims the relationship between law and capitalism is unidirectional?
    a.   structural critical theory
    b.   instrumental critical theory
    c.   left realism
    d.   feminist theory

23. Left realists are troubled by the emergence of a _____ philosophy.
    a.   strict due process
    b.   strict law and order
    c.   liberal peacemaking
    d.   liberal rehabilitative

24. A type of restorative justice based upon Native American culture is:
    a. a community circle
    b. a community court
    c. a sentencing circle
    d. a sentencing court

25. Critical criminologist claim that the motives behind _____ are the exploitation of natural resources, avoiding regulation, and taking advantage of desperate workers.
    a. restoration
    b. demystification
    c. decriminalization
    d. globalization

ESSAY QUESTIONS

1. Discuss the concept of social conflict and how it shapes behavior.

2. Discuss the difference between structural and instrumental critical theory.

3.   Discuss the concept of patriarchy.

4.   Describe feminist criminology.

5.   Describe the concept of restorative justice.

MATCHING

1. _____ Demystify
2. _____ Marginalization
3. _____ Paternalistic
4. _____ Karl Marx
5. _____ Bourgeoisie
6. _____ Surplus Value
7. _____ Conflict Theory
8. _____ Antithesis
9. _____ Role Exit Behaviors
10. _____ Left Realism

A. A branch of conflict theory that views crime as a social problem and government as incapable of creating positive social change
B. When people are thrust outside of the economic mainstream
C. Communist manifesto
D. Marx held that the laboring class produces goods that exceed wages in value.
E. The view that the inter-group conflicts and rivalry that exist in every society cause crime
F. Running away and attempting suicide
G. Leaders are seen as father figures and others are treated as children
H. People who do the actual labor
I. An opposing argument
J. To unmask the true purpose of law and justice

CHAPTER 8 ANSWER KEY

Fill in the Blank Answers

1. proletariat
2. dialectic method
3. normal
4. marginalization
5. poor
6. preemptive
7. patriarchy
8. egalitarian
9. informal
10. relationships

True/False Answers

1.	F	6.	T	11.	T
2.	F	7.	F	12.	T
3.	F	8.	T	13.	F
4.	T	9.	T	14.	T
5.	T	10.	F	15.	T

Multiple Choice Answers

1.	A	11.	D	21.	C
2.	D	12.	A	22.	A
3.	B	13.	B	23.	B
4.	A	14.	C	24.	C
5.	D	15.	A	25.	D
6.	C	16.	C		
7.	C	17.	B		
8.	B	18.	A		
9.	D	19.	D		
10.	A	20.	B		

Essay Questions

1. Pages 253-255
2. Pages 261-262
3. Page 265
4. Pages 264-266
5. Pages 270-271

Matching Answers

1.	J	6.	D
2.	B	7.	E
3.	G	8.	I
4.	C	9.	F
5.	H	10.	A

DEVELOPMENTAL THEORIES

Life Course and Latent Trait

OUTLINE

- Foundations of Developmental Theory
- Life Course Fundamentals
- The Criminological Enterprise: Desisting from Crime
- Theories of the Criminal Life Course
- The Criminological Enterprise: Shared Beginnings, Divergent Lives
- Latent Trait Fundamentals
- Evaluating Developmental Theories
- Public Policy Implications of Developmental Theory
- Policy and Practice in Criminology: The Fast Track Project

Chapter 9

Developmental Theories:
Life Course and Latent Trait

LEARNING OBJECTIVES

1. Be familiar with the concept of developmental theory

2. Know the factors that influence the life course

3. Recognize that there are different pathways to crime

4. Know what is meant by problem behavior syndrome

5. Differentiate between adolescent-limited and life course persistent offenders

6. Be familiar with the turning points in crime

7. Be able to discuss the influence of social capital on crime

8. Know what is meant by a latent trait

9. Be familiar with the concepts of impulsivity and self-control

10. Be able to discuss Gottfredson and Hirschi's General Theory of Crime

KEYWORDS AND DEFINITIONS

Desist: age out of crime as one matures.

Developmental theories: seek to identify, describe, and understand the developmental factors that explain the onset and continuation of a criminal career.

Life course theories: view criminality as a dynamic process, influenced by a multitude of individual characteristics, traits, and social experiences. As people travel through the life course, they are constantly bombarded by changing perceptions and experiences, and as a result their behavior will change directions, sometimes for the better and sometimes for the worse.

Latent trait theories: hold that human development is controlled by a "master trait," present at birth or soon after. Some criminologists believe that this master trait remains stable and unchanging throughout a person's lifetime, whereas others suggest that it can be altered, influenced, or changed by subsequent experience.

Problem behavior syndrome (PBS): crime is one among a group of antisocial behaviors that cluster together and typically involve family dysfunction, sexual and physical abuse, substance abuse, smoking, precocious sexuality and early pregnancy, educational underachievement, suicide attempts, sensation seeking, and unemployment.

Authority conflict pathway: the path to a criminal career that begins at an early age with stubborn behavior and defiance of parents (doing things one's own way, disobedience) and then progresses to authority avoidance (staying out late, truancy, running away).

Covert pathway: path to a criminal career that begins with minor, underhanded behavior (lying, shoplifting) that progresses to property damage (setting nuisance fires, damaging property). This behavior eventually escalates to more serious forms of criminality, ranging from joyriding, pocket picking, larceny, and fencing to passing bad checks, using stolen credit cards, stealing cars, dealing drugs, and breaking and entering.

Overt pathway: pathway to a criminal career that begins with minor aggression (annoying others, bullying), leads to physical fighting, and eventually escalates to violent crime.

Adolescent-limited offenders: an offender who follows the most common criminal trajectory, in which antisocial behavior peaks in adolescence and then diminishes.

Life course persisters: one of the small group of offenders whose criminal career continues well into adulthood.

Integrated theories: Models of crime causation that weave social and individual variables into a complex explanatory chain.

Turning points: according to Laub and Sampson, the life events that alter the development of a criminal career; two critical turning points are marriage and career.

Social capital: positive relations with individuals and institutions that are life sustaining.

Latent trait: a stable feature, characteristic, property, or condition, present at birth or soon after, that remains stable and unchanging throughout a person's lifetime.

Human nature theory: a belief that personal traits (such as genetic makeup, intelligence, and body build) may outweigh the importance of social variables as predictors of criminal activity.

General Theory of Crime (GTC): according to Gottfredson and Hirschi, a developmental theory that modifies social control theory by integrating concepts from biosocial, psychological, routine activities, and rational choice theories.

Self-control theory: according to Gottfredson and Hirschi, the view that the cause of delinquent behavior is an impulsive personality. Kids who are impulsive may find that their bond to society is weak.

CHAPTER OUTLINE

I.   Foundations of developmental theory
     A.   The Glueck research
          1.   One of the cornerstones of recent life course theories; integration of biological, psychological, and social factors
          2.   Followed the careers of known delinquents to determine the factors that predicted persistent offending
          3.   Focused on early onset of delinquency as a harbinger of a criminal career
          4.   Noted the stability of offending careers
          5.   Children who are antisocial early in life are most likely to continue offending careers into adulthood.
          6.   Personal and social factors related to persistent offending
               a.   The most important factor related to persistent offending was family relations.
               b.   Physical and mental factors played a role in determining persistent offenders.
                    1)   Low intelligence
                    2)   Background of mental disease
                    3)   Powerful (mesomorph) physique
          7.   Gluecks' research ignored for 30 years as focus shifted to social and social-psychological factors.
          8.   Sampson and Laub
               a.   Rediscovered the Glueck legacy during the 1990s
               b.   Reanalyzed the Glueck data
               c.   Fueled the popularity of the life course approach
          9.   Wolfgang and associates identify a small group of chronic offenders that focused attention on criminal careers..
          10. Loeber and LeBlanc – criminologists must pay attention to how a criminal career unfolds, how it begins, why it is sustained, and how it comes to an end
          11. Two distinct viewpoints
               a.   Life course view – criminality is a dynamic process, influenced by a multitude of individual characteristics, traits, and social experiences.
               b.   Latent trait view – human development is controlled by a "master trait," present at birth or soon after.

II. Life course fundamentals
     A.   Even as toddlers, people begin relationships and behaviors that will determine their adult life course.
     B.   Some individuals are incapable of maturing in a reasonable and timely fashion because of family, environmental, or personal problems.
     C.   Because the transition from one stage of life to another can be "bumpy," the propensity to commit crimes is neither stable nor constant: it is a developmental process.
          1.   A positive life experience may help some criminals desist.
          2.   A negative life experience may cause some criminals to resume.
          3.   Criminal careers are developmental because people are influenced by the behavior of those around them.
          4.   Disruptions in life's major transitions can be destructive and ultimately can promote criminality.
          5.   Those already at risk due to socioeconomic problems or family dysfunction are the most susceptible.

6. People are influenced by different factors as they mature.
7. Negative life events can become cumulative.
8. The nature of social interactions change as people mature.
    a. At first, family relations may be the most influential.
    b. In later adolescence, school and peer relations predominate.
    c. Some antisocial children manage to find stable work and to maintain intact marriages as adults.
    d. Others, who develop arrest records and get involved with the wrong crowd, may find themselves limited to menial jobs and at risk for criminal careers.
9. The factors that produce crime and delinquency at one point in the life cycle may not be relevant at another.

D. Problem behavior syndrome
1. Crime is one among a group of antisocial behaviors that cluster together and typically involve:
    a. Family dysfunction
    b. Sexual and physical abuse
    c. Smoking
    d. Precocious sexuality and early pregnancy
    e. Educational underachievement
    f. Suicide attempts
    g. Sensation seeking
    h. Unemployment
2. All forms of antisocial behavior have similar developmental patterns.
3. PBS sufferers are prone to more difficulties than the general population.
4. PBS has been linked to
    a. Individual-level personality problems
    b. Family problems
    c. Educational failure

E. Pathways to crime
1. Career criminals may travel more than a single road.
2. Loeber has identified three distinct paths to a criminal career.
    a. Authority conflict pathway
    b. Covert pathway
    c. Overt pathway
3. Each of these paths may lead to a sustained deviant career.
4. Some people enter two or even three pathways simultaneously.

F. Age of onset/continuity of crime
1. Age of onset
    a. Most life course theories assume that:
        1) The seeds of a criminal career are planted early in life.
        2) Early onset of deviance strongly predicts later and more serious criminality.
        3) The earlier the onset of crime, the longer its duration.
    b. Research supports this.
    c. Not all persistent offenders begin at an early age.
2. Continuity and desistance
    a. Poor parental discipline and monitoring are key to the early onset of criminality.
    b. Desistance is a process, not an instantaneous event.
        1) A process of cognitive change
        2) Discard old habits, begin the process of crafting a different way of life

3) "Hooks for change"
   3.   Gender similarities and differences
       a.   Males and females – age of onset related to continuity of crime
       b.   Some distinct gender differences
          1)   For males, the path runs from early onset to problems at work and substance abuse.
          2)   For females – early onset leads to relationship problems, depression, a tendency to commit suicide, and poor health in adulthood.
  G.   Adolescent-limiteds and life course persisters
     1.   Adolescent-limiteds – "typical teenagers;" rebellious teenage behavior
     2.   Life course persisters – small group; begin offending at a very early age and continue to offend well into adulthood
     3.   Supporting research
       a.   Life course persisters offend more frequently and engage in a greater variety of antisocial acts than other offenders.
       b.   The cause of early onset/life course persistent delinquency is found at the individual level.
       c.   Life course persisters manifest significantly more mental health problems.
          1)   Low verbal ability, hyperactivity, negative or impulsive personality, impaired spatial and memory functions
       d.   ADHD and life course persisters
          1)   Some with ADHD do not outgrow levels of disobedience typical of the preschool years.
          2)   Others show few symptoms of ADHD but, from an early age, are aggressive and in constant opposition to authority.

III. Theories of the criminal life course
  A.   Integrated theories
     1.   Interconnected factors
       a.   Personal factors
       b.   Social factors
       c.   Socialization factors
       d.   Cognitive factors
       e.   Situational factors
     2.   Asks not only why people enter a criminal way of life but also, once they do, why they are able to alter the trajectory of their criminal involvement
     3.   Some important life course theories
       a.   Social development model
          1)   Community-level risk factors make some people susceptible to antisocial behaviors.
          2)   A child must maintain prosocial bonds to control the risk of antisocial behavior.
       b.   Interactional theory
          1)   A deterioration of the social bond during adolescence
          2)   Weakened attachment to parents
          3)   Weakened commitment to school
          4)   Weakened belief in conventional values
       c.   General theory of crime and delinquency
          1)   Crime and social relations are reciprocal.

> 2) Engaging in crime weakens bonds with significant others and strengthens association with criminal peers.
> 3) Life domains: self, family, school, peers, work
>> d. The reinforcement (such as feedback) children perceive for their participation

B. Sampson and Laub: Age-graded theory
1. If there are various pathways to crime, are there trails back to conformity?
2. Turning points-life events that enable adult offenders to desist from crime
   a. Marriage
   b. Career
3. Social capital influences the trajectory of a criminal career
   a. Positive relations with individuals and institutions that are life sustaining
4. Testing age-graded theory
   a. Criminality appears to be dynamic; people change over the life course and factors that predict delinquency in adolescence may have less of an impact on adult crime.
   b. Of critical importance is early labeling by the justice system.
   c. Career trajectories can be reversed if life conditions improve.
   d. A number of research efforts have supported the idea that social capital reduces crime rates.
   e. High-risk adults who obtain high-quality jobs reduce their criminal activities.
5. The marriage factor
   a. People who maintain a successful marriage and become parents are the most likely to mature out of crime.
   b. The marriage benefit may also be intergenerational.
   c. Recent research: former offenders were far less likely to return to crime if they settled down into the routines of a solid marriage.
      1) Common law marriages or living with a partner did not have the same crime-reducing effect as did traditional marriages.
      2) Among non-Caucasians, parolees cohabiting without marriage actually increased recidivism rates.
6. Future research directions
   a. What is it about a military career that helps reduce future criminality?

IV. Latent trait fundamentals
   A. General
   1. Latent traits to explain the flow of crime over the life cycle

   2. People have a personal attribute or characteristic that controls their inclination or propensity to commit crimes.
   3. Trait is present at birth or established early in life and can remain stable over time.
      a. Defective intelligence, impulsive personality, genetic abnormalities, physical-chemical functioning of the brain, environmental influences on brain function
   4. Regardless of gender or environment, those with a latent trait may be at risk to crime.
   5. Because latent traits are stable, people who are antisocial during adolescence are the most likely to persist in crime.
   6. The opportunity to commit crime fluctuates over time.
   7. As people mature and develop, there are fewer opportunities to commit crimes and greater inducements to remain "straight."

B.   Crime and human nature
    1.   Personal traits outweigh the importance of social variables as predictors of criminal activity.
    2.   All human behavior, including criminality, is determined by its perceived consequences.
    3.   A criminal incident occurs when an individual chooses criminal over conventional behavior after weighing the potential gains and losses of each.

C.   General theory of crime (GTC)
    1.   Gottfredson and Hirschi: integrated the concepts of control with those of biosocial, psychological, routine activities, and rational choice theories.
    2.   The act and the offender
        a.   The criminal offender and the criminal act are separate concepts.
            1)   Criminal acts are illegal events or deeds that offenders engage in when they perceive them to be advantageous.
            2)   Criminal offenders are predisposed to commit crimes.
        b.   Crime is rational and predictable.
        c.   If targets are well guarded, crime rates diminish.
    3.   Impulsivity and crime?
        a.   The tendency to commit crime is linked to a person's level of self-control
    4.   Self-control and crime
        a.   Explains all varieties of criminal behavior
        b.   Explains all the social and behavioral correlates of crime
        c.   Self-control applies equally to all crimes.
    5.   Support for GTC
        a.   Research in the United States and abroad support GTC.
    6.   Analyzing the general theory of crime
        a.   Theory explains
            1)   Why some people who lack self-control can escape criminality
            2)   Why some people who have self-control might not escape criminality
        b.   Criticisms
            1)   Tautological – involves circular reasoning
            2)   Other research shows different classes of criminals.
            3)   Fails to address individual and ecological patterns in the crime rate
            4)   Racial and gender differences
            5)   Ignores the moral concept of right and wrong
            6)   Peer relations may either enhance or control criminal behavior.
            7)   People change.
            8)   Only a modest relationship between self-control and crime
            9)   GTC may be culturally limited.
           10)   Misreads human nature
           11)   Lack of self-control is but one of many reasons
           12)   More than one kind of impulsivity

D.   Differential coercion theory
    1.   Identifies another master trait that may guide behavioral choices – coercion
    2.   There are two sources of coercion
        a.   Interpersonal
        b.   Impersonal
    3.   A person's ability to maintain self-control is a function of the amount, type, and consistency of coercion experienced as he or she goes through the life course

4. Prosocial behavior – when the amount of coercion is minimal
5. Even more debilitating – inconsistent or erratic episodes of coercive behavior
6. Coercion and criminal careers
   a. Chronic offenders grew up in homes where parents used
      1) Erratic control
      2) Applied it in an inconsistent fashion
   b. Coercive ideation
7. Differential Social Support and Coercion Theory (DSSCT)
   a. Consistently applied social support may eventually negate or counterbalance the crime-producing influence of coercion.
   b. Social support comes in two forms
      1) Expressive
      2) Instrumental
   c. To reduce crime rates, societies must
      1) Enhance the legitimate sources of social support
      2) Reduce the forces of coercion

V. Evaluating developmental theories
   A. The theories in this chapter share some common ground.
      1. Criminal career must be understood as a passage along which people travel.
      2. The factors that affect a criminal career may include:
         a Structural factors
         b. Socialization factors
         c. Biological factors
         d. Psychological factors
         e. Opportunity factors
   B. Perspectives differ in their view of human development.

VI. Public policy implications of developmental theory
   A. Multi-systemic treatment efforts for at-risk youth
   B. Multidimensional strategies aimed at children in preschool and early elementary

CHAPTER SUMMARY

The Glueck research forms the foundation for recent life course theories that integrate biological, psychological, and social factors. This research focused on early onset of delinquency as a harbinger of a criminal career. The Gluecks identified personal and social factors associated with persistent offending, the most important being family relations. The Glueck's research came to be ignored for 30 years as criminological focus shifted to social and social-psychological factors. Sampson and Laub "rediscovered" the Glueck legacy during the 1990s.

Life course theories view transitions from one stage of life to another as sometimes "bumpy," and state that one's propensity to commit crime is neither stable nor constant; rather, it is a developmental process. This developmental process is impacted by positive and negative life experiences resulting from relationships and behaviors that begin during one's toddler years.

Problem behavior syndrome (PBS) states that crime is one among a group of antisocial behaviors that cluster together and that all forms of antisocial behavior have similar developmental patterns. PBS has been linked to individual-level personality problems, family problems, and educational failure. Pathways to crime argues that career criminals may travel more than a single road. Loeber has identified three distinct paths to a criminal career: authority conflict pathway, covert pathway, overt pathway. Each of these paths may lead to a sustained deviant career.

Integrated theories interconnect personal, social, socialization, cognitive and situational factors to examine not only why people enter a criminal way of life but also, once they do, why they are able to alter their criminal involvement. For instance, the social development model specifies that a child must maintain prosocial bonds to control the risk of antisocial behavior. Interaction theory examines the deterioration or weakening of the social bonds with parents, schools, and conventional values during the adolescent or "crime-prone" years.

The general theory of crime and delinquency proposes that the way an individual reacts to constraints and motivations are shaped by five key domains of human development: self, family, school, peers, and work, which continuously evolve and each life domain influences the others. Sampson and Laub's age-graded theory identifies the turning points in a criminal career, marriage and career. Social capital influences the trajectory of a criminal career.

Latent trait theories explain the flow of crime over the life cycle as being the result of a personal attribute or characteristic that controls one's propensity to commit crime. This trait is may be present at birth or established early and life and can remain stable over time. According to the latent trait view, because latent traits remain stable, people who are antisocial during adolescence are the most likely to persist in crime. While latent traits remain stable, it is the opportunity to commit crime that fluctuates over one's life course.

The crime and human nature view states that all human behavior, including criminality, is determined by its perceived consequences. A criminal incident occurs when an individual chooses criminal over conventional behavior after weighing the potential gains and losses of each. One aspect of human nature is self-control. Gottfredson and Hirschi's general theory of crime states that the propensity to commit crimes remains stable throughout a person's life. What makes people crime-prone is a person's level of self-control. People with limited self control tend to be impulsive, are insensitive to other people's feelings, are physical (rather than mental), risk-takers, shortsighted, and nonverbal. Those with low self-control enjoy risky, exciting, or thrilling behaviors with immediate gratification. The root cause of poor self-control is inadequate childrearing practices. Low self-control develops early in life and it remains stable into and through adulthood. While research in the United States and abroad support the general theory of crime, a variety of criticisms exist.

Differential coercion theory identifies another master trait that may guide behavioral choices – coercion. There are two sources of coercion, interpersonal and impersonal. A person's ability to maintain self-control is a function of the amount, type, and consistency of coercion experienced as he or she goes through the life course. Prosocial behavior occurs when the amount of coercion is minimal. Chronic offenders grew up in homes where parents used erratic control or applied it in an inconsistent fashion.

A variation of differential coercion is differential social support and coercion theory. This theory states that consistently applied social support may eventually negate or counterbalance the crime-producing influence of coercion. Social support comes in two forms, expressive and instrumental. To reduce crime rates, societies must enhance the legitimate sources of social support and reduce the forces of coercion. Control balance theory postulates the concept of personal control as a predisposing element for criminality. The concept of control has two distinct elements: 1) the amount of control one is subjected to by others and 2 the amount of control one can exercise over others. Conformity results when these two elements are in balance. Control imbalances produce deviant and criminal behaviors. Those who sense a deficit of control turn to three types of behavior to restore balance. Those behaviors are predation, defiance, and submission. An excess of control can also lead to deviance and crime and those who have an excess of control engage in exploitation, plunder, and decadence.

The theories in this chapter share some common ground. First, a criminal career must be understood as a passage along which people travel. Second, the factors that affect a criminal career may include structural factors, socialization factors, biological factors, psychological factors, and opportunity factors. The theories differ in their view of human development with life course theories suggesting people constantly change and latent trait theories claiming people are changeless due to a master trait. Regardless of this difference, developmental theories have prompted multi-dimensional treatment efforts and strategies designed to target at-risk children.

STUDENT EXERCISES

Exercise 1

Go online to http://www.wjh.harvard.edu/soc/faculty/sampson/2004.2.pdf and read the article, "A General Age-Graded Theory of Crime: Lessons Learned and the Future of Life-Course Criminology." After reading the article, write a two to three page paper comparing Sampson and Laub's age-graded theory to Hirschi's social bond theory.

Exercise 2

Go to http://wcr.sonoma.edu/v4n1/Manuscripts/katzarticle.pdf and read the article by Rebecca S. Katz. Then prepare a listing of five major key points contained in the article. Next, compare your results with those of one of your classmates, and then two of you are to come up with an agreement on the five most important points in the article.

CRIMINOLOGY WEB LINKS

http://www.lse.ac.uk/collections/methodologyInstitute/pdf/SKanazawa/JCCJ2002.pdf
This is website provides an interesting article on social capital, crime, and human nature. The authors state that their article demonstrates how evolutionary psychology ". . . can bridge theories on the proximate causes of crime with the "ultimate" causes of human nature and human behavior."

http://www.roxbury.net/clcwebch1.pdf
The website provides chapter 1 of *Crime and the Life Course: An Introduction* by Michael L. Benson. It provides a good insight into the book and a basic review of what life course theory is.

http://www.ncjrs.org/pdffiles1/nij/grants/184551.pdf
This website contains a research article titled "Influence of Neighborhood, Peer, and Family Context: Trajectories of Delinquent/Criminal Offending Across the Life Course" by Kenneth C. Land.

http://www.findarticles.com/p/articles/mi_m2294/is_n5-6_v28/ai_14154682
This article looks at sexual assault and stranger aggression on a Canadian university campus. The main purpose of the paper is to present exploratory Canadian incidence data collected from a sample of eastern Ontario female university students.

TEST BANK

FILL-IN THE BLANKS

1. _____ _____ _____ view criminality as a dynamic process, influenced by a multitude of individual characteristics, traits, and social experiences.

2. The view that criminality may best be understood as one of many social problems faced by at-risk youth is called _____ _____ _____.

3. Most life course theories assume that the seeds of a _____ _____ are planted early in life and that early onset of deviance strongly predicts later and more serious criminality.

4. Age of onset is associated with another key life course concept, the _____ _____ _____.

5. Moffitt finds that there is a small group of _____ _____ _____ who begin their offending career at a very early age and continue to offend well into adulthood.

6. According to the social development model, a child must maintain _____ _____ to control the risk of antisocial behavior.

7. _____ _____ states that the onset of crime can be traced to a deterioration of the social bond during adolescence, marked by weakened attachment to parents, commitment to school, and belief in conventional values.

8. Sampson and Laub's age-graded theory states that marriage and career are _____ _____ in one's life.

9. The process whereby a person reshapes his or her thought and behavior patterns into a more conventional and rewarding lifestyle is termed a _____ _____.

10. According to the general theory of crime, the propensity to commit crimes remains stable throughout a person's life. Change in the frequency of criminal activity is purely a function of change in _____ _____.

TRUE/FALSE QUESTIONS

1. T/F According to life course theory, even as toddlers, people begin relationships and behaviors that will determine their adult life course.

2. T/F The covert pathway escalates to aggressive acts beginning with aggression (annoying others, bullying), leading to physical (and gang) fighting, and then to violence (attacking someone, forced theft).

3.   T/F Not all persistent offenders begin at an early age.

4.   T/F Males, but not females, who have early experiences with antisocial behavior are the ones most likely to be continually involved in this type of behavior throughout the life course.

5.   T/F Early-onset delinquents appear to be more violent than their older peers, who are likely to be involved in nonviolent crimes such as theft.

6.   T/F Unlike Hirschi's version of control theory, which assumes that all attachments are beneficial, the social development model suggests that interaction with antisocial peers and adults promotes participation in delinquency and substance abuse.

7.   T/F The Gluecks' research has remained a mainstay of criminological thinking since their initial research in the 1930s.

8.   T/F The key idea in interactional theory is that causal influences are bidirectional.

9.   T/F Problem behavior syndrome views crime as a distinct type of antisocial behavior, separate from other antisocial behaviors that involve family dysfunction, sensation seeking, unemployment, and educational underachievement.

10. T/F According to Sampson and Laub, when adolescents achieve adulthood, those who had significant problems with the law are able to desist from crime if they become attached to a spouse who supports and sustains them, even when the spouse knows they had gotten in trouble when they were young.

11. T/F Wilson and Richard Herrnstein's human nature theory argues that personal traits—such as genetic makeup, intelligence, and body build—may outweigh the importance of social variables as predictors of criminal activity.

12. T/F Gottfredson and Hirschi attribute the tendency to commit crimes to a person's level of self-esteem.

13. T/F Colvin's differential coercion theory suggests that a person's ability to maintain self-control is a function of the amount, type, and consistency of coercion experienced as he or she goes through the life course.

14. T/F Differential social support and coercion theory posits that consistently applied social support may eventually negate or counterbalance the crime-producing influence of coercion.

15. T/F Environmental traits rather than individual traits seem to have the greatest influence on life course persistence.

MULTIPLE CHOICE QUESTIONS

1. Which theories attempt to provide a more global vision of a criminal career, encompassing its onset, continuation, and termination?
   a. latent trait theories
   b. developmental theories
   c. integrated theories
   d. life course theories

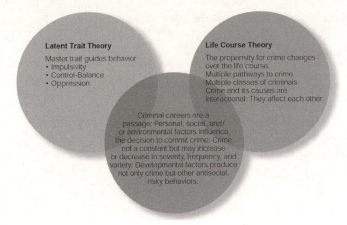

2. Which theories view criminality as a dynamic process, influenced by a multitude of individual characteristics, traits, and social experiences?
   a. latent trait theories
   b. developmental theories
   c. integrated theories
   d. life course theories

3. Those who suffer from this find themselves with a range of personal dilemmas ranging from drug abuse to being accident prone, requiring more healthcare and hospitalization, becoming teenage parents, and having mental health problems.
   a. problem behavior syndrome
   b. latent behavior syndrome
   c. antisocial behavior syndrome
   d. criminal behavior syndrome

4. Which pathway begins at an early age with stubborn behavior that leads to defiance (doing things one's own way, disobedience) and then to authority avoidance (staying out late, truancy, running away)?
   a. covert pathway
   b. overt pathway
   c. authority conflict pathway
   d. antisocial pathway

5. Which pathway involves escalation to aggressive acts - beginning with aggression (annoying others, bullying), leading to physical (and gang) fighting, and then to violence (attacking someone, forced theft)?
    a. covert pathway
    b. overt pathway
    c. authority conflict pathway
    d. antisocial pathway

6. In his important work, *Making Good: How Ex-Convicts Reform and Rebuild Their Lives*, criminologist Shadd Maruna found that desistance was a/an:
    a. instantaneous event
    b. practiced event
    c. route
    d. process

7. Males and females with antisocial behavior have many similar experiences. Which of the following is a **DISSIMILAR** behavior?
    a. high rates of mortality
    b. criminal behavior
    c. poor sexual health
    d. tendency to commit suicide

8. Referring to persistence, what do we call those who follow the path whereby the prevalence and frequency of antisocial behavior peaks in adolescence and then diminishes?
    a. adolescent-limited offenders
    b. life course persisters
    c. early-onset offenders
    d. latent-limited offenders

9. What life course theory holds that commitment and attachment to conventional institutions, activities, and beliefs insulate youths from the criminogenic influences of their environment?
    a. age-graded theory
    b. latent trait theory
    c. the social development model
    d. interactional theory

10. According to _____, the onset of crime can be traced to a deterioration of the social bond during adolescence.
    a. age-graded theory
    b. latent trait theory
    c. the social development model
    d. interactional theory

11. Which of the following is **NOT** a key element of human development that Agnew's general theory of crime and delinquency terms "life domains?"
    a. peers
    b. family
    c. church
    d. school

12. According to Sampson and Laub's age-graded theory, positive relations with individuals and institutions that are life sustaining are called:
    a. social capital
    b. life domains
    c. transitions
    d. pathways

13. A personal attribute or characteristic that controls one's inclination or propensity to commit crime is called a/an:
    a. problem behavior syndrome
    b. criminal onset
    c. antisocial potential
    d. latent trait

14. Which of the following is **NOT** a characteristic of the latent trait view?
    a. latent traits are stable
    b. the opportunity to commit crime is stable
    c. the propensity to commit crime is stable
    d. people age out of crime

15. What theory argues that personal traits, such as genetic makeup, intelligence, and body build, may outweigh the importance of social variables as predictors of criminal activity?
    a. human nature theory
    b. general theory of crime
    c. age-graded theory
    d. differential coercion theory

16. What theory considers the criminal offender and the criminal act as separate concepts?
    a. human nature theory
    b. general theory of crime
    c. age-graded theory
    d. differential coercion theory

17. Gottfredson and Hirschi attribute the tendency to commit crimes to a person's level of:
    a. testosterone
    b. self-reliance
    c. self-control
    d. education

18. Gottfredson and Hirschi trace the root cause of poor self-control to:
    a. ADHD
    b. inadequate childrearing practices
    c. inadequate education
    d. labeling

19. People who maintain a _____ and who become parents are the most likely to mature out of crime.
    a. strong religious faith
    b. strong relationship with their parents
    c. successful job
    d. successful marriage

20. Coercion that is direct, involving the use or threat of force and intimidation from parents is called:
    a. interpersonal coercion
    b. personal coercion
    c. intrapersonal coercion
    d. impersonal coercion

21. According to control balance theory, which of the following crimes would be classified as "plunder?"
    a. an arson
    b. polluting the environment
    c. child molesting
    d. hiring a contract killer

22. A criticism of Gottfredson and Hirschi's general theory of crime is that it ignores:
    a. age
    b. economics
    c. moral beliefs
    d. education

Criminal Offender

Impulsive personality
- Physical
- Insensitive
- Risk-taking
- Short-sighted
- Nonverbal

Low self-control
- Poor parenting
- Deviant parents
- Lack of supervision
- Active
- Self-centered

Weakening of social bonds
- Attachment
- Involvement
- Commitment
- Belief

+

Criminal Opportunity
- Presence of gangs
- Lack of supervision
- Lack of guardianship
- Suitable targets

=

Criminal Act
- Delinquency
- Smoking
- Drinking
- Underage sex
- Substance abuse

23. What theory states that the concept of control has two distinct elements: the amount of control one is subject to by others and the amount of control one can exercise over others?
    a. human nature theory
    b. general theory of crime
    c. control balance theory
    d. differential coercion theory

24. According to control balance theory, _____ challenges control mechanisms but stops short of physical harm, for example vandalism, curfew violations, and unconventional sex is called:
    a. defiance
    b. predation
    c. plunder
    d. exploitation

25. The Fast Track Project is designed to prevent _____ in high-risk children entering first grade.
    a. educational underachievement
    b. cognitive dysfunction
    c. ineffective parental discipline
    d. serious antisocial behavior

ESSAY QUESTIONS

1. Discuss the factors that influence the life course.

2. Discuss the differences between the three pathways to crime.

3. Explain the concept of "turning points in crime."

4. Discuss the influence of social capital on crime.

5. Discuss Gottfredson and Hirschi's general theory of crime.

MATCHING

1. _____ Adolescent-Limiteds
2. _____ Turning Points
3. _____ Social Development Model
4. _____ Authority Conflict Pathway
5. _____ Social Capital
6. _____ Wolfgang's Cohort Research
7. _____ Overt Pathway
8. _____ Latent Trait
9. _____ Developmental Theories
10. _____ Life Course Theory

A. A view that posits a number of community-level risk factors make some people susceptible to antisocial behaviors
B. Pathway to crime that escalates to aggressive acts beginning with aggression, leading to physical fighting and then to violence
C. A stable feature, characteristic, property or condition, present at birth or soon after, that makes some people crime-prone over the life course
D. Pathway to crime that begins at an early age with stubborn behavior
E. "Typical teenagers" who get into minor scrapes and engage in what might be considered rebellious teenage behavior with their friends
F. A small group of chronic offenders engage in frequent and repeated criminal activity and continue to do so across their life span.
G. Attempt to provide a more global vision of a criminal career, encompassing its onset, continuation, and termination
H. A view that even as toddlers, people begin relationships and behaviors that will determine their adult life course
I. Positive relations with individuals and institutions that are life-sustaining
J. Life events that enable adult offenders to desist from crime

CHAPTER 9 ANSWER KEY

Fill in the Blank Answers

1. life course theories
2. problem behavior syndrome
3. criminal career
4. continuity of crime
5. life course persisters
6. prosocial bonds
7. interactional theory
8. turning points
9. cognitive transformation
10. criminal opportunity

True/False Answers

1.	T	6.	T	11.	T
2.	F	7.	F	12.	F
3.	T	8.	T	13.	T
4.	F	9.	F	14.	T
5.	T	10.	T	15.	F

Multiple Choice Answers

1.	B	11.	C	21.	B
2.	D	12.	A	22.	C
3.	A	13.	D	23.	C
4.	C	14.	B	24.	A
5.	B	15.	A	25.	D
6.	D	16.	B		
7.	D	17.	C		
8.	A	18.	B		
9.	C	19.	D		
10.	D	20.	A		

Essay Questions

1. Pages 286-292
2. Pages 287-288
3. Page 294
4. Page 295
5. Pages 297-305

Matching Answers

1.	E	6.	F
2.	J	7.	B
3.	A	8.	C
4.	D	9.	G
5.	I	10.	H

VIOLENT CRIME

OUTLINE

Chapter 10

Violent Crime

LEARNING OBJECTIVES

1. Be familiar with the various causes of violent crime

2. Know the concept of the brutalization process

3. Be able to discuss the history of rape and know the different types of rape

4. Be able to discuss the legal issues in rape prosecution

5. Recognize that there are different types of murder

6. Be able to discuss the differences among serial killing, mass murder, and spree killing

7. Be familiar with the nature of assault in the home

8. Understand the careers of armed robbers

9. Be able to discuss newly emerging forms of violence such as stalking, hate crimes, and workplace violence

10. Understand the different types of terrorism and what is being done to combat terrorist activities

KEYWORDS AND DEFINITIONS

Expressive violence: acts that vent rage, anger, or frustration.

Instrumental violence: designed to improve the financial or social position of the criminal, for example, through an armed robbery or murder for hire.

Crusted over: children who have been victims of or witnesses to violence and do not let people inside, nor do the express heir feelings. They exploit others and in turn are exploited by those older and stronger; as a result, they develop a sense of hopelessness.

Subculture of violence: norms and customs that, in contrast to society's dominant value system, legitimize and expect the use of violence to resolve social conflicts.

Disputatiousness: a concept that refers to how it is considered appropriate behavior within culturally defined conflict situations for an individual who has been offended by a negative outcome in a dispute to seek reparations through violent means.

Rape: unlawful sexual intercourse with a female without her consent.

Gang rape: forcible rape involving multiple offenders, are more severe in violence and outcome.

Serial rape: involves rapists who engage in multiple rapes, sometimes increasing their use of force.

Acquaintance rape: forcible sex in which offender and victim are acquainted with each other.

Statutory rape: sexual relations between an underage individual and an adult; an underage partner is considered incapable of giving informed consent.

Marital rape: forcible sex between people who are legally married to each other.

Marital exemption: the practice in some states of prohibiting the prosecution of husbands for the rape of their wives.

Virility mystique: the belief that males must separate their sexual feelings from needs for love, respect, and affection.

Narcissistic personality disorder: a condition marked by a persistent pattern of self-importance, need for admiration, lack of empathy, and preoccupation with fantasies of unlimited success, power, brilliance, beauty, or ideal love.

Aggravated rape: rape involving multiple offenders, weapons, and victim injuries.

Consent: In prosecuting rapes cases, it is essential to prove that the attack was forced and that the victim did not give voluntary consent to her attacker. In a sense, the burden of proof is on the victim to show that her character is beyond question and that she in no way encouraged, enticed, or misled the accused rapist. Proving victim dissent is not a requirement in any other violent crime.

Shield laws: laws designed to protect rape victims by prohibiting the defense attorney from inquiring about their previous sexual relationships.

Murder: the unlawful killing of a human being with malice aforethought.

First-degree murder: the killing of another person after premeditation and deliberation.

Premeditation: consideration of a homicide before it occurs.

Deliberation: planning a homicide after careful thought, however brief, rather than acting on sudden impulse.

Felony murder: a homicide in the context of another felony, such as robbery or rape; legally defined as first-degree murder.

Second-degree murder: a homicide with malice but not premeditation or deliberation, as when a desire to inflict serious bodily harm and a wanton disregard for life result in the victim's death

Manslaughter: a homicide without malice.

Nonnegligent manslaughter: a homicide committed in the heat of passion or during a sudden quarrel; although intent may be present, malice is not; also called voluntary manslaughter.

Involuntary manslaughter: a homicide that occurs as a result of acts that are negligent and without regard for the harm they may cause others, such as driving under the influence of alcohol or drugs.

Negligent manslaughter: a homicide that occurs as a result of acts that are negligent and without regard for the harm they may cause others, such as driving under the influence of alcohol or drugs; also called involuntary manslaughter.

Feticide: endangering or killing an unborn fetus.

Infanticide: the murder of a very young child.

Filicide: the murder of an older child.

Eldercide: the murder of a senior citizen.

Serial killer: a person who kills three or more persons in three or more separate events. In between the murders, the serial killer reverts to his normal lifestyle.

Mass murder: the killing of a large number of people in a single incident by an offender who typically does not seek concealment or escape.

Familicide: the killing of one's family.

Road rage: a term used to describe motorists who assault each other.

Child abuse: any physical, sexual, or emotional trauma to a child for which no reasonable explanation, such as an accident, can be found. Child abuse can also be a function of neglecting to give proper care and attention to a young child.

Neglect: not providing a child with the care and shelter to which he or she is entitled.

Sexual abuse: the exploitation of a child through rape, incest, or molestation by a parent or other adults.

Acquaintance robbery: robbers who focus their thefts on people they know.

Hate crimes: acts of violence or intimidation designed to terrorize or frighten people considered undesirable because of their race, religion, ethnic origin, or sexual orientation.

Bias crimes: Violent acts directed toward a particular person or members of a group merely because the targets share a discernable racial, ethnic, religious, or gender characteristic; also called hate crimes.

Thrill-seeking hate crimes: violent acts committed by hatemongers who join forces to have fun by bashing minorities or destroying property; inflicting pain on others gives hatemongers a sadistic thrill.

Reactive (defensive) hate crimes: violent acts committed by perpetrators who believe they are taking a defensive stand against outsiders who they believe threaten their community or way of life.

Mission hate crimes: violent crimes committed by disturbed individuals who see it as their duty to rid the world of evil.

Retaliatory hate crimes: a hate crime motivated by revenge for another hate crime, either real or imaginary, which may spark further retaliation.

Workplace violence: violent acts committed by irate employees or former employees who attack coworkers or sabotage machinery and production lines; now considered the third leading cause of occupational injury or death.

Sufferance: the aggrieved party does nothing to rectify a conflict situation; over time, the unresolved conflict may be compounded by other events that cause an eventual eruption.

Stalking: a pattern of behavior directed at a specific person that includes repeated physical or visual proximity, unwanted communications, and/or threats sufficient to cause fear in a reasonable person.

Terrorism: the illegal use of force against innocent people to achieve a political objective.

International terrorism: terrorism involving citizens or the territory of more than one country.

Terrorist group: any group that practices, or that has significant subgroups that practice, international terrorism.

Guerilla: the term means "little war" and developed out of the Spanish rebellion against French troops after Napoleon's 1808 invasion of the Iberian Peninsula. Today the term is used interchangeably with the term terrorist.

Death squads: government troops used to destroy political opposition parties.

USA Patriot Act (USAPA): legislation giving U.S. law enforcement agencies a freer hand to investigate and apprehend suspected terrorists.

CHAPTER OUTLINE

I. The causes of violence
    A. Psychological abnormality
        1. Dorothy Otnow Lewis – kids who kill may suffer from multiple symptoms of psychological abnormality.
            a. Neurological impairment
            b. Low intelligence
            c. Psychotic symptoms
        2. Lewis finds that death row inmates have a history of
            a. Mental impairment
            b. Intellectual dysfunction
        3. Abnormal personality structures associated with violence and murderers who kill themselves shortly after committing their crimes

B. Evolutionary factors/human instinct
    1. Freud maintained that humans possess two opposing instinctual drives that interact to control behavior.
        a. Eros, the life instinct, which drives people toward self-fulfillment and enjoyment
        b. Thanatos, the death instinct, which produces self-destruction
            1) Expressed internally as suicide, alcoholism or other self-destructive behaviors
            2) Expressed externally as violence and sadism
    2. Lorenz argued that aggressive energy is produced by inbred instincts that are independent of environmental forces.
        a. Humans possess some of the same aggressive instincts as animals.
        b. Unlike lower species, where aggression is rarely fatal; humans lack a similar inhibition against fatal violence and are capable of killing their own.

C. Substance abuse
    1. Has been linked to violence in one of three ways
        a. Psychopharmacological relationship – violence may be the direct consequence of ingesting mood-altering substances.
        b. Economic compulsive behavior – drug users/dealers resort to violence to obtain the financial resources to support their habit.
        c. Systemic link – violence escalates when drug-dealing gangs flex their muscle to dominate territory and drive out rivals.

D. Socialization and upbringing
    1. Absent or deviant parents
    2. Inconsistent discipline
    3. Physical abuse
    4. Lack of supervision
    5. Physical punishment
        a. Children who are subject to even minimal amounts of physical punishment may be more likely to one day use violence.
        b. The effect of physical punishment may be neutralized, to some extent, if parents also provide support, warmth, and care.
    6. Abused children
        a. Abused children later engage in delinquent behaviors, including violence.
        b. Sexual abuse is also a constant factor in father (patricide) and mother (matricide) killings.
        c. Juvenile death row inmates have long histories of intense child abuse.
        d. Abuse may have the greatest effect if it is persistent and extends from childhood to adolescence.
        e. Abusive childhood experiences may be a key factor in the later development of relationship aggression.
    7. The brutalization process
        a. Athens finds that people can be classified into three groups based on their aggressive tendencies
            1) Nonviolent
            2) Violent (those who attack others physically with the intention of harming them)
            3) Incipiently violent (those who are willing and ready to attack but limit themselves to violent ultimatums and/or intimidating physical gestures)

       b.   Four distinct types of violent acts
          1)   Physically defensive (in which the perpetrator sees his violent act as one of self-defense)
          2)   Frustrative (in which the offender acts out of anger due to frustration when he cannot get his way)
          3)   Malefic (in which the victim is considered to be extremely evil or malicious)
          4)   Frustrative-malefic (a combined type)
       c.   To become socialized into violence, one must complete the full cycle of the "violentization process."
          1)   Brutilization process – A young victim begins the process of developing a belligerent, angry demeanor.
          2)   Violent performances – When confronted at home, school, or on the street, belligerent youth respond with angry, hostile behavior.
          3)   Virulency – Emerging criminals develop a violent identity that makes them feared; they enjoy intimidating others.
       d.   Many brutalized children do not go on to become criminals or may reject the fact they were abused as children.

E.   Exposure to violence
    1.   People who are constantly exposed to violence may adopt violent methods themselves.
    2.   People are exposed to violence when they associate with violent peers.
    3.   Children living in areas marked by extreme violence may eventually become desensitized to the persistent brutality.
    4.   Between 30 and 40 percent of the children who reported exposure to violence also displayed significant violent behavior themselves.
    5.   Exposure to gun violence, even a single exposure, doubles the chance a young person will later engage in violent behavior.
    6.   Children living in these conditions become "crusted over."
       a.   They do not let people inside, nor do they express their feelings.
       b.   They exploit others and in turn are exploited by those older and stronger.
       c.   They develop a sense of hopelessness.
       d.   They find that parents and teachers focus on their failures and problems, not their achievements.
       e.   They are vulnerable to the lure of delinquent gangs and groups.

F.   Cultural values/subculture of violence
    1.   Another theory is that violence is the product of cultural beliefs, values, and behaviors that develop in poor and disorganized neighborhoods.
    2.   Some areas contain an independent subculture of violence – a concept formulated by Wolfgang and Ferracuti.
    3.   The subculture's norms are separate from society's central, dominant value system.
    4.   Subculture members expect that violence will be used to solve social conflicts and dilemmas.
       a.   Disputatiousness – seeking reparation through violent means
    5.   Research has shown that the subculture of violence may be found in areas that experience concentrated poverty and social disorganization.
       a.   Income inequality and racial disparity may help instill a sense of hopelessness that nourishes pro-violence norms and values.

        b.   *Cultural retaliatory homicide* is common in neighborhoods that suffer economic disadvantage; people take matters into their own hands rather than calling police.

6. Peer group influences
   a. Violence rates are highest in urban areas where subcultural values support teenage gangs.
   b. Gang boys are more likely to have peers who are gun owners and are more likely to carry guns outside the home, themselves.
   c. Gang violence may be initiated for a variety of reasons.
      1) It enables new members to show toughness during initiation ceremonies.
      2) It can be used to retaliate against rivals for actual or perceived grievances.
      3) It protects ownership, such as when violence erupts when graffiti is defaced by rivals.
      4) It protects turf from incursions by outsiders.
   d. Once in gangs, boys' violent behavior quickly escalates; after leaving, it significantly decreases.
7. Regional values
   a. Some criminologists have suggested that regional values promote violence.
   b. Not all criminologists agree with the southern subculture concept.
8. National values
   a. Some nations have relatively high violence rates.
   b. National characteristics predictive of violence:
      1) High level of social disorganization
      2) Economic stress
      3) High rates of child abuse
      4) Approval of violence by the government
      5) Political corruption
      6) An inefficient justice system

II. Forcible rape
   A. From the Latin *rapere*, to take by force
   B. History of rape
      1. Rape has been a recognized crime throughout history.
      2. In early civilization rape was common.
      3. In the Middle Ages men abducted and raped wealthy women to force them into marriage.
      4. Forcible rape was outlawed in the late fifteenth century.
         a. Violation of a wealthy virgin forced a dowry to be paid.
         b. Peasant and married women were not considered rape victims until the sixteenth century.
   C. Rape and the military
      1. Rape has long been associated with military conquest.
         a. Current example: 1996 "rape ring" at Aberdeen Proving Grounds
      2. Throughout recorded history rape has been associated with armies and warfare.
         a. Soldiers of conquering armies have considered sexual possession of their enemies' women one of the spoils of war.
         b. Ancient Greeks considered rape socially acceptable within rules of warfare.
         c. During the Crusades, knights and pilgrims took time to rape.
         d. World War II: Japanese army raped Korean women.

  e. 1990: Serbian army officers raped Bosnian and Kosovar women during the civil war in Yugoslavia to deliberately impregnate these women with Serbian children.

  f. 2004: Militias in the Dafur region of Sudan used rape and sexual violence as a "weapon of war."

D. Incidence of rape
 1. UCR data
  a. About 92, 000 rapes or attempted rapes were reported to U.S. police in 2004.
  b. A rate of about 62 per 100,000 females – compare to 84 per 100,000 females in 1992
  c. Like other violent crimes, the rape rate has been in a decade-long decline.
 2. Population density influences the rape rate.
 3. The police make arrests in slightly more than half of all reported rape offenses.
 4. About half of the offenders are 25 years of age.
 5. About two-thirds of the offenders are white.
 6. Rape is a warm-weather crime.
 7. Rape is underreported.
  a. As many as ten percent of all adult women have been raped during their lifetime.
  b. According to the NCVS, less than half of all rape incidents are reported to police.
   1) Victims are embarrassed.
   2) Victims may blame themselves.
   3) Victims may believe nothing can be done.
   4) Victims may question whether they have "really" been raped.

E. Types of rape and rapists
 1. According to Groth, every rape encounter contains at least one of these three elements.
  a. Power – 55%
  b. Anger – 40%
  c. Sadism – 5%
 2. Gang versus individual rape
  a. As many as 25 percent or more of rapes involve multiple offenders.
  b. Little difference in the demographic characteristics of single- or multiple-victim rapes.
  c. Women who are attacked by multiple offenders are subject to more violence.
  d. Gang rape victims are more likely to:
   1) Resist and face injury than those attacked by single offenders
   2) Call police
   3) Seek therapy
   4) Contemplate suicide
 3. Serial rape
  a. Some rapists are one-time offenders but others engage in multiple or serial rapes.
  b. Some rapists constantly increase their use of force.
   1) Twenty-five percent of such "increasers" are white males.
   2) Increasers have a limited history for other crimes, focusing almost solely on sexual violence.
  c. Some serial rapists commit "blitz rapes," in which they attack their victims without warning.
  d. Others try to "capture" their victims by striking up a conversation or offering them a ride.
  e. Others use personal or professional relationships to gain access to their targets

   4. Acquaintance rape
    a. Involves someone known to the victim, including family members and friends
     1) Date rape
     2) Statutory rape
     3) Marital rape
    b. Estimated that 50% of rapes involve acquaintances rather than strangers
     1) Stranger rapes are typically more violent than acquaintance rapes.
     2) Stranger attackers more likely to carry a weapon, to threaten, and to physically harm the victim.
     3) Stranger rapes may be less likely to be prosecuted than acquaintance rapes.
   5. Date rape
    a. Involves people who are in some form of courting relationship
    b. No single form of date rape
    c. Believed to be frequent on college campuses
     1) 15-20% of all college women
     2) One self-report study indicated 100% of all campus rapists knew their victims beforehand.
    d. The incidence of date rape may be higher than surveys indicate.
   6. Marital rape
    a. Marital exemption – Traditionally, a legally married husband could not be charged with raping his wife.
    b. Research – Many women are raped each year by their husbands as part of an overall pattern of spousal abuse.
    c. Marital rapes are not the result of "healthy male sexuality."
    d. Many spousal rapes are accompanied by brutal, sadistic beatings.
    e. Today, almost every state recognizes marital rape as a crime.
     1) Most states do not give wives the same legal protection as they would nonmarried couples.
     2) Marital rapists are sanctioned less harshly than other rapists.
   7. Statutory rape
    a. Sexual relations between an underage minor and an adult.
    b. Although the sex is not forced or coerced, the law indicates that young people are incapable of giving informed consent.
 F. The causes of rape
   1. Evolutionary, biological aspects of the male sex drive
    a. Rape may be instinctual, developed over the ages as a means of perpetuating the species.
     1) Males have an evolutionary, sexual urge to spread genes as widely as possible.
     2) Women are more cautious and look for mates willing to make a long-term commitment to child-rearing.
     3) This difference produces sexual tension that forces men to employ forceful copulatory tactics.
    b. Rape is bound up with sexuality as well as violence because rape involves the "drive to possess and control others to whom one is sexually attracted."
   2. Male socialization
    a. Some men have been socialized to be aggressive with women and believe that the use of violence or force is legitimate if their sexual advances are rebuffed.
    b. Use of sexual violence is aggravated if pro-force socialization is reinforced by peer group members.

    c.   From an early age, boys are taught to be aggressive, forceful, tough, and dominating.

    d.   Virility mystique – the belief that males must separate their sexual feelings from needs for love, respect, and affection.

        1)   Sexual insecurity may lead some men to commit rape.

        2)   Feminists suggest that the trend toward gender equality may bring an immediate increase in rape rates because of increased threats to male virility.

3.   Psychological abnormality

    a.   Rapists suffer from some type of personality disorder or mental illness.

        1)   A significant percentage of incarcerated rapists exhibit psychotic tendencies; many other have hostile, sadistic feelings toward women.

    b.   Evidence links rape proclivity with narcissistic personality disorder.

4.   Social learning

    a.   Men learn to commit rapes much as they learn any other behavior.

        1)   Groth found 40% of rapists were sexually victimized as children.

        2)   Watching violent or pornographic films featuring women who are beaten, rapes, or tortured has been linked to sexually aggressive behavior in men.

5.   Sexual motivation

    a.   Most criminologists believe rape is a violent act that is not sexually motivated.

    b.   NCVS data reveal

        1)   Victims tend to be young.

        2)   Rapists prefer younger, presumably more attractive, victims.

        3)   There is an association between the ages of rapists and their victims.

        4)   Men choose rape targets of approximately the same age as consensual sex partners.

    c.   This pattern indicates that:

        1)   Older criminals may rape for motives of power and control.

        2)   Younger offenders may be seeking sexual gratification.

G.   Rape and the law

1.   Proving rape

    a.   Rape victims reluctant to report sexual assaults because of the sexist fashion in which rape victims are treated by police, prosecutors, and the courts.

    b.   Proving guilt in a rape case is extremely challenging for prosecutors.

        1)   Prosecutors must establish that the act was forced and violent and that no question of compliance exists.

        2)   Prosecutors concerned that a traumatized victim may identify the wrong man.

        3)   Jurors are sometimes swayed by thinking that the rape was victim precipitated.

2.   Consent

    a.   It is essential to prove that:

        1)   The attack was forced.

        2)   The victim did not give voluntary consent to her attacker.

    b.   In a sense, the burden of proof is on the victim to show that

        1)   Her character is beyond question.

        2)   She in no way encouraged, enticed, or misled the accused rapist.

    c.   Proving victim dissent is not a requirement in any other violent crime.

    d.   Even when found guilty, a rapist's punishment is significantly reduced if the victim is believe to have negative personal characteristics.

3. Reform
   a. Rape laws have been changing around the country.
   b. Sexual assault laws outlaw any type of forcible sex, including homosexual rape.
   c. Most states and the federal government have developed shield laws.
      1) Validity of shield laws upheld in 1991 case of *Michigan v. Lucas*
   d. Corroboration is no longer required except under extraordinary circumstances.
   e. The Violence Against Women Act (1994) allows rape victims to sue in federal court.

III. Murder and homicide
   A. Degrees of murder
      1. First-degree murder
         a. Premeditation
         b. Deliberation
         c. Felony murder
      2. Second-degree murder
         a. Malice aforethought, but not premeditation or deliberation
         b. Manslaughter
         c. Voluntary or nonnegligent manslaughter
         d. Involuntary or negligent manslaughter
      3. "Born and alive"
         a. Murder victim can be a fetus that has not yet been delivered – feticide.
         b. Prosecution of women for endangering or killing their unborn fetuses by their drug or alcohol abuse.
         c. *Whitner v. State*
         d. State laws allow prosecutions for murder when a third party's actions kill a fetus.
   B. The nature and extent of murder
      1. Murder rates
         a. Peaked in 1933 and then fell until 1958
         b. Doubled from mid-1960s to the late 1970sa and then peaked in 1980
         c. Brief decline, then rose again in late 1980s and early 1990s peaking in 1991
         d. Decline in the murder rate since 1991
      2. Murder tends to be an urban crime.
         a. More than half of the homicides occur in cities with a population of 100,000 or more.
      3. Almost 1/4 of homicides occur in cities with a population of more than one million.
      4. Infanticide – killing a young child
      5. Filicide – killing an older child
      6. Eldercide – killing an older adult
      7. Murder victims and offenders (90% of those arrested) are males.
      8. Approximately 1/3 of murder victims and almost 1/2 the offenders are under the age of 25.
      9. Slightly less than half of all victims are African Americans.
      10. Slightly less than half are white.
      11. African Americans are disproportionately represented as both homicide victims and offenders
      12. Murder tends to be an intraracial crime – 90% of victims slain by members of their own race.

13. Murderers typically have a long involvement in crime.
C. Murderous relations
   1. Spousal relations
      a. The rate of homicide among cohabiting couples has declined significantly during the past two decades.
      b. The number of unmarried men killed by their partners has declined.
         1) Possibly due to alternatives to abusive relationships such as battered women's shelters
      c. The number of women killed by their partners has increased dramatically.
         1) Men may kill because they fear losing control and power.
      d. Research indicates that most females who kill their mates do so after suffering repeated violent attacks.
   2. Personal relations
      a. Most murders occur among people who are acquainted.
         1) Often the result of a long-simmering dispute
      b. Homicides follow a sequential pattern.
         1) First, the victim makes what the offender considers an offensive move.
         2) The offender typically retaliates verbally or physically.
         3) An agreement to end things violently is forged with the victim's provocative response.
         4) The battle ensues, leaving the victim dead or dying.
         5) The offender's escape is shaped by his or her relationship to the victim or the reaction of the audience, if any.
   3. Stranger relations
      a. Over the past decade, the number of stranger homicides has increased.
      b. Today more than half of murderers are strangers to their victims.
      c. "Three-Strikes" laws may contribute to the increase of stranger killings.
   4. Student relations
      a. Violence in schools has become commonplace.
      b. More than 16% of schoolchildren have been bullied by other students.
      c. Approximately 30% of 6th through 10th graders report being involved in some aspect of bullying.
      d. School shootings are relatively rare but may be expected because up to ten percent of students report bringing weapons to school on a regular basis.
         1) Most school shootings occur around the start of the school day, at lunch, or at the end of the school day.
         2) In 55% of shootings, a note, threat, or other action indicating risk for violence occurred prior to the event.
         3) Shooters were likely to have expressed some form of suicidal behavior and to have been bullied by their peers.
D. Serial murder
   1. Serial killers kill in three or more separate events over a long period of time and revert to normal lifestyles between killings.
      a. Some wander the countryside killing at random.
      b. Others lure victims to their deaths.
      c. Some are sadists who gain satisfaction from torturing and killing.
      d. Psychopathic killers are motivated by a character disorder that causes an inability to experience shame, guilt, sorrow, or other normal human emotions.
   2. Fox and Levin's typology of serial killers
      a. Thrill killers strive for sexual sadism or dominance.

      b.   Mission killers want to reform the world or have a vision that drives them to kill.

      c.   Expedience killers are out for profit or want to protect themselves from a perceived threat.

   3.   Female serial killers

      a.   Ten to fifteen percent of serial killers are women.

      b.   Gender differences in serial killing

         1)   Males more likely than females to use extreme violence and torture

         2)   Males more likely to use a hands-on approach; females more likely to poison or smother victims

         3)   Male killers stalk; female killers lure

         4)   Female killers older and more likely to abuse drugs and alcohol

         5)   Male killers more often diagnosed as having antisocial personality disorders; women killers diagnosed as having histrionic, manic-depressive, borderline, dissociative, and antisocial personality disorders

      c.   Profile of a female serial killer:

         1)   Smothers or poisons someone she knows

         2)   Suffered from an abusive relationship in a disrupted family

         3)   Below average education level with a low-status job

   4.   Why do serial killers kill?

      a.   The cause of serial murder eludes criminologists.

      b.   Most experts view serial killers as sociopaths who from early childhood demonstrate bizarre behavior.

      c.   Fox and Levin – serial killers may enjoy:

         1)   The thrill

         2)   The sexual gratification

         3)   The dominance over the victim

         4)   Rarely use a gun as it would be too quick and would deprive a serial killer of exalting in his victim's suffering

         5)   Dispute the notion that serial killers have some form of biological or psychological problem

         6)   Serial killers are not insane but are "more cruel than crazy."

   5.   Controlling serial killers

      a.   Law enforcement official have been at a loss to control serial killers; catching serial killers is often a matter of luck.

      b.   FBI has developed a profiling system to identify potential suspects.

      c.   The Justice Department's Violent Criminal Apprehension Program (VICAP

E.   Mass Murder

   1.   Killing of four or more victims by one or a few assailants within a single event.

      a.   Mass murders engage in a single, uncontrollable outburst called "simultaneous killing."

   2.   Fox and Levin define four types of mass murderers

      a.   Revenge killers seek to get even with individuals or society at large

      b.   Love killers are motivated by a warped sense of devotion

      c.   Profit killers are usually trying to cover up a crime, eliminate witnesses, and carry out a criminal conspiracy

      d.   Terrorist killers are trying to send a message

   3.   Mass murder is not a phenomenon of today's society.

      a.   Mass killings nearly as common during the 1920s and 1930s

1) More of these earlier incidents involved familicide.
    b. The most significance between former and contemporary mass murders is that more killers use guns and more incidents involve drug trafficking.

F. Spree killers
    1. Spree killers engage in a rampage of violence over a period of days or weeks.
        a. Spree killing is not confined to a single outburst.
        b. Spree killers do not return to their "normal" identities in between killings.
        c. Some spree killers target a specific group or class.
        d. Some spree killers kill randomly.

IV. Assault and battery
    A. Are two separate crimes
        1. Battery requires offensive touching.
        2. Assault requires no actual touching but involves attempted battery or intentionally frightening the victim by word or deed.
    B. Nature and extent of assault
        1. The pattern of criminal assault is similar to that of homicide.
        2. Road rage
        3. Every citizen is bound by the law of assault, even police officers.
        4. In 2004 the FBI recorded 850,000 assaults, a rate of about 294 per 100,000 inhabitants.
        5. The number of assaults has been in decline, down about 25% in the past decade.
        6. Offenders are usually young, male (about 80 percent), and white.
        7. African Americans arrested for assault (33 percent) in numbers disproportionate to their representation in the population.
        8. Assault victims tend to be male.
        9. Assault rates are highest in urban areas, during summer, and in southern and western regions.
      10. NCVS indicates that only about 1/2 of all serious assaults are reported to the police.
      11. NCVS indicates a steep decline (50%) in assaults over the past decade.
    C. Assault in the home
        1. Criminologists recognize that intrafamily violence is an enduring social problem both in the United States and globally.
            a. Almost half the women who die due to homicide are killed by their current or former husbands or boyfriends.
            b. In some countries, 70% of all female deaths are domestic homicides.
            c. It is possible that nearly one in four women will experience sexual violence over time.
            d. WHO report re: women assaulted by spouse or intimate partner:
                1) 3% in the U.S., Canada, and Australia
                2) 38% in the Republic of Korea
                3) 52% of Palestinian women on the West Bank of the Gaza Strip
                4) In Egypt, 47% of women who were killed by a relative were murdered after they had been raped.
        2. Child abuse
            a. Any physical or emotional trauma to a child for which no reasonable explanation can be found
            b. Child abuse can result from actual physical beatings.
            c. Another form of abuse results from neglect.
            d. Two million reports of suspected child abuse or neglect per year

1) Two-thirds of these unfounded
2) 12.3 child victims per every 1,000 children
3) 1,400 child fatalities in 2002 or 1.98 per 100,000 children
4) Maltreatment rates lower today than a decade ago

3. Sexual abuse
   a. The exploitation of children through rape, incest, and molestation, by parents or other adults
   b. Difficult to estimate the incidence of sexual abuse
      1) Research indicates that at least one in five girls suffer sexual abuse.
   c. The number of reported cases has been in a significant decline.
      1) May be the result of prevention programs, prosecution, and public awareness
      2) May be the result of new evidentiary requirements, legal rights for caregivers, and investigative limitations
   d. Children who have been abused experience: fear, PTSD, behavior problems, sexualized behavior, and poor self-esteem.
   e. Amount of force used during abuse related to long-term effects

4. Parental abuse – Arina Ulman and Murray Straus found
   a. The younger the child, the higher the rate of child-to-parent violence (CPV).
   b. At all ages, more children were violent to mothers than to fathers.
   c. Both boys and girls hit mothers more than fathers.
   d. At all ages, slightly more boys than girls hit parents.
   e. CPV was associated with some form of violence by parents.
      1) Suggested that limiting or curtailing the use of physical punishment would decrease child-to-parent violence

5. Spousal abuse
   a. Spousal abuse has occurred throughout recorded history.
      1) Rome: men had the right to beat their wives until the later stages of the Roman Empire when the practice abated.
      2) During the Middle Ages there was a separation of love and marriage.
      3) From 1400-1900, little community objection against a man using force against a wife as long as the assault did not exceed certain limits
      4) Wife beating outlawed in England and the U.S. by the end of the nineteenth century.
      5) History's long tradition of men's physical control over wives still results in spousal abuse.
   b. The nature and extent of spousal abuse
      1) Sixty to 70 percent of evening calls to the police involve domestic disputes.
      2) Twenty to 40 percent of females experience violence while dating.

V. Robbery
  A. The taking or attempting to take anything of value from the care, custody, or control of a person or persons by force or threat of force or violence and/or putting the victim in fear
  B. Robbery is considered a violent crime because it involves the use of force to obtain money or goods.
    1. 2004: FBI recorded 400,000 robberies, a rate of about 140 per 100,000 population
    2. Robbery rate down more than 40% since 1994
    3. Ecological pattern similar to other violent crimes, except:
      a. Northeastern states have the highest robbery rates.
    4. NCVS has indicates a 63% reduction in the robbery rate since 1993, but shows a recent increase in 2003.

5. Types of robbers
   a. Professional robbers
   b. Opportunist robbers
   c. Addict robbers
6. Typologies indicate the typical robber is likely to be an amateur offender, diverted by modest defensive measures.

C. Acquaintance robbery
   1. Victims may be reluctant to report crimes because they do not want to get involved with the police.
   2. Some robberies are motivated by street justice.
   3. Because the robber knows the victims personally, the robber has inside information that there will be a "good take."
   4. When in desperate need for immediate cash, robbers may target those in close proximity because they are convenient targets.
   5. Victims are more likely to be injured than in stranger robberies.
   6. Robberies of family members more likely to have a bigger payoff than stranger robberies.

D. Rational robbery
   1. Patterns of robbery suggest that it is not merely a random act.
   2. Robberies seem to peak during the winter months.
      a. Cold weather may allow for greater disguise.
      b. Robbers attracted to large amounts of cash carried during the Christmas shopping season.
      c. Because days are shorter, robbers are afforded greater concealment by the dark.
   3. Robbers choose vulnerable victims.
   4. Decker and Wright suggest that robbers are rational decision makers.

VI. Emerging forms of interpersonal violence
   A. Hate crimes or bias crimes
      1. Violent acts directed toward a particular person or members of a group merely because the targets share a discernible racial, ethnic, religious, or gender characteristic
      2. Can include the desecration of a house of worship or cemetery, harassment of a minority group family that has moved into a previously all-white neighborhood, or a racially motivated murder
      3. Usually involves convenient, vulnerable targets who are incapable of fighting back
      4. Factors that produce hate crimes
         a. Poor or uncertain economic conditions
         b. Racial stereotypes in films and on television
         c. Hate-filled discourse on talk shows or in political advertisements
         d. The use of racial code language such as "welfare mothers" and "inner-city thugs"
         e. An individual's personal experiences with members of particular minority groups
         f. Scapegoating
      5. The roots of hate
         a. McDevitt and Levin identify three motivations for hate crimes.
            1) Thrill-seeking hate crimes (66%)
            2) Reactive (defensive) hate crimes (25%)
            3) Mission hate crimes (few)

      b.   McDevitt and Levin with Susan Bennett uncovered a new category of hate crime: retaliatory hate crimes (8%).

      c.   Hate crimes can be committed by "dabblers."

          1)   People who are not committed to hate but drift in and out of active bigotry

      d.   Some people are "sympathizers."

          1)   May not attack a minority but think nothing of telling jokes with racial themes or agreeing with people who despise gays

      e.   Some people are "spectators."

          1)   May not actively participate in bigotry but who do noting to stop its course

6.   Nature and extent of hate crime

      a.   During 2004, there were 9,528 victims.

      b.   Racial bigotry was the motivation for more than half the crimes.

      c.   Twenty percent caused by religious intolerance

      d.   Sixteen percent the result of a sexual-orientation bias

      e.   Almost thirteen percent triggered by an ethnicity/national origin bias

      f.   Sixty percent involved a violent act

      g.   Forty percent involved property crimes

      h.   Intimidation the most common form of hate crime in 2004 but five bias-motivated murders recorded by the FBI

      i.   Most victims reported that they were acquainted with their attackers.

      j.   Most hate crimes are perpetrated in public settings.

7.   Controlling hate crimes

      a.   Today, almost every state jurisdiction has enacted some form of legislation designed to combat hate crimes.

          1)   39 states have enacted laws against bias-motivated violence and intimidation

          2)   19 states have mandated collection of hate crime data

      b.   Critics argue it is unfair to punish hate crime offenders more severely than offenders motivated by revenge, anger, or greed.

      c.   Lawrence argues that a "society dedicated to equality of all its peoples must treat bias crimes differently from other crimes and…enhance the punishment."

          1)   Bias crimes are different.

          2)   More likely to be violent and involve serious physical injury

          3)   Have significant emotional and psychological impact on the victim

          4)   Harm not only the victim but also the "target community"

          5)   Violate the shared value of equality among citizens and racial and religious harmony in a heterogeneous society

8.   Legal controls

      a.   Are symbolic acts of hate protected by the free speech clause of the First Amendment?

      b.   *Virginia v. Black* (2003) – The Supreme Court upheld Virginia's law that criminalized cross burning.

B.   Workplace violence

1.   Creating workplace violence

      a.   A management style that appears cold and insensitive to workers

      b.   Refusing romantic relationships with the assailants or reporting them for sexual harassment

      c.   Coworkers killed because they received a job the assailant coveted

      d.   Irate clients and customers who receive poor service or perceive slights

      e.   Responses to workplace provocations – disgruntled employees may

          1)   Take out anger and aggression by attacking supervisors to punish the company – "murder by proxy"

          2)   Misdirect rage by attacking family members or friends

          3)   Sabotage company equipment

          4)   Doing nothing, such inaction is termed "sufferance"

  2.   The extent of workplace violence

      a.   Cost of workplace violence runs more than $4 billion annually.

      b.   On average, violence in the workplace accounts for about 18 percent of all violent crime.

      c.   Whose occupation is riskiest?

          1)   Police officers

          2)   Correctional officers

          3)   Taxicab drivers

          4)   Private security workers

          5)   Bartenders

  3.   Can workplace violence be controlled?

      a.   One approach is to use third parties to mediate disputes.

      b.   Restorative justice techniques may work particularly well in the workplace.

      c.   Human resource approach

          1)   Aggressive job retraining and continued medical coverage provided after layoff

          2)   Using objective and fair hearings to thwart unfair or biased terminations

          3)   Rigorous screening to identify violence-prone workers

          4)   Establish policies restricting weapons in the workplace

C. Stalking

  1.   A course of conduct directed at a specific person that involves repeated physical or visual proximity, nonconsensual communication, or verbal, written, or implied threats sufficient to cause fear in a reasonable person

  2.   Stalking affects an estimated 1.4 million victims annually.

  3.   College women at particular risk of being victims of stalking.

  4.   Most victims know their stalker.

  5.   Women are most likely to be stalked by an intimate partner.

      a.   Stalked because her assailant wants to control her

  6.   Men are typically stalked by a stranger or an acquaintance..

  7.   Stalkers behave in ways that induce fear.

  8.   Stalkers do not always make overt threats against their victims.

  9.   Stalkers who make verbal threats are the ones most likely to later attack their victims.

  10. Many stalking cases dropped by the courts even if the stalker had an extensive criminal history.

  11. Victims experience long-term social and psychological consequences.

VII. Terrorism

  A. What is terrorism?

    1.   An act must carry with it the intent to disrupt and change the government and must not be merely a common-law crime committed for greed or egotism.

    2.   Most experts agree that terrorism generally involves the illegal use of force against innocent people to achieve a political objective.

    3.   International terrorism

4. Terrorist group
5. Terrorism usually involves a type of political crime that emphasizes violence as a mechanism to promote change.
6. Not all terrorist actions are aimed at political change.
   a. Some terrorists may try to bring about what they consider to be economic or social reform.
7. Terrorism requires secrecy and clandestine operations.
8. Terrorist and guerilla
   a. Guerilla – Spanish term meaning "little war"
   b. Terrorists have an urban focus; guerillas are located in rural areas.
   c. Guerillas may infiltrate urban areas in small bands.

B. A brief history of terrorism
   1. Acts of terrorism have been known throughout history.
   2. When rulers had absolute power, terrorist acts were viewed as one of the only means of gaining political rights.
   3. American privateers who attacked the British during the American Revolution considered heroes, not terrorists.
   4. The term terrorist first became popular during the French Revolution.
   5. World War I started by the assassination of Archduke Franz Ferdinand.
   6. Between the world wars, terrorism existed in Germany, Spain, and Italy.
   7. During World War II, the Germans considered resistors to be terrorists.

C. Contemporary forms of terrorism
   1. Revolutionary terrorists use violence to frighten those in power.
      a. Jemaah Islamiyah
   2. Political terrorists direct their acts at people or groups who oppose the terrorists' political ideology.
      a. Ku Klux Klan, the Arian Nation, the Posse Comitatus
   3. Nationalist terrorism promotes the interests of a minority ethnic or religious group that believes it has been persecuted under majority rule.
      a. Palestinian Liberation Organization, Hamas, Hezbollah
      b. Sufi Islam rebels in China
      c. Chechen terrorists in Russia
   4. Cause-based terrorists espouse a particular social or religious cause and use violence to attract followers to their standard.
      a. Anti-abortion groups
   5. Environmental terrorism is aimed at slowing down individuals, organizations, or developers who are believed to be threatening the environment or harming animals.
      a. Animal Liberation Front and Earth Liberation Front
   6. State-sponsored terrorism occurs when a repressive government regime forces its citizens into obedience, oppresses minorities, and stifles political dissent.
      a. Death squads
   7. Criminal terrorism occurs when terrorist groups become involved in crimes. Such terrorism may involved organized crime groups working in close cooperation with guerillas.
      a. Arms trading
      b. Theft and transportation of nuclear material
      c. Drug dealing
      d. Kidnapping

D. What motivates terrorists?

1. One view is that terrorists are emotionally disturbed individuals who act out their psychosis within the confines of violent groups.
2. Another view is that terrorists hold extreme ideological beliefs that prompt their behavior.
    a. Heightened perceptions of oppressive conditions
    b. Conclude they must resort to violence to effect change
    c. The violence need not be aimed at a specific goal.
    d. "Successful" terrorists believe that their "self-sacrifice" outweighs the guilt created by harming innocent people.
3. Many terrorists appear to be educated members of the upper class.
    a. Modern terrorism involves using the Internet, logistically complex and expensive assaults, and complex writings – all which require the training and education of the social elite, not the oppressed poor.

E. Responses to terrorism
    1. Post 9/11
        a. Critics failed to comprehend the difficulty of gathering intelligence about closed, highly secretive groups.
        b. Difficulty of sealing the nation's borders from nuclear attack
    2. Legal responses
        a. The 1994 Violent Crime Control Act authorized the death penalty for international terrorists who kill U.S. citizens abroad.
        b. USA Patriot Act – sweeping legislation that provides law enforcement agencies a freer hand to investigate and apprehend suspected terrorist.
            1) Expanded traditional tools of surveillance
            2) Expanded the Foreign Intelligence Surveillance Act
            3) Gave greater power to the FBI
            4) Expanded law enforcement monitoring of the Internet
            5) Allowed enforcement agencies to monitor cable operators and to obtain access to cable operator's records and systems.
            6) Expanded the definition of terrorism and enabled the government to monitor, more closely, those people suspected of "harboring" and giving "material support" to terrorists.
            7) Increased the authority of the attorney general to detain and deport noncitizens with little or no judicial review
            8) Is not limited to true terrorism investigations
    3. Judicial responses
        a. Revamped existing agencies, such as mission of the FBI
        b. Homeland Security Act of 2002
            1) Established the Department of Homeland Security
        c. Creation of the office of Director of National Intelligence
            1) Coordinates data from the nation's primary intelligence-gathering agencies
            2) Serves as principle advisor to the president
            3) Statutory intelligence advisor to the National Security Council

CHAPTER SUMMARY

The causes of violence are many and varied. Among the explanations for it are psychological abnormality, evolutionary factors and human instinct, substance abuse, socialization and upbringing, exposure to violence, cultural values, and the subculture of violence.

Forcible rape has been a recognized crime throughout history. Uniform Crime Report data indicate that approximately 92,000 rapes or attempted rapes were reported to U.S. police in 2004, a rate of about 62 per 100,000 females. The National Crime Victimization Survey (NCVS) indicates that half of all rape incidents are reported to the police. Every rape encounter contains at least one of three elements: power, anger, or sadism. As many of 25% of rapes are gang rapes. Other categories of rape are serial rape, acquaintance rape, date rape, marital rape and statutory rape. The causes of rape include evolutionary or biological aspects of the male sex drive, male socialization, psychological abnormality, social learning, and sexual motivation. Proving guilt in a rape case is extremely challenging for prosecutors. The most difficult issue is consent because it is essential to prove that the attack was forced and that the victim did not give voluntary consent to her attacker. Proving victim dissent is not a requirement in any other violent crime.

Murder and homicide tend to be urban crimes and occur in cities with a population of 100,000 or more. The murder rate has declined since 1991. Murder victims and offenders tend to be males and under the age of 25. African Americans are disproportionately represented as both homicide victims and offenders. The rate of homicide among cohabitating couples has declined significantly during the past two decades but the number of women killed by their partners has increased dramatically. Most murders occur among people who are acquainted. Over the past decade, the number of stranger homicides has increased and today more than half of murderers are strangers to their victims. Violence in schools has become commonplace, but school shootings are relatively rare.

Serial killers operate over a long period of time, while mass murderers kill many victims in a single, violent outburst. Female serial killers are somewhat older than their male counterparts, are more likely to poison and smother their victims, and, unlike males, lure rather than stalk their victims. Male serial killers are more likely to use extreme violence and torture, are often diagnosed with antisocial personality disorder, and are less likely to abuse drugs and alcohol. Most experts view serial killers as sociopaths who from early childhood demonstrate bizarre behavior. For law enforcement officials, catching serial killers is more a matter of luck than expertise.

The pattern of criminal assault is similar to that of homicide. In 2004, the FBI recorded 850,000 assaults, a rate of about 294 per 100,000 inhabitants. The number of assaults has been in decline over the past decade. The offenders are typically young, male, and white. However, African Americans are arrested for assault in numbers that are disproportionate to their representation in the population. Assault rates are highest in urban areas, during the summer, and in southern and western regions. The National Crime Victimization Survey indicates that only about half of all serious assaults are reported to the police.

Criminologists recognize that intrafamily violence (assault in the home) is an enduring social problem in the United States and globally. Almost half the women who die due to homicide are killed by their current or former husbands or boyfriends. There are two million suspected reports of child abuse per year with 12.3 child victims per every 1,000 children. Research indicates that at least one in five girls suffer sexual abuse in the home. Children who have been abused experience fear, PTSD, behavior problems, socialization problems, sexualized behavior, and poor self-esteem. Children may also abuse their parents and, at all ages, children are more violent to mothers than to fathers. Spousal abuse has occurred throughout recorded history. Approximately 60 to 70 percent of evening calls to the police involve domestic disputes.

There are three types of robbers: professional robbers, opportunist robbers, and addict robbers. Patterns of robbery suggest that it is not merely a random act and it seems to peak during the winter months. Female armed robbers are likely to choose female targets, but when robbing males, women "set them up" in order to catch them off guard. Decker and Wright suggest that robbers are rational decision makers.

Hate crimes are violent acts directed toward a particular person or members of a group merely because the targets share a discernible racial, ethnic, religious, or gender characteristic. Factors that produce hate crimes are poor or uncertain economic conditions, racial stereotypes in films and on television, hate-filled discourse on talk shows or in political advertisements, the use of racial code language such as "welfare mothers" and "inner-city thugs," an individual's personal experiences with members of particular minority groups, or scapegoating. McDevitt and Levin identify three motivations for hate crimes: thrill-seeking hate crimes, reactive (defensive) hate crimes, and mission hate crimes. McDevitt, Levin, and Bennett uncovered a new category of hate crime called retaliatory hate crimes. Hate crimes can also be committed by "dabblers," and "sympathizers" and "spectators" contribute to bigotry. During 2004, there were 9,528 victims of hate crimes, with racial bias being the motivation for more than half the crimes. Today, almost every state jurisdiction has enacted some form of legislation designed to combat hate crimes. Critics argue it is unfair to punish hate crime offenders more harshly than offenders motivated by revenge, anger or greed. Lawrence argues for enhanced punishment.

There are two factors that tend to create workplace violence: a management style that appears cold and insensitive to workers and refusing romantic relationships with the assailants or reporting them for sexual harassment. The cost of workplace violence runs more than $4 billion annually and, on average, violence in the workplace accounts for about 18 percent of all violent crime. Controlling workplace violence involves mediating disputes and other restorative justice techniques along with human resource approaches – these include job retraining and continued medical coverage after layoffs, fair hearings for terminations, rigorous screening to identify violence-prone employees, and restricting weapons in the workplace.

Another form of interpersonal violence is stalking. Stalking affects an estimated 1.4 million victims annually. College women are at particular risk of being victims of stalking. Most victims know their stalker. Stalkers behave in ways that induce fear, but they do not always make overt threats against their victims; however, stalkers who make verbal threats are the most likely to later attack their victims. Victims of stalking experience long-terms social and psychological consequences.

Terrorism is an act that carries with it the intent to disrupt and change the government and is not merely a common-law crime committed for greed or egotism. Most experts agree that terrorism generally involves the illegal use of force against innocent people to achieve a political objective, although not all terrorism is aimed at political change. Terrorism usually involves a type of political crime that emphasizes violence as a mechanism to promote change. Acts of terrorism have been known throughout history with contemporary forms including revolutionary terrorism, political terrorism, nationalist terrorism, cause-based terrorism, environmental terrorism, state-sponsored terrorism, and criminal terrorism. Some criminologists feel that terrorists are emotionally disturbed individuals who act out their psychosis within the confines of violent groups. Another view is that terrorists hold extreme ideological beliefs that prompt their behavior. Since the attacks of September 11th, responses to terrorism have included the USA Patriot Act, revamping of existing federal agencies such as the FBI, and creation of new agencies such as the Department of Homeland Security.

STUDENT EXERCISES

Exercise 1

Go online to http://www.ojp.usdoj.gov/bjs/homicide/homtrnd.htm and read about homicide trends in the United States. Pick out one topic listed in the contents, browse that topic, and write a one or two page summary on that aspect of homicide trends.

Exercise 2

Go to http://www.ncjrs.org/pdffiles1/nij/grants/193800.pdf and read the paper by Richard Wright and Scott H. Decker. The paper discusses robbery from the point of view of offenders themselves. Make a listing of those points concerning robbery that are different from or not included in what the author of the text has said concerning robbery. Be prepared to present your answer in class.

CRIMINOLOGY WEB LINKS

http://www.ojp.usdoj.gov/BJA/pubs/SniperRpt.pdf
This is website contains a document addressing the problems of managing a multijurisdictional case like the sniper investigation involving John Lee Malvo and John Allen Muhammad. The large document contains a wealth of information on a major case that kept Americans glued to the television for a long period of time.

http://www.ncjrs.org/pdffiles1/bja/205263.pdf
The website provides information concerning Project Safe Neighborhoods, a national program designed to reduce gun violence in America.

http://www.ojp.usdoj.gov/bjs/pub/pdf/vvcs00.pdf
This website contains a Bureau of Justice Statistics document concerning violent victimization of college students.

http://www.mencanstoprape.org/
This is the official website of Men Can Stop Rape, a non-profit organization dedicated to changing the attitudes of men toward rape and sexual violence.

http://www.vaw.umn.edu/documents/vawnet/mrape/mrape.html
This website contains a thoughtful article on marital rape by Raquel Kennedy Bergen.

TEST BANK

FILL-IN THE BLANKS

1. Acts that vent rage, anger, or frustration are called _____ _____.

2. Children who are "_____ _____" do not let people inside, nor do they express their feelings; they exploit others and in turn are exploited by those older and stronger.

3. Date rape is believed to be frequent on _____ _____.

4. _____ means the killing was planned after careful thought rather than carried out on impulse.

5. _____ _____ want to reform the world or have a vision that drives them to kill.

6. At all ages, more children were violent to _____ than to _____.

7. Robbers show evidence of being highly _____ offenders.

8. _____ _____ is now considered the third leading cause of occupational injury or death.

9. _____ terrorism promotes the interests of a minority ethnic or religious group that believes it has been persecuted under majority rule and wishes to carve out its own independent homeland.

10. In the wake of the 9/11 attacks, the United States has moved to freeze the _____ assets of groups it considers to engage in or support terrorist activities.

TRUE/FALSE QUESTIONS

1. T/F An estimated 20 to 25% of serial killers are women.

2. T/F Absent or deviant parents, inconsistent discipline, physical abuse, and lack of supervision have all been linked to persistent violent offending.

3. T/F All criminologists agree with the southern subculture concept.

4. T/F Like other violent crimes, the rape rate has been in a decade-long decline.

5. T/F In some states, defendants can claim they mistakenly assumed their victims were above the age of consent, whereas in others, "mistake-of-age" defenses are ignored.

6. T/F Jurors are sometimes swayed by the insinuation that a rape was victim precipitated.

7.   T/F The rate of homicide among cohabiting couples has risen significantly during the past two decades.

8.   T/F The cause of serial murder eludes criminologists.

9.   T/F The behavior of abusive parents can often be traced to negative experiences in their own childhood.

10. T/F The typical armed robber is likely to be a professional who carefully studies targets while planning a crime.

11. T/F Hate crimes usually involve convenient, vulnerable targets who are incapable of fighting back.

12. T/F Spouse abuse among men who have served in the military service is extremely high.

13. T/F Most victims know their stalker.

14. T/F Contemporary transnational terrorists rely solely on violence to achieve their goals.

15. T/F Many terrorists are uneducated members of the lower class.

MULTIPLE CHOICE QUESTIONS

1.   Violence designed to improve the financial or social position of the criminal, for example, through an armed robbery or murder for hire is what kind of violence?
     a.   radical
     b.   expressive
     c.   mission-oriented
     d.   instrumental

2.   Freud believed that _____ can be expressed externally as violence and sadism or internally as suicide, alcoholism, or other self-destructive habits.
     a.   thanatos
     b.   eros
     c.   evolutionary instinct
     d.   sexual instinct

3.   Evolutionary theories in criminology suggest that violent behavior is committed predominantly by:
     a.   whites
     b.   females
     c.   males
     d.   minorities

4. Violence that may be the direct consequence of ingesting mood-altering substances is called:
    a. psychopharmacological relationship
    b. economic compulsive behavior
    c. systemic link
    d. drug altered violence

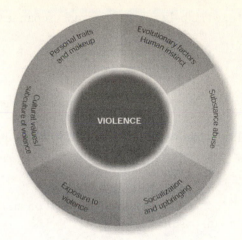

5. In her study of juvenile death row inmates, Lewis found that all inmates had long histories of intense:
    a. drug abuse
    b. child abuse
    c. behavioral problems
    d. gang involvement

6. Empirical evidence shows that violence rates are highest in urban areas where subcultural values support.
    a. school dropouts
    b. patriarchy
    c. single female headed households
    d. teenage gangs

7. Like other violent crimes, the rape rate has been in a decade-long:
    a. incline
    b. steady pace
    c. decline
    d. steep increase

8. The type of rape that involves an attacker who does not want to harm his victim as much as he wants to possess her sexually is called:
    a. anger rape
    b. power rape
    c. sadistic rape
    d. thrill rape

9. What type of rape constitutes the bulk of sexual assaults?
    a. acquaintance rape
    b. serial rape
    c. gang rape
    d. date rape

10. The belief that males must separate their sexual feelings from needs for love, respect, and affection is called:
    a. hypermasculinity
    b. virility mystique
    c. marital exemption
    d. narcissistic personality disorder

11. What protects women from being questioned about their sexual history unless it directly bears on the case?
    a. gender equality
    b. public outrage
    c. the Violence Against Women Act
    d. shield laws

12. What term means that a killing was planned after careful thought rather than carried out on impulse?
    a. premeditation
    b. malice
    c. deliberation
    d. manslaughter

13. What refers to a killing committed in the heat of passion or during a sudden quarrel that provoked violence?
    a. nonnegligent manslaughter
    b. involuntary manslaughter
    c. negligent manslaughter
    d. felony murder

14. Today, more than half of murderers are _____ to their victims.
    a. strangers
    b. related
    c. allied
    d. known

15. Violence in schools has become _____ but school shootings are _____.
    a. focused on females; focused on males
    b. isolated; gang-related
    c. more hidden; more visible
    d. commonplace; relatively rare

16. Killers who are out for profit or want to protect themselves from a perceived threat are called:
    a. expedience killers
    b. serial killers
    c. mission killers
    d. thrill killers

17. Killers who are usually trying to cover up a crime, eliminate witnesses, or carry out a criminal conspiracy are called:
    a. revenge killers
    b. love killers
    c. profit killers
    d. terrorist killers

18. What requires offensive touching, such as slapping, hitting, or punching a victim?
    a. assault and battery
    b. assault
    c. battery
    d. simple assault

19. Obsession with a wife's behavior, however trivial, can result in violent assaults. This obsession is called:
    a. compulsive perception
    b. excessive brooding
    c. estrangement
    d. hostility toward dependency

20. These robbers steal to obtain small amounts of money when an accessible target presents itself are called:
    a. opportunist robbers
    b. professional robbers
    c. addict robbers
    d. alcoholic robbers

21. Those disturbed individuals who see it as their duty to rid the world of evil commit what type of hate crime?
    a. a mission hate crime
    b. a reactive (defensive) hate crime
    c. a thrill-seeking hate crime
    d. a retaliatory hate crime

22. Which of the following is **not** true of terrorism?
    a. It is a political crime.
    b. The act must carry with it the intent to disrupt and change the government.
    c. The act must not be merely a common-law crime committed for greed or egotism.
    d. The act must achieve worldwide press coverage.

23. What kind of terrorists use violence to frighten those in power and their supporters in order to replace the existing government with a regime that holds acceptable political or religious views?
    a. cause-based terrorists
    b. international terrorists
    c. revolutionary terrorists
    d. political terrorists

24. Who is the typical workplace violence offender?
    a. a middle-aged minority female who faces termination
    b. a middle-aged white male who faces termination
    c. a young black male who faces termination
    d. a young white male who faces termination

25. Which of the following is **NOT** a mission of the Department of Homeland Security?
    a. coordinating state and local antiterrorism efforts
    b. reducing America's vulnerability to terrorism
    c. minimizing the damage and recovery from attacks that do occur
    d. preventing terrorist attacks within the United States

ESSAY QUESTIONS

1. Discuss the various causes of violent crime.

2. Discuss the history of rape and explain the different types of rape.

3.   Discuss the differences among serial killing, mass murder, and spree killing.

4.   Discuss the various types of assault in the home.

5.   Explain the different types of terrorism and what is being done to combat terrorists.

MATCHING

1. _____ Date Rape
2. _____ Eros
3. _____ Felony Murder
4. _____ Guerilla
5. _____ Neglect
6. _____ Martial Rape
7. _____ Rape
8. _____ Serial Murder
9. _____ Sexual Abuse
10. _____ Shield Laws

A. Laws that protect women from being questioned about their sexual history unless it directly bears on the case
B. The killing of a large number of people over time by an offender who seeks to escape detection
C. In common law, "the carnal knowledge of a female forcibly and against her will"
D. Not providing children with the care and shelter to which they are entitled
E. A killing accompanying a felony, such as robbery or rape, usually constitutes first-degree murder.
F. Rape involving people in some form of courting relationship
G. The most basic human drive present at birth; the instinct to preserve and create life
H. Located in rural areas and attack the military, the police and government officials
I. Rape of a woman by her husband
J. The exploitation of children through rape, incest, and molestation by parents or other adults

CHAPTER 10 ANSWER KEY

Fill in the Blank Answers

1. expressive violence
2. crusted over
3. college campuses
4. deliberation
5. mission killers
6. mothers; fathers
7. rational
8. workplace violence
9. nationalist
10. financial

True/False Answers

1.	F	6.	T	11.T
2.	T	7.	F	12.T
3.	F	8.	T	13.T
4.	T	9.	T	14.F
5.	T	10.	F	15.F

Multiple Choice Answers

1.	D	11.	D	21.	A
2.	A	12.	C	22.	D
3.	C	13.	A	23.	C
4.	A	14.	D	24.	B
5.	B	15.	D	25.	A
6.	D	16.	A		
7.	C	17.	C		
8.	B	18.	C		
9.	A	19.	B		
10.	B	20.	A		

Essay Questions

1. Pages 320-323
2. Pages 324-329
3. Pages 336-338
4. Pages 339-341
5. Pages 349-356

Matching Answers

1.	F	6.	I
2.	G	7.	C
3.	E	8.	B
4.	H	9.	J
5.	D	10.	A

PROPERTY CRIME

OUTLINE

Chapter 11

Property Crime

LEARNING OBJECTIVES

1. Be familiar with the history of theft offenses

2. Recognize the differences between professional and amateur thieves

3. Know the similarities and differences between the various types of larceny

4. Understand the different forms of shoplifting

5. Be able to discuss the concept of fraud

6. Know what is meant by a confidence game

7. Understand what it means to burgle a home

8. Know what it takes to be a good burglar

9. Understand the concept of arson

KEYWORDS AND DEFINITIONS

Fence: a buyer and seller of stolen merchandise.

Street crime: common, theft-related offenses.

Economic crime: an act in violation of the criminal law that is designed to bring financial gain to the offender.

Skilled thieves: thieves who typically work in the larger cities, such as London and Paris. This group includes pickpockets, forgers, and counterfeiters, who operate freely.

Flash houses: public meeting places in England, often taverns, that served as headquarters for gangs. Here, deals were made, crimes were plotted, and the sale of stolen goods was negotiated.

Smugglers: thieves who move freely in sparsely populated areas and transport goods, such as spirits, gems, gold, and spices, without bothering to pay tax or duty.

Poachers: early English thieves who typically lived in the country and supplemented their diet and income with game that belonged to a landlord.

Occasional criminals: offenders who do not define themselves by a criminal role or view themselves as committed career criminals.

Professional criminals: offenders who make a significant portion of their income from crime. Professionals pursue their craft with vigor attempting to learn from older, experienced criminals the techniques that will earn them the most money with the least risk.

Situational inducement: short-term influence on a person's behavior, such as financial problems or peer pressure that increases risk taking.

Professional fence: an individual who earns his or her living solely by buying and reselling stolen merchandise.

Constructive possession: in the crime of larceny, willingly giving up temporary physical possession of property but retaining legal ownership.

Petit (petty) larceny: theft of a small amount of money or property, it is punished as a misdemeanor.

Grand larceny: theft of money or property of substantial value, punished as a felony.

Shoplifting: a common form of theft involving taking goods from retail stores.

Boosters: professional shoplifters who steal with the intention of reselling stolen merchandise.

Heels: professional shoplifters who steal with the intention of reselling stolen merchandise to pawnshops or fences, usually at half the original price.

Snitches: amateur shoplifters who do not self-identify as thieves but who systematically steal merchandise for personal use.

Target removal strategies: putting dummy or disabled goods on display, as a means of preventing shoplifting, while the real merchandise is kept under lock and key

Target hardening strategies: making one's home or business crime proof through the use of locks, bars, alarms, and other devices.

Naive check forgers: amateurs who cash bad checks because of some financial crisis but have little identification with a criminal subculture.

Closure: a term used by Lemert to describe the condition resulting when people from a middle-class background who have little identification with a criminal subculture cash bad checks because of a financial crisis that demands an immediate resolution.

Systematic forgers: professional offenders who make a living by passing bad checks.

Carjacking: theft of a car by force or threat of force.

False pretenses: illegally obtaining money, goods, or merchandise from another by fraud or misrepresentation.

Fraud: taking the possession of another through deception or cheating, such as selling a person a desk that is represented as an antique but is known to be a copy.

Confidence game: a swindle, usually involving a get-rich-quick scheme, often with illegal overtones, so that the victim will be afraid or embarrassed to call the police.

Mark: the target of a con man or woman.

Pigeon drop: a con game in which a package or wallet containing money is "found" by a con man or woman. A passing victim is stopped and asked for advice about what to do and soon another "stranger," who is part of the con, approaches and enters the discussion. The three decide to split the money; but first one of the swindlers goes off to consult a lawyer. The lawyer claims the money can be split up, but each party must prove he or she has the means to reimburse the original owner, should one show up. The victim is then asked to give some good-faith money for the lawyer to hold. When the victim goes to the lawyer's office to pick up a share of the loot, he or she finds the address to be bogus and the money gone. In the new millennium, the pigeon drop has been appropriated by corrupt telemarketers who typically contact elderly victims over the phone to bilk them out of their savings.

Embezzlement: a type of larceny that involves taking the possessions of another (fraudulent conversion) that have been placed in the thief's lawful possession for safekeeping, such as a bank teller misappropriating deposits or a stockbroker making off with a customer's account.

Good burglar: professional burglars use this title to characterize colleagues who have distinguished themselves as burglars. Characteristics of the good burglar include technical competence, maintenance of personal integrity, specialization in burglary, financial success, and the ability to avoid prison sentences.

Arson for profit: people looking to collect insurance money, but who are afraid or unable to set the fire themselves hire professional arsonists. These professionals have acquired the skills to set fires yet make the cause seem accidental.

Arson fraud: involves a business owner burning his or her property or hiring someone to do it, to escape financial problems.

Flashover: an effect in a fire when heat and gas at the ceiling of a room reach 2,000 degrees and clothes and furniture burst into flame, duplicating the effects of arsonists' gasoline or explosives. It is possible that many suspected arsons are actually the result of flashover

CHAPTER OUTLINE

I.   A brief history of theft
      A.   Self-report studies show that property crime among the young, in every social class, is widespread.
      B.   Theft is not a phenomenon unique to modern times.
      C.   By the eighteenth century, three separate groups of property criminals were active.
           1.   Skilled thieves
           2.   Smugglers
           3.   Poachers

II.   Modern thieves
      A.   Occasional criminals
           1.   Most thefts are committed by occasional criminals.
           2.   Other theft-offenders are in fact skilled professional criminals.
           3.   The great majority of economic crimes are the work of amateur criminals.
                a.   Whose decision to steal is spontaneous
                b.   Whose acts are unskilled, impulsive, and haphazard
           4.   There are the millions of adults whose behavior may occasionally violate the criminal law.
           5.   Occasional property crime occurs when there is an opportunity or situational inducement to commit crime.
                a.   Short-term influences on a person's behavior that increase risk taking
                b.   Opportunity and situational inducements are not the cause of crime, they are the occasion for crime.
                c.   The opportunity to commit crime and the short-run inducements to do so are not randomly situated.
                d.   Some people, typically poor young males, have an ample supply of both.
           6.   Occasional criminals have little group support for their acts.
      B.   Professional criminals
           1.   Professional criminals make a significant portion of their income from crime.
           2.   Professionals pursue their craft with vigor.
           3.   They attempt to learn from older, experienced criminals.
           4.   Professional theft traditionally refers to nonviolent forms of criminal behavior.
                a.   Undertaken with a high degree of skill for monetary gain
                b.   That exploit interests tending:
                     1)   To maximize financial opportunities
                     2)   To minimize the possibilities of apprehension
           5.   Three career patterns of professional thieves and criminals
                a.   Youth come under the influence of older, experienced criminals who teach them the trade.
                b.   Juvenile gang members continue their illegal activities at a time when most of their peers have "dropped out" in order to:
                     1)   Marry
                     2)   Raise families
                     3)   Take conventional jobs
                c.   Youth sent to prison for minor offenses learn the techniques of crime from more experienced thieves.
      C.   Sutherland's professional criminal
           1.   The Professional Thief
           2.   Conwell and Sutherland's concept of professional theft has two critical dimensions.

    a. Professional thieves engage in limited types of crime.

    b. The exclusive use of wits, front (a believable demeanor), and talking ability

   3. In their world, "thief" is a title worn with pride.

   4. Sutherland and Conwell view professional theft as an occupation with much the same internal organization as legitimate professions.

   5. Professional thieves have changed their behavior over time in response to crime control technology.

 D. The professional fence

   1. Some experts have argued that Sutherland's view of the professional thief may be outdated because:

    a. Modern thieves often work alone.

    b. They are not part of a criminal subculture.

    c. They were not tutored early in their careers by other criminals.

   2. Research efforts show that the principles set down by Sutherland still have value.

    a. The fence's critical role in criminal transactions has been recognized since the eighteenth century.

    b. They act as middlemen who purchase stolen merchandise and resell it to merchants who market them to legitimate customers.

   3. According to Goodman, to be successful, a fence must meet the following criteria:

    a. Upfront cash

    b. Knowledge of dealing

    c. Connections with suppliers of stolen goods

    d. Connections with buyers

    e. Complicity with law enforcers

   4. Fencing seems to contain many of the elements of professional theft as described by Sutherland.

 E. The nonprofessional fence

   1. A significant portion of all fencing is performed by amateur or occasional criminals.

   2. One type of occasional fence is the part-timer who, unlike professional fences, has other sources of income.

   3. Some merchants become actively involved in theft either by specifying the merchandise they want the burglars to steal or by "fingering" victims.

   4. Associational fences

   5. Neighborhood hustlers

   6. Amateur receivers

III. Larceny/Theft

 A. Larceny today

   1. Larceny is usually separated by state statute into:

    a. Petit (petty) larceny

    b. Grand larceny

   2. Larceny/theft is probably the most common criminal offense.

   3. Some larcenies involve complex criminal conspiracies.

 B. Shoplifting

   1. Retail security measures add to the already high cost of this crime, all of which is passed on to the consumer.

2. Profile of a shoplifter
   a. Cameron found that about 10 percent of all shoplifters were professionals who derived the majority of their income from shoplifting.
   b. Cameron found that the majority of shoplifters are amateur pilferers, called snitches in thieves' argot.
   c. Criminologists view shoplifters as people who are likely to reform if apprehended.
3. Controlling shoplifting
   a. Many states encourage the arrest of shoplifters.
   b. Many states have passed merchant privilege laws designed to protect retailers and their employers from litigation from improper or false arrests of suspected shoplifters.
   c. Privilege laws require:
      1) That arrests be made on reasonable grounds or probable cause
      2) That detention be of short duration
      3) That store employees or security guards conduct themselves in a reasonable fashion
4. Prevention strategies
   a. Target removal strategies
   b. Target hardening strategies
   c. Situational measures
      1) Place the most valuable goods in the least vulnerable places
      2) Use warning signs to deter potential thieves
      3) Use closed-circuit cameras
C. Bad checks
   1. Lemert
      a. Found that the majority of check forgers are amateurs who do not believe their actions will hurt anyone.
      b. Lemert calls them naive check forgers.
   2. Naïve check forgers cash bad checks because of a financial crisis that demands an immediate resolution.
   3. Naive check forgers are often socially isolated people who have been unsuccessful in their personal relationships.
   4. They are risk prone when faced with a situation that is unusually stressful for them.
   5. Check fraud schemes and techniques
   6. Lemert found that a few professionals (systematic forgers) make a substantial living by passing bad checks.
D. Credit card theft
   1. Fraud has been responsible for a billion-dollar loss in the credit card industry.
   2. Compounded by thieves who set up bogus internet sites
   3. Congress passed a law in 1971 limiting a person's liability to $50 per stolen card.
E. Auto Theft
   1. Motor vehicle theft is another common larceny offense.
   2. Detailed typologies developed by Charles McCaghy and his associates
      a. Joyriding
      b. Short-term transportation
      c. Long-term transportation
      d. Profit
      e. Commission of another crime

3. Which cars are stolen the most?
    a. Car thieves show signs of rational choice in their target selections.
    b. Typically choose vehicles because of the high profit potential after stripping the component parts, which are then sold on the black market.
    c. Car models that have been in production for a few years without many design changes stand the greatest risk of theft.
4. Carjacking
    a. Both victims and offenders in carjackings tend to be young black men.
    b. Weapons were used in about three-quarters of all carjacking victimizations.
5. Combating auto theft
    a. One approach to theft deterrence – increase the risks of apprehension
    b. The Lojack® system
    c. Other prevention efforts involve making it more difficult to steal cars – publicity campaigns, closed-circuit television, and security systems in autos.
F. False pretenses or fraud
    1. False pretense differs from traditional larceny because the victims willingly give their possessions to the offender.
    2. Fraud may also occur when people conspire to cheat a third party or institution.
G. Confidence games
    a. Pigeon drop
    b. Telemarketers
    c. Pyramid schemes
    d. Shady contractors
H. Embezzlement
    1. Embezzlement was first codified in law by the English Parliament during the sixteenth century.
    2. The number of people arrested for embezzlement has increased more than 40 percent since 1991.
    3. Rash of embezzlement-type crimes around the world

IV. Burglary
  A. The nature and extent of burglary
    1. State jurisdictions have changed the legal requirements of burglary and most have discarded the necessity of forced entry.
    2. Many legal requirements now protect all structures, not just dwelling houses.
    3. The nature and extent of burglary
  B. Residential burglary
    1. Some burglars are crude thieves.
    2. Others plan out a strategy.
    3. Burglary has been a crime long associated with professional thieves who carefully learn their craft.
    4. Gender differences in burglary
        a. Men typically become involved in burglary with male peers.
        b. Women are more often introduced to crime by their boyfriends.
        c. Men prefer to commit residential burglaries alone.
        d. Women commit residential burglaries with others.
  C. Commercial burglary
    1. Some burglars prefer to victimize commercial property rather than private homes.
    2. Retail stores are burglars' favorite targets.

3. Establishments located within three blocks of heavily traveled thoroughfares have been found to be less vulnerable to burglary than those located farther away.
4. Alarms
    a. Have been found to be an effective deterrent to burglary
    b. Are less effective in isolated areas
    c. Burglary of non-alarmed properties is 4.57 times higher than that of similar property with alarms.
D. Careers in burglary
    1. Some criminals make burglary their career.
    2. They continually develop new and specialized skills to aid their profession.
    3. Characteristics of the good burglar
        a. Technical competence
        b. Maintenance of personal integrity
        c. Specialization in burglary
        d. Financial success
        e. The ability to avoid prison sentences
    4. Shover found that novices must develop four key requirements of the trade.
        a. They must learn the many skills needed to commit lucrative burglaries.
        b. The good burglar must be able to team up to form a criminal gang.
        c. The good burglar must have inside information.
        d. The good burglar must cultivate fences or buyers for stolen goods.
    5. The burglary "career ladder"
        a. Begin as young novices
        b. The journeyman stage
        c. Become professional burglars
    6. Repeat burglary
        a. Research suggests that burglars may in fact return to the scene of the crime to repeat their offenses.
        b. Research shows that some burglars repeat their acts to steal these replacement goods.

V. Arson
    A. There are several motives for arson.
        1. Adult arsonists may be motivated by severe emotional turmoil.
        2. Some psychologists view fire starting as a function of a disturbed personality.
        3. It is alleged that arsonists often experience sexual pleasure from starting fires.
        4. Fires are started by angry people looking for revenge against property owners.
        5. Fires are started by teenagers out to vandalize property.
    B. Juvenile fire setting has long been associated with conduct problems.
        1. The "playing with matches" fire setter
        2. The "crying for help" fire setter
        3. The "delinquent" fire setter
        4. The "severely disturbed" fire setter
    C. Arsons are set by professional arsonists who engage in arson for profit.
    D. Another form is arson fraud.
    E. It is possible that many suspected arsons are actually the result of flashover.

CHAPTER SUMMARY

Self-report studies show that property crime among the young in every social class is widespread. Most thefts are committed by occasional criminals, but other theft-offenders are, in fact, skilled professional criminals. The great majority of economic crimes are the work of amateur criminals whose decision to steal is spontaneous. Their acts are unskilled, impulsive, and haphazard. Professional criminals make a significant portion of their income from crime, so they pursue their craft with vigor. There are three career patterns of professional thieves and criminals. First, a youth may come under the influence of older, experienced criminals who teach them the trade. Second, a juvenile gang member may continue their illegal activities at a time when most of their peers have "dropped out" to marry, raise families, and take conventional jobs. Third, a youth sent to prison for minor offenses may learn the techniques of crime from more experienced thieves. The most renowned work on the professional criminal is Sutherland's *The Professional Thief*.

Larceny is usually separated by state statute into petit (petty) larceny and grand larceny. Larceny/theft is probably the most common criminal offense. Cameron found that about 10 percent of all shoplifters were professionals who derived the majority of their income from shoplifting. She also found that the majority of shoplifters are amateur pilferers, called snitches in thieves' argot. Criminologists view shoplifters as people who are likely to reform if apprehended. Many states encourage the arrest of shoplifters by passing merchant privilege laws designed to protect retailers and their employers from litigation due to improper or false arrests of suspected shoplifters.

Lemert found that the majority of check forgers are amateurs who do not believe their actions will hurt anyone, he called them naïve check forgers. Naïve check forgers cash bad checks because of a financial crisis that demands an immediate resolution and they are often socially isolated people who have been unsuccessful in their personal relationships. Lemert also found that a few professionals (systematic forgers) make a substantial living by passing bad checks.

Motor vehicle theft is another common larceny offense. Detailed categories developed by Charles McCaghy and his associates include joyriding, short-term transportation, long-term transportation, profit, and commission of another crime. Car thieves show signs of rational choice in their target selections as they typically choose vehicles that have high profit potential after stripping the component parts, which are then sold on the black market.

False pretense differs from traditional larceny because the victims willingly give their possessions to the offender. Fraud may occur when people conspire to cheat a third party or institution. A confidence game is another form of fraud. The number of people arrested for embezzlement has increased more than 40 percent since 1991. In fact, there has been a global rash of embezzlement-style crimes.

State jurisdictions have changed the legal requirements of burglary and most have discarded the legal necessity of forced entry. Some residential burglars are crude thieves, while others plan out a strategy. Burglary has been a crime long associated with professional thieves who carefully learn their craft. Some burglars prefer to victimize commercial property rather than private homes. Retail stores tend to be burglars' favorite targets. Alarms have been found to be an effective deterrent to burglary but they are less effective in isolated areas. However, burglary of non-alarmed properties is 4.57 times higher than that of similar property containing alarms. The characteristics of the good burglar are technical competence, maintenance of personal integrity, specialization in burglary, financial success, and the ability to avoid prison sentences. Burglars progress through a "career ladder." They begin as young novices, go through the journeyman stage, and finally, they become professional burglars.

There are several motives for arson. First, adult arsonists may be motivated by severe emotional turmoil. Second, some psychologists view fire starting as a function of a disturbed personality. Third, it is alleged that arsonists often experience sexual pleasure from starting fires. Fourth, fires are started by angry people looking for revenge against property owners. Fifth, fires are started by teenagers out to vandalize property. Juvenile fire setting has long been associated with conduct problems such as playing with matches, as a cry for help, being delinquent, or being severely disturbed. Some arson is committed by professional arsonists who engage in arson for profit. Another form is arson fraud. It is possible that many suspected arsons are actually the result of flashover.

STUDENT EXERCISES

Exercise 1

Go online to policing burglary in Australia. The website for the article to read is at http://jratcliffe.net/papers/Ratcliffe%20(2001)%20Policing%20urban%20burglary.pdf. Be prepared to present in class an analysis of how burglary in Australia compares with burglary as presented in the textbook.

Exercise 2

Go to http://samsara.law.cwru.edu/comp_law/10-shoplifting.html and read the information provided by an anonymous writer concerning how to commit shoplifting. Prepare a one to two page analysis of the article and how it compares with the information provided by the textbook.

CRIMINOLOGY WEB LINKS

http://www.auto-theft.info/
This is the official website for the online Auto-Theft Information Clearing House. Take a look around this website that contains a wealth of information on auto theft.

http://www.iii.org/media/hottopics/insurance/test4/
This is the official website for the Insurance Information Institute and provides a great deal of information on auto theft.

http://www.ftc.gov/bcp/conline/pubs/credit/cards.pdf
This website contains a brochure published by the Federal Trade Commission on how to avoid credit and charge card fraud.

http://www.aafp.org/fpm/970900fm/suite_1.html
This is an article on how to prevent embezzlement in a physician's office. It offers some tips that can be of value to anyone who owns their own business and has employees.

http://www.ncjrs.org/pdffiles1/nij/181584.pdf
This website contains a Department of Justice publication on fire and arson investigation.

TEST BANK

FILL-IN THE BLANKS

1. As a group, _____ _____ can be defined as acts in violation of the criminal law designed to bring financial reward to an offender.

2. _____ _____ are short-term influences on a person's behavior that increase risk taking.

3. _____ _____ are amateur fences who barter stolen goods for services.

4. A significant portion of all fencing is performed by _____ or _____ criminals.

5. _____ was one of the earliest common-law crimes created by English judges to define acts in which one person took for his or her own use the property of another.

6. Retail security measures add to the already high cost of _____, all of which is passed on to the consumer.

7. The condition that drives someone to cash bad checks because of a financial crisis that demands an immediate resolution is called _____.

8. _____ do not steal cars for profit or gain but to experience, even briefly, the benefits associated with owning an automobile.

9. _____ _____ are run by swindlers who aspire to separate a victim (or "sucker") from his or her hard-earned money.

10. Both residential and commercial burglaries have underwent steep _____ since 1994.

TRUE/FALSE QUESTIONS

1. T/F Many theft offenses are committed by school-age youths who are likely to enter into a criminal career.

2. T/F Manual dexterity and physical force are of little importance to professional thieves.

3. T/F According to Goodman, to be successful, a fence must insure that all deals are cash transactions.

4. T/F Petit (petty) larceny is a felony.

5. T/F Cameron found that most shoplifters were professionals.

6. T/F Lemert found that the majority of check forgers are professionals.

7. T/F Most credit card abuse is the work of amateurs who acquire stolen cards through theft or mugging and then use them for two or three days.

8. T/F Motor vehicle theft has increased during the past decade.

9. T/F Auto theft is the most highly reported of all major crimes.

10. T/F Both victims and offenders in carjackings tend to be young white men.

11. T/F Embezzlement occurs when someone who is trusted with property fraudulently converts it; that is, keeps it for his or her own use or the use of others.

12. T/F The FBI's definition of burglary is not restricted to burglary from a person's home; it includes any unlawful entry of a structure to commit theft or felony.

13. T/F Burglars show a preference for corner houses because they are easily observable and offer the maximum number of escape routes.

14. T/F Of all business establishments, gas stations are burglars' favorite targets.

15. T/F Although some arsonists may be aroused sexually by their activities, there is little evidence that most arsonists are psychosexually motivated.

MULTIPLE CHOICE QUESTIONS

1. Acts in violation of the criminal law designed to bring financial reward to an offender are called:
    a. economic crime
    b. street crime
    c. monetary crime
    d. fiscal crime

2. Those that do not define themselves by a criminal role or view themselves as committed career criminals are called:
    a. felons
    b. misdemeanant criminals
    c. occasional criminals
    d. professional criminals

3. A professional shoplifter is called a:
    a. cannon
    b. booster
    c. prowl
    d. pennyweighter

4. A sneak thief from stores, banks, and offices is called:
    a. heel
    b. booster
    c. con artist
    d. pennyweighter

5. Those who buy and sell stolen property as one of the many ways they make a living are called:
    a. professional hustlers
    b. amateur receivers
    c. associational fences
    d. neighborhood hustlers

6. Those who are approached in a public place by complete strangers offering a great deal on valuable commodities are called:
    a. professional hustlers
    b. amateur receivers
    c. associational fences
    d. neighborhood hustlers

7. The legal fiction applied to situations in which persons voluntarily and temporarily give up custody of their property but still believe the property is legally theirs is called:
    a. economic crime
    b. situational inducement
    c. constructive possession
    d. petit larceny

8. To combat losses from credit card theft, Congress passed a law in 1971 limiting a person's liability to _____ per stolen card.
    a. $50
    b. $75
    c. $100
    d. $150

9. Lemert calls the majority of check forgers who are amateurs and who do not believe their actions will hurt anyone:
    a. closure check forgers
    b. naïve check forgers
    c. immature check forgers
    d. pennyweighters

10. Most naïve check forgers come from:
    a. dysfunctional backgrounds
    b. upper class backgrounds
    c. middle class backgrounds
    d. lower class backgrounds

11. Thieves stealing cars for their personal use is what type of auto theft transaction?
    a. long-term transportation
    b. joyriding
    c. short-term transportation
    d. profit

12. Car thefts motivated by teenagers' desires to acquire the power, prestige, sexual potency, and recognition associated with an automobile are what type of auto theft transaction?
    a. long-term transportation
    b. joyriding
    c. short-term transportation
    d. profit

13. The auto theft transaction that involves stealing an auto in hope of monetary gain is called:
    a. long-term transportation
    b. joyriding
    c. short-term transportation
    d. profit

14. The auto theft transaction that involves the theft of a car simply to go from one place to another is called:
    a. long-term transportation
    b. joyriding
    c. short-term transportation
    d. profit

15. Carjacking is legally consider a type of:
    a. robbery
    b. theft
    c. larceny
    d. burglary

16. Which of the following is **not** a characteristic of a good burglar?
    a. technical competence
    b. maintenance of personal integrity
    c. generalization in crimes
    d. financial success

17. The target of a con game is called a:
    a. pigeon
    b. mark
    c. drop
    d. chump

18. Youth who set fires to school property or surrounding areas to retaliate for some slight experienced at school are known as a:
    a. "playing with matches" fire setter
    b. "crying for help" fire setter
    c. "delinquent" fire setter
    d. "severely disturbed" fire setter

19. The youngest fire starter, usually between the ages of 4 and 9, who sets fires because parents are careless with matches and lighters is known as:
    a. "playing with matches" fire setter
    b. "crying for help" fire setter
    c. "delinquent" fire setter
    d. "severely disturbed" fire setter

20. False pretense differs from traditional larceny because:
    a. The victims share in the criminal intent.
    b. The victims need not file legal charges to regain ownership of their property.
    c. The victims tend to be elderly.
    d. The victims willingly give their possessions to the offender.

21. In early Greek culture, Aristotle alluded to theft by road commissioners and other government officials. He was describing what we, today, call:
    a. a confidence game
    b. embezzlement
    c. false pretenses
    d. fraud

22. Fires set by professionals who engage in arson are known as:
    a. arson for profit
    b. flashover
    c. felony arson
    d. premeditated arson

23. During the course of an ordinary fire, heat and gas at the ceiling of a room can reach 2,000 degrees. This is known as:
    a. blazeover
    b. flareover
    c. flashover
    d. burnover

24. Research on gender differences in burglary indicates:
    a. Males become involved in burglary to provide necessities for their children.
    b. Females become involved in burglary for money to pursue sexual conquests.
    c. Females typically become involved in burglary with female peers
    d. Men typically become involved in burglary with male peers

25. Which of the following is a motive for arson?
    a. conduct problems
    b. profit
    c. severe emotional turmoil
    d. all of the above

ESSAY QUESTIONS

1. Explain the differences between professional and amateur thieves.

2. Discuss the different forms of shoplifting.

3. Explain what is meant by a confidence game.

4. Discuss what it takes to be a "good burglar."

5.   Discuss the difference between arson for profit and arson fraud.

MATCHING

1. _____ Systematic Forgers
2. _____ Street Crimes
3. _____ Snitches
4. _____ Situational Inducements
5. _____ Professional Criminals
6. _____ Pigeon Drop
7. _____ Occasional Criminals
8. _____ Naive Check Forgers
9. _____ Joyriding
10. _____ Heels

A. Common theft-related offenses which include larceny, embezzlement and theft by false pretenses
B. Short-term influences on a person's behavior that increase risk taking
C. A method of swindling money out of an innocent victim
D. The majority of check forgers who do not believe their actions will hurt anyone
E. Professional shoplifters who steal with the intention of reselling stolen merchandise to pawnshops or fences
F. Professionals who make a substantial living by passing bad checks
G. Usually respectable persons who do not conceive of themselves as thieves, but are systematic shoplifters who steal merchandise for their own use
H. Criminals who make a significant portion of their income from crime
I. Amateur criminals whose decision to steal is spontaneous and whose acts are unskilled, unplanned and haphazard
J. Car theft usually motivated by a teenager's desire to acquire the power, prestige, sexual potency, and recognition associated with an automobile

CHAPTER 11 ANSWER KEY

Fill in the Blank Answers

1. economic crime
2. situational inducements
3. associational fences
4. amateur; occasional
5. larceny/theft
6. shoplifting
7. closure
8. joyriders
9. confidence games
10. declines

True/False Answers

1.	F	6.	F	11.	T
2.	T	7.	T	12.	T
3.	T	8.	F	13.	T
4.	F	9.	T	14.	F
5.	F	10.	F	15.	T

Multiple Choice Answers

1.	A	11.	A	21.	B
2.	C	12.	B	22.	A
3.	B	13.	D	23.	C
4.	A	14.	C	24.	D
5.	D	15.	A	25.	D
6.	B	16.	C		
7.	C	17.	B		
8.	A	18.	C		
9.	B	19.	A		
10.	C	20.	D		

Essay Questions

1. Pages 369-370
2. Pages 375-376
3. Pages 381-382
4. Pages 385-386
5. Pages 386-388

Matching Answers

1.	F	6.	C
2.	A	7.	I
3.	G	8.	D
4.	B	9.	J
5.	H	10.	E

ENTERPRISE CRIME

White Collar and Organized Crime

OUTLINE

Chapter 12

Enterprise Crime: White-Collar and Organized Crime

LEARNING OBJECTIVES

1. Understand the concept of enterprise crime

2. Be familiar with the various types of white-collar crime

3. Be familiar with the various types of corporate crime

4. Recognize the extent and various causes of white-collar crime

5. Be able to discuss the different approaches to combating white-collar crime

6. List the different types of illegal behavior engaged in by organized crime figures

7. Describe the evolution of organized crime

8. Explain how the government is fighting organized crime

KEYWORDS AND DEFINITIONS

Enterprise crime: the use of illegal tactics to gain profit in the marketplace. Enterprise crimes can involve both the violation of law in the course of an otherwise legitimate occupation or the sale and distribution of illegal commodities.

White-collar crime: illegal activities of people and institutions whose acknowledged purpose is profit through legitimate business transactions.

Organized crime: illegal activities of people and organizations whose acknowledged purpose is profit through illegitimate business enterprise.

Corporate crime: white-collar crime involving a legal violation by a corporate entity, such as price fixing, restraint of trade, or hazardous waste dumping.

Sting (or swindle): a white-collar crime in which people use their institutional or business position to cheat others out of their money.

Chiseling: crimes that involve using illegal means to cheat an organization, its consumers, or both, on a regular basis.

Churning: a white-collar crime in which a stockbroker makes repeated trades to fraudulently increase commissions.

Front running: a form of stockbroker chiseling I which brokers place personal orders ahead of a large order from a customer to profit from the market effects of the trade.

Bucketing: a form of stockbroker chiseling in which brokers skim customer trading profits by falsifying trade information.

Insider trading: illegal buying of stock in a company based on information provided by someone who has a fiduciary interest in the company, such as an employee or an attorney or accountant retained by the firm. Federal laws and the rules of the Securities and Exchange Commission require that all profits from such trading be returned and provide for both fines and a prison sentence.

Exploitation: forcing victims to pay for services to which they have a clear right.

Influence peddling: using an institutional position to grant favors and sell information to which their co-conspirators are not entitled.

Pilferage: theft by employees through stealth or deception.

Check kiting: a scheme whereby a client with accounts in two or more banks takes advantage of the time required for checks to clear in order to obtain unauthorized use of bank funds.

Organizational crime: crime that involves large corporations and their efforts to control the marketplace and earn huge profits through unlawful bidding, unfair advertising, monopolistic practices, or other illegal means.

Actual authority: the authority a corporation knowingly gives to an employee.

Apparent authority: the authority that a third party, like a customer, reasonably believes the agent has to perform the act in question.

Sherman Antitrust Act: law that subjects to criminal or civil sanctions any person "who shall make any contract or engage in any combination or conspiracy" in restraint of interstate commerce.

Division of markets: firms divide a region into territories and each firm agrees not to compete in the others' territories.

Tying arrangement: a corporation requires customers of one of its services to use other services it offers.

Group boycott: a company's refusal to do business with retail stores that do not comply with its rules or desires.

Price fixing: a conspiracy to set and control the price of a necessary commodity.

Alien conspiracy theory: the view that organized crime was imported to the United States by Europeans and that crime cartels have a policy of restricting their membership to people of their own ethnic background.

Mafia: a criminal society that originated in Sicily, Italy, and is believed to control racketeering in the United States.

La Cosa Nostra: a national syndicate of 25 or so Italian-dominated crime families that control crime in distinct geographic areas.

Racketeer Influenced and Corrupt Organization Act (RICO): federal legislation that enables prosecutors to bring additional criminal or civil charges against people whose multiple criminal acts constitute a conspiracy. RICO features monetary penalties that allow the government to confiscate all profits derived from criminal activities. Originally intended to be used against organized criminals, RICO has been used against white-collar criminals.

Enterprise theory of investigation (ETI): a standard investigation tool of the FBI that focuses on criminal enterprise and investigation attacks on the structure of the criminal enterprise rather than on criminal acts viewed as isolated incidents.

CHAPTER OUTLINE

I.   Enterprise crime
    A.   Two categories
        1.   White-collar crime
        2.   Organized crime
    B.   Crimes of business enterprise
        1.   White-collar and organized crime are linked and often overlap.
        2.   These organizational crimes taint and corrupt the free market system
        3.   Enterprise crime can involve violence
            a.   Corporate violence annually kills and injures more people than all street crimes combined.

II. White-collar crime
    A.   General
        1.   Edwin Sutherland first used the phrase "white-collar crime" to describe the criminal activities of the rich and powerful.
            a.   "A crime committed by a person of respectability and high social status in the course of his occupation"
        2.   White-collar crime involved conspiracies by members of the wealthy classes to use their position in commerce & industry for personal gain without regard to law.
        3.   Sutherland believed the great majority of white-collar criminals did not become the subject of criminological study because their crimes were handled by civil courts and injured parties were more concerned with recouping losses rather than punishment of offenders.
    B.   Redefining white-collar crime
        1.   Contemporary definitions of white-collar crime are typically much broader than Sutherland's including:
            a.   Offenses of those who are not members of the upper class
            b.   Tax evasion, credit card and bankruptcy frauds, embezzlement, violations of trust, swindles, and corporate crime
        2.   Difficult to judge the extent of harm to victims
        3.   In addition to monetary losses, white-collar crime:
            a.   Damages property and kills people

       b.   Destroys confidence and saps the integrity of commercial life

       c.   Has potential for devastating destruction

III.   Components of white-collar crime

    A.   Stings and swindles

       1.   People use their institutional or business position to trick others out of their money.

       2.   Swindlers have little shame when defrauding people out of their money.

       3.   Swindlers are usually charged with embezzlement or fraud.

       4.   Religious swindles

           a.   Fake religious organizations bilk people out of an estimated $100 million per year.

              1)   Fraudulent charitable organizations

              2)   Religious television and radio shows

    B.   Chiseling

       1.   Involves regularly cheating an organization, its consumers, or both

           a.   May be individuals who own their business or employees of large companies

           b.   Charging for bogus auto repairs, zapping cab meters with magnet-loaded pens

       2.   Professional chiseling – Pharmacists have been known to

           a.   Alter prescriptions

           b.   Substitute low-cost generic drugs for more expensive name brands

       3.   Securities fraud

           a   A great deal of chiseling takes place on the commodities and stock markets

           b.   California scheme that defrauded elderly and retired victims out of $1.7 million.

           c.   Churning, front running, and bucketing

           d.   Insider training

              1)   Originally defined as corporate employees with direct knowledge of market-sensitive information using that information for their own benefit

              2)   Definition has since been expanded by the federal courts

    C.   Individual exploitation of institutional position

       1.   Exploiting one's power or position in organizations to take advantage of other individuals who have an interest in how that power is used.

       2.   Exploitation at the local level

              1)   Fire inspectors, liquor license board members, food inspectors

       3.   Exploitation in private industry

              1)   Purchasing agents, fraudulent contracts for work never performed

              2)   In some foreign countries, soliciting bribes to do business is common.

    D.   Influence peddling and bribery

       1.   Individuals holding important institutional positions sell power, influence, and information.

           a.   Government employees taking kickbacks

           b.   Political leaders accepting bribes to rig elections

           c.   Difference between influence peddling and exploitation

              1)   Exploitation involves forcing victims to pay for services to which they have a clear right.

              2)   Influence peddling and bribery involve using institutional positions to grant favors and sell information to those not entitled to it.

       2.   Influence peddling in government

           a.   Federal officials

           b.   State officials

           c.   Agents of the criminal justice system

1) Knapp Commission – corruption in NYPD

3. Influence peddling in business

    a. 1970s: multinational companies regularly made payoffs to foreign officials to secure business contracts.

    b. 1977: Congress passed the Foreign Corrupt Practices Act making it a criminal offense to bribe foreign officials.

E. Embezzlement and employee fraud

  1. Individual's use of their positions to embezzle company funds or appropriate company property for themselves

    a. The company or the organization is the victim.

  2. Blue collar fraud

    a. Pilferage – theft of company property

    b. Explained by factors relevant to the work setting:

      1) Job dissatisfaction

      2) Workers' beliefs they are being exploited

      3) Strain and conflict

    c. Employee theft may amount to nearly $35 billion per year and perhaps $1,500 per year, per employee.

  3. Management fraud

    a. Converting company assets for personal benefit

    b. Fraudulently receiving increases in compensation

    c. Fraudulently increasing personal holdings of company stock

    d. Retaining one's position by manipulating accounts

    e. Concealing unacceptable performance from stockholders

F. Client fraud

  1. Theft by an economic client from an organization that advances credit to its clients or sometimes reimburses them for services rendered

    a. Involve cheating an organization

    b. Insurance fraud, welfare fraud

  2. Healthcare fraud

    a. Doctors who violate ethical standards

      1) Medical professionals who set up Medicaid fraud schemes

      2) Ping-ponging

      3) Gang visits

    b. Estimated that $100 billion spent annually on federal healthcare is lost to fraudulent practices.

    c. State and federal governments have been reluctant to prosecute Medicaid fraud but have tightened controls.

  3. Bank fraud

    a. Check kiting

    b. Check forgery

    c. False statements on loan applications

    d. Bank credit card fraud

  4. Tax evasion

    a. The victim is the government.

    b. Particularly challenging because so many citizens regularly underreport their income

    c. Legal elements of tax fraud

      1) The government must find that the taxpayer either underreported income or did not report taxable income.

        2)   Willfulness – voluntary, intentional violation

        3)   The government must show that the taxpayer purposely attempted to evade or defeat a tax payment.

    d.   The majority of major tax cheats are not prosecuted because the IRS lacks the money to enforce the law.

        1)   13 million cases per year; IRS pursues one-fifth

G.   Corporate crime

   1.   Powerful institutions or their representatives willfully violate the laws that restrain these institutions from doing social harm or require them to do social good.

   2.   Interest in corporate crime first emerged in the early 1900s

    a.   Monopolistic business practices of John D. Rockefeller targeted

    b.   Ross's "criminaloid" business leader

    c.   Sutherland focus of theoretical attention on corporate crime

   3.   Corporate crimes are socially injurious acts committed by people who control companies to further their business interests.

    a.   Actual authority – a corporation knowingly gives authority to an employee

    b.   Apparent authority – a third party reasonably believes the agent has the authority to perform some act

   4.   Illegal restraint of trade and price fixing

    a.   Involves a contract or conspiracy designed to stifle competition, create a monopoly, artificially maintain prices, or otherwise interfere with free market competition

    b.   Sherman Antitrust Act has defined as illegal:

        1)   Division of markets

        2)   Tying arrangement

        3)   Group boycott

        4)   Price fixing

   5.   Deceptive pricing

    a.   Occurs when contractors provide the government or a corporation with incomplete or misleading information on how much it will actually cost to fulfill a contract on which they are bidding or use mischarges once the contracts are signed.

    b.   Lockheed C-5 cargo plane example

   6.   False claims and advertising

    a.   Illegal to knowingly and purposely advertise a product as possessing qualities that the manufacturer realizes it does not have

    b.   Supreme Court has held that states may charge fraud when fundraisers make false or misleading representations designed to deceive donors about how their donations will be used.

   7.   Worker safety/environmental crimes

    a.   Many different types of environmental crimes

    b.   Estimated that 20 million workers exposed to hazardous materials while on the job

    c.   Occupational Safety and Health Administration (OSHA) oversees worker safety

    d.   Environmental Protection Agency (EPA) enforces environmental crimes

        1)   Granted full law enforcement authority in 1988

        2)   Criminal Investigation Division (EPA CID) investigates criminal allegations of criminal wrongdoings prohibited by various environmental statues, including:

            a.   Illegal disposal of hazardous wastes

    b. Illegal discharge of pollutants into a water of the U.S.
    c. Illegal importation of restricted or regulated chemicals
    d. Tampering with a drinking water supply
    e. Mail and wire fraud
    f. Conspiracy and money laundering relating to environmental criminal activities

IV. Causes of white-collar crime
  A. Greedy or needy?
    1. Greed and need play important roles.
      a. Executives may tamper with company books because they feel a need to keep or improve their jobs, to satisfy their egos, or to support their children.
      b. Blue-collar workers may pilfer because they need to keep pace with inflation.
      c. Women convicted of white-collar crime typically work in lower-echelon positions, and their acts seem more motivated by economic survival than greed.
      d. For some, such as Boesky, scars from an earlier needy period in life can only be healed via accumulating ever-greater amounts of money.
      e. According to Donald Cressey, embezzlement is caused by a "nonshareable financial problem."

V. Theories of white-collar crime
  A. Rationalization/neutralization view
    1. People develop rationalizations for white-collar crime
    2. Offenders use rationalizations to resolve the conflict they experience over engaging in illegal behavior.
    3. Medicare/Medicaid fraud study found offenders used three techniques of neutralization.
      a. Everyone else does it.
      b. It's not my fault or responsibility.
      c. No one is hurt except wealthy insurance companies.
  B. Corporate culture view
    1. Some business organizations promote white-collar criminality in the same way that lower-class culture encourages the development of juvenile gangs and street crime.
    2. Some business organizations cause crime by placing excessive demands on employees while at the same time maintaining a business climate tolerant of employee deviance.
    3. Can be used to explain the collapse of Enron.
  C. Self-control view
    1. Hirschi and Gottfredson maintain the motives that produce white-collar crimes – quick benefits with minimal effort – are the same as those that produce any other criminal behaviors.
    2. White-collar offenders have low self-control and are inclined to follow momentary impulses without considering the long-term costs of such behavior.
    3. White-collar crime is relatively rare because business executives tend to hire people with self-control.
    4. Data indicate that the demographic distribution of white-collar crime is similar to other crimes.

VI. White-collar law enforcement systems
  A. General
    1. On the federal level, detection of white-collar crime is primarily in the hands of administrative departments and agencies.
    2. The number of state-funded technical assistance offices to help local prosecutors has increased significantly.
      a. Local agencies rarely have the funds necessary for effective enforcement..
      b. Local prosecutors pursue white-collar criminals more vigorously if they are a part of a team effort involving a network of law enforcement agencies.
      c. Relatively few prosecutors participate in interagency task forces.
  B. Controlling white-collar crime
    1. Prevailing belief is that many white-collar offenders avoid prosecution, and those who are prosecuted receive lenient punishment.
    2. Compliance strategies
      a. Aim for law conformity without the necessity of detecting, processing, or penalizing individual violators
        1) Set up administrative agencies to oversee business activities
          a. Food and Drug Administration
      b. Ask for cooperation and self-policing among the business community
      c. Attempt to create conformity by giving companies economic incentives to obey the law
      d. Post-Enron Sarbanes-Oxley (SOX) legislation limits the nonaudit services auditing firms can provide for publicly traded companies
      e. Enforcing compliance with civil penalties is on the upswing.
        1) Between 1997 and 2003, over $2 billion in criminal fines levied on business violators
    3. Deterrence strategies
      a. Involve detecting criminal violations, determining who is responsible, and penalizing the offenders to deter future violations
      b. Deterrence strategies should and have worked because white-collar crime, by its nature, is a rational act.
      c. Obstacles to deterrence:
        1) Federal agencies have traditionally been reluctant to throw corporate executives in jail.
        2) Courts have limited the application of criminal sanctions.
        3) The government seeks criminal indictments in corporate violations "only in instances of outrageous conduct of undoubted illegality."
  C. Is the tide turning?
    a. Growing evidence that white-collar crime deterrence strategies have become normative
    b. The government has stepped up investigations against senior executives and financial reporting personnel.
    c. The government has continued to pass legislation increasing penalties for business-related crimes.
      1) Antitrust Criminal Penalty Enhancement and Reform Act of 2004 imposes significantly higher criminal antitrust penalties
    d. In the wake of Enron and WorldCom crimes, white-collar crime has become a significant focus of government interest.

VII. Organized crime
    A.   Ongoing criminal enterprise groups whose ultimate purpose is personal economic gain through illegitimate means.
    B.   Characteristics of organized crime
        1.   Organized crime is a conspiratorial activity.
        2.   Organized crime has economic gain as its primary goal, although power and status may also be motivating factors.
        3.   Organized crime activities are not limited to providing illicit services.
        4.   Organized crime employs predatory tactics such as intimidation, violence, and corruption.
        5.   Organized crime's conspiratorial groups are usually very quick and effective in controlling and disciplining their members, associates, and victims.
        6.   Organized crime is not synonymous with the Mafia.
        7.   Organized crime does not include terrorists dedicated to political change.
    C.   Activities of organized crime
        1.   Most organized crime income comes from narcotics distribution, loan sharking, and prostitution.
        2.   Additional billions from gambling, theft rings, pornography, and other illegal enterprises
        3.   Control of union pension funds and dues
        4.   Hijacking shipments and cargo theft
        5.   Computer crime and other white-collar activities
        6.   Stock market manipulation
    D.   The concept of organized crime
        1.   Alien conspiracy theory concept purports that organized crime is a direct offshoot of a criminal society – the Mafia – that first originated in Italy and Sicily and now controls racketeering in major U.S. cities.
            a.   Many criminologist view the alien conspiracy theory as a figment of the media's imagination.
        2.   Another view: organized crime is a group of ethnically diverse groups who compete for profit in the sale of illegal goods and services and who use force and violence to extort money from legitimate enterprises.
    E.   Alien conspiracy theory
        1.   National syndicate of 25 or so Italian-dominated crime families that call themselves La Cosa Nostra
        2.   Major families
             a.   Membership of 1,700 "made men"
             b.   Another 17,000 "associates"
             c.   Control crime in distinct geographic areas
             d.   New York, the most important crime area, contains five families
             e.   Families are believed to be ruled by a "commission" of family heads and bosses who settle personal problems and jurisdiction conflicts.
    F.   Contemporary organized crime groups
        1.   A loose confederation of ethnic and regional crime groups, bound together by a commonality of economic and political objectives
            a.   Some groups located in fixed, geographic areas
            2.   One important contemporary change in organized crime is the interweaving of ethnic groups into the traditional structure.
        2.   Eastern European crime groups
            a.   Massive buildup in organized crime since the fall of the Soviet Union

   b. Transnational crime cartels
       1) Trading in illegal arms
       2) Narcotics
       3) Pornography
       4) Human trafficking and prostitution
3. Sex trade
   a. Estimated that 700,000 women are transported over international borders
       per year
   b. European enforcement operation resulted in the arrest of 293 traffickers in
       September, 2002.
   c. Complicity of local authorities with criminal organizations hinders enforcement
4. Since 1970, Russian and other Eastern European organized crime groups have been
   operating on U.S. soil.
   a. Some groups formed by immigrants
   b. Estimated that 2,500 Russian immigrants involved in criminal activity in Russian
       enclaves in New York City
       1) Have cooperated with Mafia families in narcotics trafficking, fencing stolen
           goods, money laundering, and other organized crime schemes
5. The Russian Mob is believed to have moved at least $7.5 billion from Russia into the
   Bank of New York.

G. The evolution of organized crime
   1   Emerging organized crime groups may or may not develop the degree of organization
       corruption associated with traditional crime families.
   2. It is simplistic to view organized crime in the U.S. as a national syndicate that controls
       all illegitimate rackets in an orderly fashion.

H. Controlling organized crime
   1. George Vold argued that the development of organized crime parallels early capitalist
       enterprises.
   2. Organized crime employs ruthless monopolistic tactics to maximize profits.
   3. Difficult to control organized crime

   4. Foreign Travel or Transportation in Aid of Racketeering Enterprises Act (Travel Act).
   5. Racketeer Influenced and Corrupt Organization Act (RICO) prohibits acts
       intended to:
       a. Derive income from racketeering or the unlawful collection of debts and use
           or investment of such income
       b. Acquire, through racketeering, an interest in or control over any enterprise
           engaged in interstate or foreign commerce
       c. Conduct business through a pattern of racketeering
       d. Conspire to use racketeering as a means of making income, collecting loans,
           or conducting business
   6. Enterprise theory of investigation (ETI)
       a. ETI model focus is on criminal enterprise and investigation attacks on the
           structure of the criminal enterprise rather than on criminal acts viewed as isolated
           incidents.
       b. ETI focuses on subsystems of the criminal enterprise that are considered the most
           vulnerable.

I. The future of organized crime
   1. Indications are that the traditional organized crime syndicates are in decline.
       a. Reigning family heads are quite old.

       b.   The younger generation of mob leaders seems to lack the skill and leadership of the older bosses.

       c.   Government policies have halved what the estimated mob membership was twenty-five years ago.

       d.   Pressure from newly emerging ethnic gangs

       e.   Changing values in U.S. society

       f.   Code of silence now regularly broken by younger mob members

       g.   Younger members are better educated and capable of seeking fortunes through legitimate means.

2.   If traditional organized crime syndicates are in decline that does not mean the end of organized crime.

       a.   Russian, Caribbean, and Asian gangs thriving

       b.   Internet gambling a tempting target for organized crime.

       c.   Continuing demand for illegal goods and services

CHAPTER SUMMARY

Enterprise crime refers to two categories of crime: white-collar crime and organized crime. Edwin Sutherland first used the phrase "white-collar crime" to describe the criminal activities of the rich and powerful. Sutherland argued that white-collar crime involved conspiracies by members of the wealthy classes to use their positions in commerce and industry for personal gain without regard to the law. Contemporary definitions of white-collar crime are typically much broader. The components of white-collar crime are stings and swindles, chiseling, individual exploitation of institutional position, influence peddling and bribery, embezzlement and employee fraud, client fraud, and corporate crime. Many criminologists have studied the causes of white-collar crime and asked if the cause was greed or need. The three major theoretical perspectives are the rationalization/neutralization view, the corporate culture view, and the self-control view.

Law enforcement efforts aimed at white collar crime have generally been more reactive rather than proactive. However, the number of state-funded technical assistance offices to help local prosecutors convict white collar criminals has increased significantly. In years past, it was rare for a corporate or white-collar criminal to receive a serious criminal penalty because white-collar criminals were often considered non-dangerous offenders. Major compliance strategies to deter white collar crime have included setting up administrative agencies to oversee business activity, forcing corporate boards to police themselves and take oversight responsibility, and enforcing compliance with civil penalties. Research indicates that the tide is turning on white collar crime. Sentencing guidelines for convicted criminals have assisted deterrence efforts and this get-tough deterrence approach appears to be affecting all classes of white-collar criminals.

There are seven major characteristics of organized crime. First, organized crime is a conspiratorial activity. Second, it has economic gain as its primary goal; although, power and status may also be motivating factors. Third, organized crime activities are not limited to providing illicit services. Fourth, it employs predatory tactics, such as intimidation, violence, and corruption. Fifth, organized crime's conspiratorial groups are usually very quick and effective in controlling and disciplining their members, associates, and victims. Sixth, organized crime is not synonymous with the Mafia. Last, organized crime does not include terrorists dedicated to political change.

Contemporary organized crime groups are a loose confederation of ethnic and regional crime groups, bound together by common economic and political objectives. One important contemporary change in organized crime is the interweaving of ethnic groups into the traditional structure. Organized crime employs ruthless monopolistic tactics to maximize profits, is secretive, protective of its operations, and is defensive against any outside intrusion. The Racketeer Influenced and Corrupt Organization Act (RICO) prohibits acts intended: a) to derive income from racketeering or the unlawful collection of debts and use or investment of such income; b) to acquire through racketeering an interest in or control over any enterprise engaged in interstate or foreign commerce; c) to conduct business through a pattern of racketeering; and d) to conspire to use racketeering as a means of making income, collecting loans, or conducting business.

STUDENT EXERCISES

Exercise 1

Go online to http://www.fbi.gov/ucr/whitecollarforweb.pdf and read the document, The Measurement of White-Collar Crime Using Uniform Crime Reporting (UCR) Data, by Cynthia Barnett. Write a summary of the article.

Exercise 2

Go to http://www.heritage.org/Research/LegalIssues/lm14.cfm and read the article, The Sociological Origins of "White-Collar Crime," by John S. Baker, Jr. Prepare a one to two page analysis of the article and critique of the author's position on who are white collar criminals and how we should prosecute them.

CRIMINOLOGY WEB LINKS

http://www.unodc.org/pdf/crime/forum/forum3_Art1.pdf
This URL contains an article titled *Controlling Organized Crime and Corruption in the Public Sector* authored by Buscaglia and van Dijk. The authors present a world-wide perspective on the interdependent factors shaping the growth of corruption and organized crime.

http://www.unodc.org/unodc/en/organized_crime.html
This is the official website of the United States/United Nations on global organized crime and provides a great deal of information on the subject.

http://www.sec.gov
This is the website for the United States Securities and Exchange Commission. Peruse the website for a vast array of information and to find out how a citizen can file a complaint or provide a tip on potential securities law violations or the latest fraud.

http://lawprofessors.typepad.com/whitecollarcrime_blog/
This website contains a blog called White Collar Crime Prof Blog which is edited by two law professors, Peter J. Henning and Ellen S. Podgor.

TEST BANK

FILL-IN THE BLANKS

1. The use illegal tactics to make a profit is referred to as _____ _____.

2. Some white-collar criminals use their positions of _____ in business or government to commit crimes.

3. _____ involves forcing victims to pay for services to which they have a clear right.

4. Federal law prohibits physicians and other healthcare providers from referring beneficiaries in federal healthcare programs to clinics or other facilities in which the physician or healthcare provider has a _____ interest.

5. _____ authority is satisfied if a third party, like a customer, reasonably believes the agent has the authority to perform the act in question.

6. The _____ _____ view is that some business organizations promote white-collar criminality in the same way that lower-class culture encourages the development of juvenile gangs and street crime.

7. According to Hirschi and Gottfredson, white-collar criminals have _____ _____ and are inclined to follow momentary impulses without considering the long-term costs of such behavior.

8. Compliance strategies attempt to create conformity by giving companies _____ _____ to obey the law.

9. Some criminologists view the alien conspiracy theory as a figment of the _____ imagination.

10. RICO's success has shaped the way the FBI attacks organized crime groups; they now use the _____ _____ of investigation.

TRUE/FALSE QUESTIONS

1. T/F Martha Stewart, who dumped her shares of ImClone stock just prior to the negative press announcement concerning FDA approval of the cancer drug, was accused of insider trading.

2. T/F A sting is a white-collar crime in which people use their institutional or business position to cheat others out of their money.

3. T/F Sutherland first used the term "white-collar crime" to describe the criminal activities of the rich and powerful.

4. T/F Exploitation cannot occur in private industry.

5. T/F "Gang visits" means referring patients to other physicians in the same office.

6. T/F Many white collar offenders feel free to engage in business crime because they can easily rationalize its effects.

7. T/F According to the corporate culture view, new employees learn the attitudes and techniques needed to commit white-collar crime from their business peers.

8. T/F Local prosecutors pursue white-collar criminals more vigorously if they are part of a team effort involving a network of law enforcement agencies.

9. T/F Compliance strategies aim for law conformity, but require detecting, processing, or penalizing individual violators.

10. T/F Leniency is given as part of a confession or plea arrangement in a white collar crime case.

11. T/F When proving tax fraud, the government requires no minimum dollar amount be stated before fraud exists.

12. T/F Division of markets is a type of false advertising.

13. T/F Organized crime activities are limited to providing illicit services.

14. T/F The traditional sources of income are for organized crime derived from providing illicit materials and using force to enter into and maximize profits in legitimate businesses.

15. T/F In sum, the alien conspiracy theory sees organized crime as being run by an ordered group of ethnocentric criminal syndicates, maintaining unified leadership and shared values.

MULTIPLE CHOICE QUESTIONS

1. Selling stock based on privileged knowledge not available to the general public is known as:
   a. white collar crime
   b. cybercrime
   c. enterprise crime
   d. insider trading

2. Illegal activities of people and institutions whose acknowledged purpose is profit through legitimate business transactions are called:
   a. organized crime
   b. blue-collar crime
   c. white-collar crime
   d. corporate crimes

3. When a corporation requires customers of one of its services to use other services it offers, this is called:
   a. price fixing
   b. tying arrangement
   c. group boycott
   d. division of markets

4. Swindlers have _____ _____ when defrauding people out of their money.
   a. little shame
   b. needy motivations
   c. covert assistants
   d. economic advantages

5. Compared to street crime, corporate violence kills and injures:
   a. approximately the same amount of people as all street crimes combined
   b. less people than any single type of street crime
   c. more people than all street crimes combined
   d. no people

6. The first person to use the term "white collar crime" was:
   a. Michael Gottfredson
   b. Travis Hirschi
   c. Mark Moore
   d. Edwin Sutherland

7. The type of white-collar crime, which includes antitrust violations, price fixing, and false advertising, is known as:
   a. organized crime
   b. corporate crime
   c. enterprise crime
   d. insider trading

8. A white-collar crime in which people use their institutional or business position to cheat others out of their money is known as:
   a. a sting or swindle
   b. bucketing
   c. chiseling
   d. churning

9. A type of client fraud that involves having accounts in two or more banks and taking advantage of the time required for checks to clear in order to obtain unauthorized use of bank funds is called:
   a. check hanging
   b. check running
   c. check kiting
   d. check floating

10. Repeated, excessive, and unnecessary buying and selling of stock is known as:
    a. front running
    b. bucketing
    c. chiseling
    d. churning

11. The act in which brokers place personal orders ahead of a large customer's order to profit from the market effects of the trade is called:
    a. front running
    b. bucketing
    c. chiseling
    d. churning

12. Skimming customer trading profits by falsifying trade information is known as:
    a. front running
    b. bucketing
    c. chiseling
    d. churning

13. Exploitation involves forcing victims to pay for services to which they have:
    a. a specific interest
    b. no right
    c. no interest
    d. a clear right

14. Referring patients to other physicians in the same office is known as:
    a. "gang visits"
    b. "steering"
    c. "ping-ponging"
    d. "pilferage"

15. Billing for multiple medical services is known as:
    a. "gang visits"
    b. "steering"
    c. "ping-ponging"
    d. "pilferage"

16. It is estimated that religious swindles bilk people out of:
    a. $500,000 a year
    b. $100 million a year
    c. $500 million a year
    d. $4 billion a year

17. Systematic theft of company property by employees is known as:
    a. "bucketing"
    b. "steering"
    c. "ping-ponging"
    d. "pilferage"

18. The process by which firms divide a region into territories and each firm agrees not to compete in the others' territories is known as:
    a. price fixing
    b. group boycott
    c. division of markets
    d. tying arrangements

19. The process by which a corporation requires customers of one of its services to use other services it offers is known as:
    a. price fixing
    b. group boycott
    c. division of markets
    d. tying arrangements

20. The process by which an organization or company boycotts retail stores that do not comply with its rules or desires is known as:
    a. price fixing
    b. group boycott
    c. division of markets
    d. tying arrangements

21. A fire inspector who demands that the owner of a restaurant pay him to be granted an operating license is exploiting his:
    a. social relationship with the owner
    b. agency's power
    c. institutional position
    d. business relationship with the owner

22. In West Germany, corporate bribes are
    a. tax deductible
    b. nonexistent
    c. misdemeanors
    d. felonies

23. Which of the following does not explain employee theft?
    a. job dissatisfaction
    b. lack of a retirement program
    c. strain and conflict
    d. workers' belief they are being exploited

24. In recent years, organized crime syndicates have branched into:
    a. theft rings
    b. narcotics distribution
    c. prostitution
    d. computer crime

25. The Racketeer Influenced and Corrupt Organization Act (RICO) created:
    a. new law enforcement agencies
    b. new sentencing guidelines for organized crime offenders
    c. new categories of offenses in racketeering activity
    d. new courts for prosecuting organized crime

ESSAY QUESTIONS

1. Explain the concept of enterprise crime.

2. Discuss the various causes of white-collar crime.

3.   Explain the different approaches to combating white-collar crime.

4.   Discuss the alien conspiracy theory.

5.   Explain how the government is fighting organized crime.

MATCHING

1. _____ Pilferage
2. _____ OSHA
3. _____ Chiseling
4. _____ The Geritol Gang
5. _____ Front Running
6. _____ White-Collar Crime
7. _____ Alien Conspiracy Theory
8. _____ Compliance
9. _____ Churning
10. _____ Insider Trading

A. The practice of buying large blocks of stock in companies that are believed to be the target of corporate buyouts or takeovers

B. Strategies that aim for law conformity without the necessity of detecting, processing, or penalizing individual violators

C. Illegal activities of people and institutions whose acknowledged purpose is profit through legitimate business transactions.

D. New York cab drivers routinely tapping the dashboards of their cabs with magnet loaded pens to zap their meters and jack up fares

E. Controls worker safety

F. Elderly generation of reigning mob bosses

G. Theft by employees through stealth or deception

H. When a broker places a personal order ahead of a large customer's order to profit from the market effects of the trade

I. Organized crime is made up of a national syndicate of 25 or so Italian-dominated crime families that call themselves La Cosa Nostra

J. A white-collar crime in which a stockbroker makes repeated trades to fraudulently increase commissions

CHAPTER 12 ANSWER KEY

Fill in the Blank Answers

1. enterprise crime
2. trust
3. exploitation
4. financial
5. apparent
6. corporate culture
7. low self-control
8. economic incentives
9. media's
10. enterprise theory

True/False Answers

1.	F	6.	T	11.	T
2.	T	7.	T	12.	F
3.	T	8.	T	13.	F
4.	F	9.	F	14.	T
5.	F	10.	F	15.	T

Multiple Choice Answers

1.	D	11.	A	21.	C
2.	A	12.	B	22.	A
3.	B	13.	D	23.	B
4.	A	14.	C	24.	D
5.	C	15.	A	25.	C
6.	D	16.	B		
7.	B	17.	D		
8.	A	18.	C		
9.	C	19.	D		
10.	D	20.	B		

Essay Questions

1. Page 396
2. Page 408
3. Pages 410-412
4. Pages 414-415
5. Pages 416-417

Matching Answers

1.	G	6.	C
2.	E	7.	I
3.	D	8.	B
4.	F	9.	J
5.	H	10.	A

PUBLIC ORDER CRIME

OUTLINE

Chapter 13

Public Order Crime

LEARNING OBJECTIVES

1. Be familiar with the association between law and morality

2. Be able to discuss the legal problems faced by gay people

3. Know what is meant by paraphilias

4. Be able to discuss the various types of prostitution

5. Describe the relationship between obscenity and pornography

6. Know the various techniques being used to control pornography

7. Discuss the history and extent of drug abuse

8. Be able to discuss the cause of substance abuse

9. Describe the different types of drug users

10. Identify the various drug control strategies

KEYWORDS AND DEFINITIONS

Public order crimes: acts that are considered illegal because they threaten the general well-being of society and challenge its accepted moral principles. Prostitution, drug use, and the sale of pornography are considered public order crimes.

Victimless crimes: crimes that violate the moral order but in which there is no actual victim or target. In these crimes, which include drug abuse and sex offenses, it is society as a whole and not an individual who is considered the victim.

Social harm: a view that behaviors harmful to other people and society in general must be controlled. Acts that are believed to be extremely harmful to the general public are usually outlawed; those that may only harm the actor are more likely to be tolerated. Some acts that cause enormous amounts of social harm are perfectly legal, such as tobacco and alcohol.

Vigilantes: do-gooders who take it on themselves to enforce the law, battle evil, and personally deal with those whom they consider immoral.

Moral crusaders: rule creators who have an absolute certainty that their way is right and that any means are justified to get their way; "the crusader is fervent and righteous, often self-righteous."

Gay bashing: violent acts directed at people because of their sexual orientation.

Homosexuality: erotic interest in members of one's own sex.

Sodomy: deviant intercourse.

Homophobia: extremely negative overreaction to homosexuals.

Paraphilias: bizarre or abnormal sexual practices involving recurrent sexual urges focused on (1) nonhuman objects (such as underwear, shoes, or leather), (2) humiliation or the experience of receiving or giving pain (such as in sadomasochism or bondage), or (3) children or others who cannot grant consent.

Brothels: a house of prostitution, typically run by a madam who sets prices and handles "business" arrangements.

Prostitution: the granting of nonmarital sexual access for remuneration.

Madam: a woman who employs prostitutes, supervises their behavior, and receives a fee for her services; her cut is usually 40 to 60 percent of the prostitute's earnings.

Call girls: prostitutes who make dates via the phone and then service customers in hotel rooms or apartments. Call girls typically have a steady clientele who are repeat customers.

Skeezers: prostitutes who trade sex for drugs, usually crack.

Pornography: sexually explicit books, magazines, films, or tapes intended to provide sexual titillation and excitement for paying customers.

Obscenity: material deeply offensive to morality or decency and designed to incite lust or depravity.

Temperance movement: an effort to prohibit the sale of liquor in the United States that resulted in the passage of the Eighteenth Amendment to the Constitution in 1919, which prohibited the sale of alcoholic beverages.

Gateway model: an explanation of drug abuse that posits users fall into drug abuse slowly, beginning with alcohol and then following with marijuana and more serious drugs as the need for a more powerful high intensifies.

CHAPTER OUTLINE

I.   Law and morality
     A.   Debating morality
          1.   Some scholars argue that acts like pornography, prostitution, and drug use erode the moral fabric of society and therefore should be prohibited and punished.
          2.   According to this view, so-called victimless crimes are prohibited because one of the functions of criminal law is to express a shared sense of public morality.
          3.   Some influential legal scholars have questioned the propriety of legislating morals.

4. Gusfield argues that the purpose of outlawing immoral acts is to show the moral superiority of those who condemn the acts over those who partake of them.
5. Cultural clashes may ensue when behavior that is considered normative in one society is deplored by those living in another.

B. Social harm
1. Immoral acts can be distinguished from crimes on the basis of the social harm they cause.
2. Acts that are believed to be extremely harmful to the general public are usually outlawed.
3. Those acts that may only harm the actor are more likely to be tolerated.
4. Some acts that cause enormous amounts of social harm are perfectly legal.

C. Moral crusaders
1. Vigilantes held a strict standard of morality that, when they caught their prey, resulted in sure and swift justice.
2. The assumption that it is okay to take matters into your own hands if the cause is right and the target is immoral
3. Moral crusaders run the risk of engaging in immoral conduct in their efforts to protect society from those they consider immoral.

II. Homosexuality
A. Attitudes toward homosexuality
1. Throughout much of Western history, homosexuals have been subject to discrimination, sanction, and violence.
2. Intolerance continues today.

B. Homosexuality and the law
1. Homosexuality is no longer a crime in the United States.
2. The Defense of Marriage Act
   a. Massachusetts allows same-sex marriage.
   b. States are not obligated to recognize single-sex marriages performed in other states.

C. Is the tide turning?
1. All sodomy laws in the United States are now unconstitutional and unenforceable.
2. The *Romer* and *Lawrence* decisions have heralded a new era of legal and civil rights for gay men and women.

III. Paraphilias
A. Bizarre or abnormal sexual practices involving recurrent sexual urges focused on
1. Nonhuman objects (such as underwear, shoes, or leather)
2. Humiliation or the experience of receiving or giving pain (such as in sadomasochism or bondage)
3. Children or others who cannot grant consent

B. Behaviors subject to criminal penalties
1. Asphyxiophilia
2. Frotteurism
3. Voyeurism
4. Exhibitionism
5. Sadomasochism
6. Pedophilia

C. Paraphilias that involve unwilling or underage victims are illegal.

IV. Prostitution
  A. General
      1. Prostitution has been known for thousands of years.
      2. These conditions are usually present in a commercial sexual transaction
          a. Activity that has sexual significance for the customer
          b. Economic transaction
          c. Emotional indifference
  B. Incidence of prostitution
      1. Rates of arrest for prostitution have declined.
      2. The sexual revolution has liberalized sexuality so that men are less likely to use prostitutes because legitimate alternatives for sexuality are now available.
  C. International sex trade
      1. Sex tourism
      2. There has also been a soaring demand for pornography, strip clubs, lap dancing, escorts, and telephone sex in developing countries.
      3. Countries with large sex industries create the demand for women.
      4. Countries where traffickers easily recruit women provide the supply.
      5. In the sex industry today, the most popular and valuable women are from Russia and the Ukraine.
  D. Types of prostitutes
      1. Street walkers
          a. Many are young runaways who gravitate to major cities to find a new, exciting life and escape from sexual and physical abuse at home.
          b. The street life is very dangerous.
      2. Bar girls
          a. B-girls are served diluted drinks or water colored with dye or tea, for which the customer is charged an exorbitant price.
          b. It is common to find B-girls in towns with military bases and large transient populations.
      3. Brothel prostitutes
          a. A madam is in charge of the brothel.
          b. Despite their decline, some madams and their brothels have achieved national prominence.
      4. Call girls
          a. The aristocrats of prostitution
          b. Either entertain clients in their own apartments or visit clients' hotels and apartments
      5. Escort services/Call houses
          a. Some escort services are fronts for prostitution rings.
          b. Both male and female sex workers can be sent out after the client calls in response to an ad in the yellow pages.
          c. A relatively new phenomenon, call houses, combines elements of the brothel and call girl rings.
      6. Circuit travelers
          a. Prostitutes known as circuit travelers move around in groups of two or three to lumber, labor, and agricultural camps.
          b. Sometimes young girls are forced to become circuit travelers by unscrupulous pimps.

7. Skeezers
   a. A significant portion of female prostitutes have substance abuse problems.
   b. Not all drug-addicted prostitutes barter sex for drugs.
8. Massage parlors/photo studios
9. Cyber prostitute

E. Becoming a prostitute
   1. Both male and female street-level sex workers often come from troubled homes.
      a. Marked by extreme conflict and hostility
      b. From poor urban areas or rural communities
   2. Most prostitutes grew up in homes with absent fathers.
   3. Women engaging in prostitution have limited educational backgrounds.
   4. Most did not complete high school.
   5. Lower-class girls who get into "the life" report
      a. Conflict with school authorities
      b. Poor grades
      c. An overly regimented school experience
   6. A significant portion of lower class girls have long histories of drug abuse.
   7. Young girls who frequently use drugs and begin using at an early age are most at risk for prostitution to support their habits.
   8. Child sexual abuse and prostitution
      a. Child prostitution is not a recent development.
      b. In contemporary society, child prostitution has been linked to sexual trauma experienced at an early age.
      c. Many prostitutes
         1) Were initiated into sex by family members at ages as young as 10 to 12 years
         2) Have long histories of sexual exploitation and abuse

F. Controlling prostitution
   1. Prostitution is considered a misdemeanor, punishable by a fine or a short jail sentence.
   2. Law enforcement is uneven and aims at confining illegal activities to particular areas in the city.
   3. Prostitution is illegal in all states except Nevada.
   4. The Child Sexual Abuse Prevention Act made it a criminal offense to travel abroad for the purpose of engaging in sexual activity with a minor.

G. Legalize prostitution?
   1. Feminists have staked out conflicting views of prostitution.
      a. One position is that women must become emancipated from male oppression and reach sexual equality.
      b. The sexual equality view considers the prostitute a victim of male dominance.
      c. The free choice view is that prostitution, if freely chosen, expresses women's equality and is not a symptom of subjugation.
   2. Advocates of both positions
      a. Argue that the penalties for prostitution should be reduced (decriminalized)
      b. Neither side advocates outright legalization.

V. Pornography
  A. General
     1. The Internet contains at least 200,000 websites offering pornographic material.
     2. The purpose of this material is to provide sexual titillation and excitement for paying customers.
  B. Child pornography
     1. Child pornography has become widespread on the Internet.
     2. Most sites are short-lived entities whose addresses are passed around to users.
  C. Does pornography cause violence?
     1. Some studies indicate that viewing sexually explicit material actually has little effect on sexual violence.
     2. Even high levels of exposure to pornography do not turn nonaggressive men into sexual predators.
     3. The pornography–violence link seems modest.
     4. Men exposed to violent pornography are more likely to act aggressively and hold aggressive attitudes toward women.
     5. James Fox and Jack Levin find it common for serial killers to collect and watch violent pornography.
  D. Pornography and the law
     1. All states and the federal government prohibit the sale and production of pornographic material.
     2. Obscene material and the First Amendment
     3. The basic guidelines for obscenity
        a. Whether the average person applying contemporary community standards would find that the work taken as a whole appeals to the prurient interest
        b. Whether the work depicts or describes, in a patently offensive way, sexual conduct specifically defined by the applicable state law
        c. Whether the work, taken as a whole, lacks serious literary, artistic, political or scientific value
  E. Controlling pornography
     1. Controlling sex for profit is difficult because of the public's desire to purchase sexually related material and services.
     2. An alternative approach has been to restrict the sale of pornography within acceptable boundaries.
     3. The state has the right to regulate adult films as long as the public has the right to view them.
  F. Technological change
     1. The First Amendment right to free speech makes legal control of pornography, even "kiddie porn," quite difficult.
     2. Problems with the Child Pornography Prevention Act (CPPA)

VI. Substance abuse
  A. When did drug use begin?
  B. Alcohol and its prohibition
     1. The temperance movement was fueled by the belief that the purity of the U.S. agrarian culture was being destroyed by the growth of the city.
     2. What doomed Prohibition?
        a. One factor was the use of organized crime to supply illicit liquor.
        b. The law made it illegal only to sell alcohol, not to purchase it.

      c.   Law enforcement agencies were inadequate and officials were likely to be corrupted by wealthy bootleggers.

C.   The extent of substance abuse

    1.   Monitoring the Future

        a.   Conducted by the Institute of Social Research (ISR) at the University of Michigan

        b.   This survey is based on the self-report responses of nearly 50,000 high school students in the 8th, 10th, and 12th grades in almost 400 schools across the United States.

        c.   Drug use declined from a high point around 1980 until 1990, when it began once again to increase until 1996; since then teenage drug use has either stabilized or declined.

    2.   National Survey on Drug Use and Health

        a.   Conducted by the Substance Abuse and Mental Health Services Administration (SAMHSA), a division of the Department of Health and Human Services

        b.   The NSDUH collects information from all U.S. residents of households, noninstitutional group quarters, and civilians living on military bases.

        c.   In 2003, an estimated 19.5 million Americans aged 12 or older (about 8 percent of the population) were current illicit drug users.

    3.   National Center on Addiction and Substance Abuse (CASA) Survey

        a.   Alcohol abuse begins at an early age and remains an extremely serious problem over the life course.

        b.   The age at which children begin drinking is dropping.

    4.   Are surveys accurate?

        a.   Self-report evidence is subject to error.

        b.   National surveys overlook important segments of the drug-using population.

        c.   There is evidence that reporting may be affected by social and personal traits.

        d.   These surveys also use statistical estimating methods to project national use trends from relatively small samples.

D.   AIDS and drug use

    1.   Intravenous (IV) drug use is closely tied to the threat of AIDS.

    2.   It is now estimated that as many as one-third of all IV drug users are AID carriers.

    3.   One reason for the AIDS–drug use relationship is the widespread habit of needle sharing among IV users.

    4.   Needle sharing has been encouraged by efforts to control drugs by outlawing the over-the-counter sale of hypodermic needles.

    5.   The threat of AIDS may be changing the behavior of recreational and middle-class users.

E.   What causes substance abuse?

    1.   Subcultural view

        a.   The onset of drug use can be tied to such factors as racial prejudice, devalued identities, low self-esteem, poor socioeconomic status, and the high level of mistrust, negativism, and defiance found in impoverished areas.

        b.   Residents feel trapped in a cycle of violence, drug abuse, and despair.

        c.   Research shows that peer influence is a significant predictor of drug careers that actually grow stronger as people mature.

    2.   Psychological view

        a.   Not all drug abusers reside in lower-class slum areas; the problem of middle-class substance abuse is very real.

        b.   Some experts have linked substance abuse to psychological deficits that can strike people in any economic class such as:
- 1) Impaired cognitive functioning
- 2) Personality disturbance
- 3) Emotional problems

        c.   Drugs may help people deal with unconscious needs and impulses and relieve dependence and depression.

        d.   Research does in fact reveal the presence of a significant degree of personal pathology.

   3.   Genetic factors

        a.   Research shows that substance abuse may have a genetic basis.

        b.   People whose parents were alcoholic or drug dependent have a greater chance of developing a problem than the children of non-abusers.

        c.   This relationship occurs regardless of parenting style or the quality of the parent–child relationship.

   4.   Social learning

        a.   Social psychologists suggest that drug abuse may also result from observing parental drug use.

        b.   People who learn that drugs provide pleasurable sensations may be the most likely to experiment with illegal substances.

        c.   A habit may develop if the user experiences lower anxiety, fear, and tension levels

   5.   Problem behavior syndrome

        a.   Longitudinal studies show that drug abusers are maladjusted, alienated, and emotionally distressed.

        b.   Having a deviant lifestyle begins early in life and is punctuated with:
- 1) Criminal relationships
- 2) Family history of substance abuse
- 3) Educational failure
- 4) Alienation

        c.   There is robust support for the interconnection of problem drinking and drug abuse and other similar social problems.

   6.   Rational choice

        a.   Some may use drugs and alcohol because they want to enjoy their effects.

        b.   Substance abuse may be a function of the rational but mistaken belief that drugs can benefit the user.

        c.   Adolescents may begin using drugs because they believe their peers expect them to do so.

F.   Is there a drug gateway?

   1.   A number of research efforts have confirmed the gateway model.

   2.   Drinking with an adult present, presumably a parent, was a significant precursor of future substance abuse and delinquency.

   3.   The most serious drug users have a history of alcohol abuse.

   4.   Not all research efforts find that users progress to ever-more potent drugs.

   5.   Some research shows that many hard-core drug abusers never actually smoked pot or used alcohol.

G.   Types of drug users

   1.   Adolescents who distribute small amounts of drugs

   2.   Adolescents who frequently sell drugs

   3.   Teenage drug dealers who commit other delinquent acts

4. Adolescents who cycle in and out of the justice system
5. Drug-involved youth who continue to commit crimes as adults
6. Outwardly respectable adults who are top-level dealers
7. Smugglers
8. Adult predatory drug users who are frequently arrested
9. Adult predatory drug users who are rarely arrested
10. Less predatory drug-involved adult offenders
11. Women who are drug-involved offenders

H. Drugs and crime
1. One of the main reasons for the criminalization of particular substances is the assumed association between drug abuse and crime.
2. Research suggests that many criminal offenders have extensive experience with drug use.
3. Drug users commit an enormous amount of crime.
4. The true relationship between drug users and crime is still uncertain.
5. Many users have had a history of criminal activity before the onset of their substance abuse.
6. User surveys
   a. People who take drugs have extensive involvement in crime.
   b. Violent adolescents report histories of alcohol abuse.
   c. Adults with long histories of drinking are also more likely to report violent offending patterns.
7. Surveys of known criminals
   a. Youths who self-reported delinquent behavior during the past year were also more likely to use illicit drugs in the past month than other youths.
   b. Surveys of prison inmates disclose that many (80 percent) are lifelong substance abusers.
   c. Arrestee Drug Abuse Monitoring Program (ADAM)
      1) Approximately two-thirds of both female and male arrestees tested positive for at least one drug.
      2) Marijuana was the drug most commonly used by male arrestees.
      3) Cocaine was the drug most commonly used by female arrestees.
   d. The drug-crime connection
      1) Most criminals are not actually drug users.
      2) A second interpretation is that most criminals are in fact substance abusers.
      3) Even if the crime rate of drug users were actually half that reported in the research literature, users would be responsible for a significant portion of the total criminal activity in the United States.

I. Drugs and the law
1. The federal government first initiated legal action to curtail the use of some drugs early in the twentieth century.
2. Since then, various federal laws have attempted to increase penalties imposed on drug smugglers and limit the manufacture and sale of newly developed substances.

J. Drug control strategies
1. Source control
   a. One approach to drug control is to deter the sale and importation of drugs
   b. Designed to capture and punish known international drug dealers and deter those who are considering entering the drug trade.
   c. The drug trade is an important source of foreign revenue.

d. United States has little influence in some key drug-producing areas such as Vietnam, Cambodia, and Myanmar.

2. Interdiction strategies
   a. Law enforcement efforts have also been directed at intercepting drug supplies as they enter the country.
   b. Border patrols and military personnel using sophisticated hardware have been involved in massive interdiction efforts.

3. Law enforcement strategies
   a. Local, state, and federal law enforcement agencies have been actively fighting against drugs.
   b. The long-term consequence has been to decentralize drug dealing and encourage young independent dealers to become major suppliers.

4. Punishment strategies
   a. Once convicted, drug dealers can get very long sentences.
   b. Courts are so backlogged that prosecutors are anxious to plea bargain.
   c. Prisons have become jammed with inmates.

5. Community strategies
   a. Another type of drug-control effort relies on the involvement of local community groups to lead the fight against drugs.
   b. Citizen-sponsored programs attempt to restore a sense of community in drug-infested areas, reduce fear, and promote conventional norms and values.
   c. Another tactic is to use the civil justice system to harass offenders.
   d. There are also community-based treatment efforts in which citizen volunteers participate in self-help support programs.
   e. Drug prevention efforts designed to enhance the quality of life, improve interpersonal relationships, and upgrade the neighborhood's physical environment
   f. D.A.R.E.

6. Drug testing programs
   a. Drug testing of private employees, government workers, and criminal offenders is believed to deter substance abuse.
   b. Drug testing is also common in government and criminal justice agencies.
   c. Criminal defendants are now routinely tested at all stages of the justice system, from arrest to parole.

7. Treatment strategies
   a. One approach rests on the assumption that users have low self-esteem and treatment efforts must focus on building a sense of self.
   b. There are also residential programs for the more heavily involved, and a large network of drug treatment centers has been developed.
   c. Other therapeutic programs attempt to deal with the psychological causes of drug use.
   d. Supporters of treatment argue that many addicts are helped by intensive in- and out-patient treatment.

8. Employment programs
   a. Research indicates that drug abusers who obtain and keep employment will end or reduce the incidence of their substance abuse.
   b. One approach is the supported work program, which typically involves job-site training, ongoing assessment, and job-site intervention.

    K.   Drug legalization
1. Despite the massive effort to control drugs through prevention, deterrence, education, and treatment strategies, the fight against substance abuse has not proved successful.
2. Legalization is warranted because the use of mood-altering substances is customary in almost all human societies.
3. Banning drugs creates networks of manufacturers and distributors, many of whom use violence as part of their standard operating procedures.
4. When drugs were legal and freely available in the early twentieth century, the proportion of Americans using drugs was not much greater than today.
5. If drugs were legalized, the government could control price and distribution
6. The consequences of legalization.
    a.   Critics argue that legalization
        1) Might have the short-term effect of reducing the association between drug use and crime.
        2) Might also have grave social consequences such as increasing the nation's rate of drug use.
    b.   Drug users might significantly increase their daily intake.
    c.   Might encourage drug smuggling to avoid tax payments
7. The lesson of alcohol
    a.   The problems of alcoholism should serve as a warning of what can happen when controlled substances are made readily available.
    b.   Drunk-driving fatalities might be matched by deaths due to driving under the influence of pot or crack.

CHAPTER SUMMARY

When discussing the issue of law and morality, some scholars argue that acts like pornography, prostitution, and drug use erode the moral fabric of society and should therefore be prohibited and punished. According to this view, so-called victimless crimes are prohibited because one of the functions of criminal law is to express a shared sense of public morality.

Throughout much of Western history, homosexuals have been subject to discrimination, sanction, and violence. In fact, much intolerance continues today even though homosexuality is no longer a crime in the United States. Massachusetts is the only state that allows same-sex marriage, but under The Defense of Marriage Act, individual states are not obligated to recognize single-sex marriages performed in other states. All sodomy laws in the United States are now unconstitutional and unenforceable and Supreme Court decisions such as those in *Romer* and *Lawrence* have heralded a new era of legal and civil rights for gay men and women.

Paraphilias are defined as bizarre or abnormal sexual practices involving recurrent sexual urges focused on nonhuman objects (such as underwear, shoes, or leather), humiliation or the experience of receiving or giving pain (such as in sadomasochism or bondage), or children or others who cannot grant consent. Behaviors subject to criminal penalties include asphyxiophilia, frotteurism, voyeurism, exhibitionism, sadomasochism, and pedophilia. Paraphilias that involve unwilling or underage victims are also illegal.

Prostitution has been known for thousands of years. The following conditions are usually present in a commercial sexual transaction: sexual significance for the customer, an economic transaction, and emotional indifference. In the international sex trade, sex tourism is a booming business. There has also been a soaring demand for pornography, strip clubs, lap dancing, escorts, and telephone sex in developing countries. Both male and female street-level sex workers often come from troubled homes marked by extreme conflict and hostility and from poor urban areas or rural communities. In contemporary society, child prostitution has been linked to sexual trauma experienced at an early age. Prostitution is illegal in all states except Nevada. The Child Sexual Abuse Prevention Act made it a criminal offense to travel abroad for the purpose of engaging in sexual activity with a minor.

The Internet contains at least 200,000 websites offering pornographic material. The purpose of this material is to provide sexual titillation and excitement for paying customers. Child pornography has become widespread on the Internet. Some studies indicate that viewing sexually explicit material has little effect on sexual violence. However, men exposed to violent pornography are more likely to act aggressively and hold aggressive attitudes toward women. According to the Supreme Court, the basic guidelines for obscenity include 1) whether the average person applying contemporary community standards would find that the work taken as a whole appeals to the prurient interest, 2) whether the work depicts or describes, in a patently offensive way, sexual conduct specifically defined by the applicable state law, and 3) whether the work, taken as a whole, lacks serious literary, artistic, political or scientific value.

Substance abuse is a global problem and the drug-crime link in the United States is a strong one. Several studies concerning the extent of substance abuse in the United States are conducted throughout the year. Among those studies are Monitoring the Future, the National Survey on Drug Use and Health, and the National Center on Addiction and Substance Abuse Survey. Intravenous (IV) drug use is closely tied to the threat of AIDS and it is now estimated that as many as one-third of all IV drug users are AIDS carriers. One reason for the AIDS–drug use relationship is the widespread habit of needle sharing among IV users. There are six major theories concerning what causes substance abuse. They include the subcultural view, the psychological view, genetic factors, social learning, problem behavior syndrome, and rational choice. A number of research efforts have confirmed that there is a drug gateway. The most serious drug users have a history of alcohol abuse, but not all research efforts find that users progress to more potent drugs. One of the main reasons for the criminalization of particular substances is the assumed association between drug abuse and crime. Despite the massive effort to control drugs through prevention, deterrence, education, and treatment strategies, the fight against substance abuse has not proved successful and so some scholars propose legalization as a solution.

STUDENT EXERCISES

Exercise 1

Go online to http://www.city-journal.org/html/7_2_a1.html and read the document, *Don't Legalize Drugs*, by Theodore Dalrymple. Next, go to http://www.lp.org/issues/relegalize.html and read the document, *Should We Re-Legalize Drugs?*, by the Libertarian Party. Now write a short paper on which drugs should be legalized and which should be not. Justify your answer.

Exercise 2

Go online to http://www.whitehousedrugpolicy.gov/publications/policy/ndcs04/2004ndcs.pdf and scan the *2004 National Drug Control Strategy*. Prepare a one to two page analysis of our government's strategy to deal with drugs. In your response, address the major law enforcement, treatment, and international efforts that are being taken.

CRIMINOLOGY WEB LINKS

http://www.psychdirect.com/forensic/Criminology/para/paraphilia.htm#types
This is the official website for PsychDirect. Take a look around the website which has a wealth of information on paraphilias.

http://www.dianarussell.com/porntoc.html
This is an article by Diana Russell on the relationship between pornography and rape.

http://www.impactresearch.org/documents/sistersspeakout.pdf
This publication by Jody Raphael and Deborah L. Shapiro from the Center for Impact Research is a study on prostitutes in Chicago. It provides "helpful information for understanding the lives of women in prostitution, and what can be done to assist them."

http://www.ojp.usdoj.gov/ovc/publications/bulletins/internet_2_2001/NCJ184931.pdf
This is a publication from the Office for Victims of Crime that deals with internet crimes against children. Although only eight pages long, it provides a great deal of information.

http://www.ncjrs.org/pdffiles1/ojjdp/203946.pdf
This website contains a document from the Office of Juvenile Justice and Delinquency Prevention called *Prostitution of Juveniles: Patterns from NIBRS*. It provides demographic data on juveniles arrested by the police for prostitution.

TEST BANK

FILL-IN THE BLANKS

1. _____ _____ _____ involve acts that interfere with the operations of society and the ability of people to function efficiently.

2. In our society, _____ _____ can be distinguished from crimes on the basis of the social harm they cause.

3. _____ is rubbing against or touching a nonconsenting person in a crowd, elevator, or other public area.

4. Modern commercial sex appears to have its roots in ancient _____.

5. A _____ is a woman who employs prostitutes, supervises their behavior, and receives a fee for her services.

6. Philip Jenkins suggests that kiddie porn is best combated by more effective law enforcement. Instead of focusing on users efforts should be directed against _____.

7. The eventual prohibition of the sale of alcoholic beverages was brought about by ratification of the _____ Amendment in 1919.

8. Those who adhere to the subcultrual view of substance abuse view drug abuse as having an environmental basis and concentrate on _____ addiction.

9. For many people substance abuse is just one of many _____ behaviors.

10. Although the drug–crime connection is powerful, the true relationship between them is still _____ because many users have had a history of criminal activity before the onset of their substance abuse.

TRUE/FALSE QUESTIONS

1. T/F There is little debate that the purpose of criminal law is to protect society and reduce social harm.

2. T/F Acts that are believed to be extremely harmful to the general public are always outlawed.

3. T/F It is possible to be a homosexual but not to engage in sexual conduct with members of the same sex.

4. T/F All paraphilias activity is outlawed.

5. T/F The sexual exchange in prostitution is simply for economic consideration.

6.   T/F The aristocrats of prostitution are brothel prostitutes.

7.   T/F The free choice view considers the prostitute a victim of male dominance.

8.   T/F Allowing for individual judgments regarding what is obscene makes the Constitution's guarantee of free speech unworkable.

9.   T/F In the case of *Young v. American Mini Theaters*, the Supreme Court permitted a zoning ordinance that restricted theaters to showing erotic movies in only one area of the city, even though it did not find any of the movies that were shown to be obscene.

10. T/F Marijuana accounted for most of the increase in overall illicit drug use during the 1990s but use is now in decline and more youth view it as dangerous.

11. T/F One of the strengths of national surveys on drug usage is that they include all the important segments of the drug-using population.

12. T/F Needle sharing has been encouraged by efforts to control drugs by outlawing the over-the-counter sale of hypodermic needles.

13. T/F Research shows that substance abuse may have a genetic basis.

14. T/F Most research shows that most people fall into drug abuse slowly, beginning with alcohol and then following with marijuana and more serious drugs as the need for a more powerful high intensifies.

15   T/F Women are far less likely than men to use addictive drugs.

MULTIPLE CHOICE QUESTIONS

1.   Crimes for which laws have been enacted to control behaviors involving sexuality and morality are often referred to as:
     a.   misdemeanors
     b.   public order crimes
     c.   social harms
     d.   felonies

2.   Rule creators who have an absolute certainty that their way is right and that any means are justified to get their way are known as:
     a.   vigilantes
     b.   entrepreneurs
     c.   law makers
     d.   moral crusaders

3.   Violent acts directed at people because of their sexual orientation are called:
    a.   gay bashing
    b.   homophobia
    c.   paraphilias
    d.   sodomy

4.   In which case did the U.S. Supreme Court determine that people could not be criminally prosecuted because of their status (such as drug addict or homosexual) ?
    a.   *Romer v. Evans*
    b.   *Robinson v. California*
    c.   *Bowers v. Hardwick*
    d.   *Lawrence v. Texas*

5.   In which case did the U.S. Supreme Court rule six to three that Colorado's Amendment 2, which prohibited state and local governments from protecting the civil rights of gay people, was unconstitutional?
    a.   *Romer v. Evans*
    b.   *Robinson v. California*
    c.   *Bowers v. Hardwick*
    d.   *Lawrence v. Texas*

6.   Which Supreme Court case made it impermissible for states to criminalize oral and anal sex and all other forms of intercourse that are not heterosexual under statutes prohibiting sodomy, deviant sexuality, or buggery?
    a.   *Romer v. Evans*
    b.   *Robinson v. California*
    c.   *Bowers v. Hardwick*
    d.   *Lawrence v. Texas*

7.   Rubbing against or touching a nonconsenting person in a crowd, elevator, or other public area is known as:
    a.   asphyxiophilia
    b.   exhibitionism
    c.   frotteurism
    d.   voyeurism

8.   Obtaining sexual pleasure from spying on a stranger while he or she disrobes or engages in sexual behavior with another is known as:
    a.   asphyxiophilia
    b.   exhibitionism
    c.   frotteurism
    d.   voyeurism

9.   Which of the following conditions are usually **NOT** present in a commercial sexual transaction?
    a.   sexual significance for the customer
    b.   curiosity
    c.   economic transaction
    d.   emotional indifference

10. Which of the following is correct concerning prostitution?
    a.   The number of arrests for prostitution has remained stable for the past two decades.
    b.   The number of men who hire prostitutes has increased sharply.
    c.   The prevalence of sexually transmitted diseases has not caused many men to avoid visiting prostitutes.
    d.   We have accurate statistics on the number of prostitutes operating in the U.S.

11. Women who barter drugs for sex are called:
    a.   boozers
    b.   ticketeros
    c.   skeezers
    d.   working girls

12. The "Natasha Trade" refers to:
    a.   juvenile prostitution
    b.   the smuggling of heroin from Eastern Europe
    c.   Russian prostitution
    d.   international trafficking in prostitution

13. Which of the following is **not** correct concerning pornography and violence?
    a.   The pornography–violence link is strong.
    b.   People exposed to material that portrays violence, sadism, and women enjoying being raped and degraded are also likely to be sexually aggressive toward female victims.
    c.   Men exposed to violent pornography are more likely to act aggressively and hold aggressive attitudes toward women.
    d.   Fox and Levin find it common for serial killers to collect and watch violent pornography.

14. Which Supreme Court decision is currently the standard for the concept of obscenity?
    a.   *Memoirs v. Massachusetts*
    b.   *Miller v. California*
    c.   *Roth v. United States*
    d.   *Alberts v. California*

15. Which law restricted importation, manufacture, sale, and dispensing of narcotics?
    a.   Harrison Narcotics Act
    b.   Boggs Act of 1951
    c.   Marijuana Tax Act
    d.   Durham-Humphrey Act of 1951

16. Which law made it illegal to dispense barbiturates and amphetamines without a   prescription?
    a.   Harrison Narcotics Act
    b.   Boggs Act of 1951
    c.   Marijuana Tax Act
    d.   Durham-Humphrey Act of 1951

17. The annual self-report survey of drug abuse among high school students conducted by the Institute of Social Research (ISR) at the University of Michigan that is an important source of information on drug use is called:
    a. National Survey on Drug Use and Health (NSDUH)
    b. National Center on Addiction and Substance Abuse (CASA) Survey
    c. Arrestee Drug Abuse Monitoring Program (ADAM)
    d. Monitoring the Future (MTF)

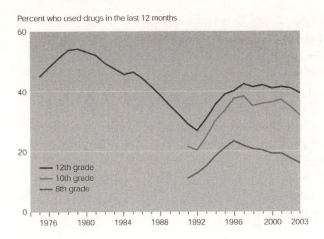

Percent who used drugs in the last 12 months

18. The view that drug abuse has an environmental basis is called:
    a. problem behavior syndrome
    b. rational choice
    c. subcultural view
    d. social learning

19. Those who suggest that drug abuse may result from observing parental drug use follow which view?
    a. problem behavior syndrome
    b. rational choice
    c. subcultural view
    d. social learning

20. Those who argue that some may use drugs and alcohol because they want to enjoy their effects subscribe to which view?
    a. problem behavior syndrome
    b. rational choice
    c. subcultural view
    d. social learning

21. The consequences of drug legalization might include:
    a. a decrease in a drug user's daily intake of drugs
    b. a decrease in drug smuggling
    c. an increase in the nation's rate of drug usage
    d. a decrease in the nation's rate of drug usage

22. The approach to drug control that deters the sale and importation of drugs through the systematic apprehension of large-volume drug dealers, coupled with the enforcement of strict drug laws that carry heavy penalties is called a/an:
    a. source control strategy
    b. interdiction strategy
    c. community strategy
    d. law enforcement strategy

23. Directing efforts at large-scale drug rings is a/an:
    a. source control strategy
    b. interdiction strategy
    c. community strategy
    d. law enforcement strategy

24. A drug prevention effort designed to enhance the quality of life, improve interpersonal relationships, and upgrade the neighborhood's physical environment is called a/an:
    a. source control strategy
    b. interdiction strategy
    c. community strategy
    d. law enforcement strategy

25. Which of the following is **NOT** part of the D.A.R.E. program?
    a. teaching students techniques to resist peer pressure
    b. teaching students to report drug users
    c. teaching students respect for the law and law enforcers
    d. giving students ideas for alternatives to drug use

ESSAY QUESTIONS

1. Explain the association between law and morality.

2. Discuss the various types of prostitution.

3. Explain the various techniques being used to control pornography.

4. Describe the causes of substance abuse.

5.   Explain the various drug control strategies.

MATCHING

1. _____   Addict
2. _____   Brothels
3. _____   Call Girls
4. _____   Paraphilias
5. _____   Gay Bashing
6. _____   Homosexuality
7. _____   Madam
8. _____   Mann Act
9. _____   Massage Parlors
10. _____   Moral Crusades

A.   Base of some prostitutes where massage and some prostitution services are for sale
B.   A woman who employs prostitutes, supervises their behavior, and receives a fee for her services
C.   Violent acts directed at people because of their sexual orientation
D.   Prostitutes who service upper-class customers and earn large sums of money
E.   A person with an overpowering physical and psychological need to continue taking a particular substance or drug by any means possible
F.   Efforts by special interest-group members to stamp out behavior they find objectionable
G.   The Federal Act which prohibited bringing women into the country or transporting them across state lines for the purposes of prostitution
H.   Refers to erotic interest in members of one's own sex
I.   Bizarre or abnormal sexual practices involving recurrent sexual urges focused on nonhuman objects, humiliation or the experience of receiving or giving pain, or children or others who cannot grant consent
J.   Also known as bordellos, cathouses, sporting houses, and houses of ill repute

CHAPTER 13 ANSWER KEY

Fill in the Blank Answers

1. public order crimes
2. immoral acts
3. frotteurism
4. Greece
5. madam
6. suppliers
7. Eighteenth
8. lower-class
9. problem
10. uncertain

True/False Answers

1.	T	6.	F	11.	F
2.	F	7.	F	12.	T
3.	T	8.	T	13.	T
4.	F	9.	T	14.	F
5.	T	10.	T	15.	T

Multiple Choice Answers

1.	B	11.	C	21.	C
2.	D	12.	D	22.	A
3.	A	13.	A	23.	D
4.	B	14.	B	24.	C
5.	A	15.	A	25.	B
6.	D	16.	D		
7.	C	17.	D		
8.	D	18.	C		
9.	B	19.	D		
10.	A	20.	B		

Essay Questions

1. Pages 426-429
2. Pages 431-435
3. Page 439
4. Pages 446-447
5. Pages 451-456

Matching Answers

1.	E	6.	H
2.	J	7.	B
3.	D	8.	G
4.	I	9.	A
5.	C	10.	F

CYBER CRIME AND TECHNOLOGY

OUTLINE

Chapter 14

Cyber Crime and Technology

LEARNING OBJECTIVES

1. Understand the concept of cyber crime and why it is becoming so important

2. Distinguish among cyber theft, cyber vandalism, and cyber terrorism

3. Know the various types of computer crimes such as computer frauds, illegal copyright infringement, and Internet securities fraud

4. Be familiar with the terms *identity theft* and *phishing*

5. Know the differences among worms, viruses, Trojan horses, logic bombs, and spam

6. Discuss how the Internet can be used for spying

7. Be able to debate the issue of cyber terrorism

8. Be familiar with the various methods being used to control cyber crime

9. Discuss the role technology now plays in the criminal justice system

10. Understand both sides of the debate over the use of technology and civil liberties

KEYWORDS AND DEFINITIONS

Cyber crime: the use of modern technology for criminal purpose; a new breed of offenses that can be singular or ongoing but typically involve the theft and/or destruction of information, resources, or funds utilizing computers, computer networks, and the Internet.

Information technology: the widespread use of computers and the Internet to access information.

Globalization: the process of creating transnational markets, politics, and legal systems in an effort to form and sustain a global economy.

Cyber theft: schemes ranging from illegal copying of copyrighted material to using technology to commit traditional theft-based offenses such as larceny and fraud.

Cyber vandalism: technological destruction; malicious attacks aimed at disrupting, defacing, and destroying technology that is deemed to be offensive.

Cyber terrorism: acts that are aimed at undermining the social, economic, and political system of an enemy by destroying its electronic infrastructure and disrupting its economy.

Automatic teller machines (ATMs): self-operated kiosks that allow banking customers to withdraw and deposit money.

Denial of service attack: an attempt to extort money from legitimate users of an Internet service by threatening to prevent the users from having access to the service.

Warez: a term computer hackers and software pirates use to describe a game or application that is made available for use on the Internet in violation of its copyright protection.

Identity theft: a type of cyber crime that entails using the Internet to steal someone's identity and/or impersonate the victim to open a new credit card account or conduct some other financial transaction.

Phishing (carding or spoofing): a scam where the perpetrator sends out e-mails appearing to come from legitimate web enterprises such as eBay and PayPal, from credit card companies, or from financial institutions in an effort to get the recipient to reveal personal and financial information.

E-tailing fraud: a cyber scam involving the use of the Internet for both illegally buying and selling merchandise.

Computer virus: one type of malicious software program (also called malware) that disrupts or destroys existing programs and networks, causing them to perform the task for which the virus was designed.

Malware: Internet argot meaning a malicious software program.

Computer worm: a malware similar to viruses but that use computer networks or the Internet to self-replicate and "send themselves" to other users, generally via e-mail, without the aid of the operator.

Trojan horse: a type of malware that hackers introduce into a computer system that looks like a benign application but contains illicit codes that can damage the system operations. While destructive, Trojan horses do not replicate themselves as do computer worms.

Logic bomb: also called a *slag* code; it is a type of delayed-action virus that is set off when a program user unwittingly inputs a specific command or makes an inputting error.

Spam: unsolicited advertisement or promotional material that typically comes in the form of an unwanted e-mail message.

Web defacement: a type of cyber vandalism that occurs when a computer hacker intrudes on another person's website by inserting or substituting codes that expose site visitors to misleading or provocative information.

Cyber stalking: using the Internet, e-mail, or other electronic communication devices to stalk another person.

Cyber spying: illegally using the Internet to gather information that is considered private and confidential.

Data mining: a process used by law enforcement agencies to conduct analysis of behavior patterns via sophisticated computer software.

Automated fingerprinting identification systems (AFIS): a computerized fingerprint identification and classification process (and databank) used by law enforcement.

Biometrics: automated methods of recognizing a person based on a physiological or behavioral characteristic.

Technocorrections: the use of information and electronic technologies within the correctional system.

CHAPTER OUTLINE

I.   Cyber theft: cyber crimes for profit
   A.   General
      1.   Since the industrial revolution, every technological breakthrough has created new opportunities for criminal wrongdoing.
      2.   Computer-based technology allows criminals to operate more efficiently and effectively.
         a.   Luxury of remaining anonymous
         b.   No geographic or time limitations
         c.   Whole world can be their target – wider number of potential victims
      3.   Cyber thieves use cyber space to:
         a.   Distribute illegal goods and services
         b.   Defraud people for quick profits
   B.   Computer fraud
      1.   A common-law crime committed using technology
      2.   Many computer crimes prosecuted under traditional larceny and fraud statues
      3.   Recent trends in computer fraud
         a.   Shift from external to internal Internet attacks at the world's largest financial institutions
            1)   2005 security survey: 35% of financial institutions encountered attacks from inside their organization within the past twelve months
         b.   Growing trend to commit fraud using devices that rely on IT for their operations
            1)   ATMs attracting cyber criminals looking for easy profits
   C.   Distributing illegal sexual material
      1.   IT revolution has revitalized the porn industry.
      2.   Estimated that the number of pornography web pages has soared during the past six years
         a.   1.3 million sites; 260 pages of erotic content
      3.   The number of visits to pornographic sites surpasses those made to Internet search engines.
         a.   Some individual sites report 50 million hits per year.
      4.   How do adult sites operate?
         a.   Large firms charge annual subscriptions for unlimited access.
         b.   Password services charge an annual fee to deliver access to small sites.
         c.   Large firms provide free content to smaller "affiliate" sites.

      d.   Webmasters forward traffic to another porn site in exchange for a small per-consumer fee – "mousetrapping"

      e.   Adult sites cater to niche audiences looking for specific kinds of adult content.

  5.   Some sites peddle access to obscene material or kiddie porn.

  6.   Landslide Productions – Internet based pornography ring

      a.   Offered, per monthly fee, access to porn websites in Russia and Indonesia.

      b.   One owner sentenced to life in prison

  7.   Difficult to control Internet pornography

      a.   Communications Decency Act – 1996

      b.   Child Online Protection Act – 1998

      c.   Children's Internet Protection Act – 2000

      d.   Filtering devices in schools and libraries

      e.   Unlikely that any law enforcement efforts will put a dent in the Internet porn industry.

D. Denial of service attack

  1.   An attempt to extort money from legitimate users of an Internet service by threatening to prevent the users from having access to the service

      a.   Attempts to flood a network

      b.   Attempts to disrupt connections

      c.   Attempts to prevent a particular individual from accessing a service

      d.   Attempts to disrupt service to a specific system or person

  2.   Unless a site owner pays extortion, the attackers threaten to keep up interference until real consumers become frustrated and abandon the site.

  3.   Online gambling casinos particularly vulnerable to attacks

E. Illegal copyright infringement

  1.   "Warez" – offenders illegally obtain software and then "crack" or "rip" its copyright protection before posting it on the Internet for members of the group to use.

  2.   Pirated copies reach the Internet days or weeks before legitimate products are commercially available.

  3.   Some member of the Warez community convicted under:

      a.   Computer Fraud and Abuse Act – criminalized accessing computer systems without authorization to obtain information

      b.   Digital Millennium Copyright Act (DMCA) – made it a crime circumvent antipiracy measures built into most commercial software

  4.   File sharing

      a.   File-sharing programs that allow Internet users to download music an other copyright material without paying royalties

      b.   Estimated to cost U.S. industries $19 billion worldwide, each year

          1)   U.S. Criminal Code for first-time offenders: five years incarceration and a $250,000 fine

      c.   Operation Digital Gridlock

          1)   First criminal enforcement action against peer-to-peer copyright piracy

  5.   Media piracy

      a.   Using the Internet to sell illegally copied films

      b.   Family Entertainment and Copyright Act of 2005 and its sub-statute, the Artists' Rights and Theft Prevention Act of 2005 (ART)

          1)   Criminalized the use of recording equipment to make copies of films while in movie theatres

          2)   Made it illegal to copy a work in production and put it on the Internet

F. Internet securities fraud

1. Three major types of Internet securities fraud
    a. Market manipulation
    b. Fraudulent offerings of securities
    c. Illegal touting
G. Identity theft
    1. Using the Internet to someone's identity and/or impersonate the victim to open a new credit card account or conduct some other financial transaction
        a. Can destroy people's lives
        b. Identity thieves use a variety of techniques to steal information.
        c. Some identity theft schemes are elaborate
    2. Phishing (or carding and spoofing)
        a. Phony e-mails or websites that entice victims to provide personal and financial information
        b. Once phishers have a victim's information, they can do one of three things:
            1) Gain access to preexisting accounts
            2) Use the information to open new bank and credit card accounts
            3) Implant viruses into the victim's software that forwards the phishing e-mail to other recipients
        c. Common phishing scams
            1) Account verification scams
            2) Sign-in rosters
            3) The Nigerian 419 scam
            4) Canadian/Netherlands lottery
            5) Free credit report
            6) "You have won a free gift."
            7) E-mail chain letters/pyramid scams
            8) "Find out everything on everyone"
            9) Job advertisement scams
            10) VISA/MasterCard scam
        d. Cyber criminals can easily copy corporate letterheads and logos making e-mails look authentic.
        e. Identity Theft and Assumption Deterrence Act (Identity Theft Act)
            1) Federal crime to "knowingly transfer or use, without lawful authority, a means of identification of another person with intent to commit...any unlawful activity"
            2) Violations investigated by U.S. Secret Service, FBI, U.S. Postal Inspection Service
        f. Identity Theft Penalty Enhancement Act – 2004
            1) Extra prison term of two years with no possibility of probation
            2) Committing identity theft while engaged in crimes associated with terrorism enhances a sentence by five years.
H. E-tailing fraud
    1. Using the Internet for both illegally buying and selling merchandise
    2. Selling frauds
        a. Failure to deliver on promised purchases
        b. Substitution of cheaper or used material for higher quality purchases
    3. Buying frauds
        a. Purchase expensive item; purchase a similar-looking cheaper model of the same brand; return the cheaper item after switching bar codes and boxes with the more expensive unit

        b.   "Shoplisting"- a thief purchases an unexpired receipt, shoplifts the items on the receipt, and returns them for a refund or gift card

II.   Cyber vandalism: cyber crime with malicious intent
    A.   General
        1.   Cyber vandalism ranges from sending destructive viruses and worms to terrorist attacks designed to destroy important computer networks.
        2.   Cyber vandals are motivated more by malice than by greed.
           a.   Some cyber vandals target computers and networks seeking revenge for some perceived wrong.
           b.   Some desire to exhibit their technical prowess and superiority.
           c.   Some wish to highlight the vulnerability of computer security systems.
           d.   Some desire to spy on other people's private financial and personal information ("computer voyeurism").
           e.   Some want to destroy computer security because they believe in a philosophy of open access to all systems and programs.
    B.   Worms, viruses, Trojan horses, logic bombs, and spam
        1.   A computer virus is one type of malicious software program (also called malware) that disrupts or destroys existing programs and networks.
           a.   The virus is then spread from one computer to another when a user sends an infected file via e-mail, a network, or a disk.
        2.   Computer worms similar to viruses but use computer networks or the Internet to self-replicate and "send themselves."
        3.   Damage caused by viruses and worms considerable
           a.   Melissa virus: More than $80 million
           b.   MS Blaster worm: Infected over 120,000 computers worldwide
        4.   Trojan horses
           a.   Malware that looks like a benign application but contains illicit codes that can damage the system operations
           b.   Do not replicate themselves like viruses but are destructive
        5.   Logic bombs
           a.   A program that is secretly attached to a computer system, monitors the network's output, and waits for a particular signal to appear – also called *slag code*
           b.   Is activated upon the signal, causing various problems including corruption of data
        6.   Spam
           a.   An unsolicited advertisement or promotional material
           b.   E-mail is the most common form of spam.
           c.   Can also be sent via instant messaging, usenet newsgroup, mobile phone messaging
           d.   A malicious form of spam contains a Trojan horse disguised as an e-mail attachment.
           e.   Sending spam can be a crime when it causes serious harm to a computer or network.
    C.   Web defacement
        1.   A type of cyber vandalism that occurs when a computer hacker intrudes on another person's website by inserting or substituting codes that expose site visitors to misleading or provocative information.
           a.   Can range from installing humorous graffiti to sabotaging or corrupting the site.

   b. Defacement is not always easily noticeable.
  2. Almost all defacement attacks are designed to vandalize rather than to bring profits or gain.
   a. Some defacers may eventually extort money from targets.
   b. Some defacers are trying to impress the hacking community with their skills.
   c. Some defacers have political goals.
    1) Analysis indicates 70% of defacements are pranks, 30% have a political motive.
  3. Major threat to online businesses and government agencies
   a. Can harm credibility and reputation
   b. Clients lose trust and become reluctant to share personal and financial information.
   c. An e-tailer may lose business if clients believe the site is not secure.
   d. Financial institutions particularly vulnerable
 D. Cyber stalking
  1. Using the Internet, e-mail, or other electronic communication devices to stalk another person
   a. Some stalkers pursue minors through online chat rooms, eventually making contact for the purpose of engaging in criminal sexual activities.
   b. Some stalkers harass victims electronically.
   c. A cyber stalker may trick others into harassing or threatening a victim by impersonating the victim on Internet bulletin boards and/or chat rooms.
 E. Cyber spying
  1. Illegally using the Internet to gather information that is considered private and confidential
   a. Lovespy computer program example
   b. Cyber spies have a variety of motivations.
    1) Marital disputes
    2) Business rivals hire disgruntled employees to steal information.
   c. Commercial cyber spies
    1) Used by businesses
    2) Used by foreign competitors seeking trade secrets
 F. Cyber espionage
  1. Cyber spying by intelligence agencies, around the world, that employ hackers to penetrate secure computer networks in order to steal important data
   a. Titan Rain spy ring is among the most pervasive cyber espionage threats to the United States.
    1) Believed that Titan Rain agents have compromised secure networks
     a. Redstone Army Arsenal
     b. NASA
     c. The World Bank
   b. Hundreds of Defense Department computer systems have been penetrated.
   c. Similar cyber espionage attacks in Britain, Canada, Australia, New Zealand

III. Cyber terrorism: cyber crime with political motives
 A. General
  1. Cyber terrorism can be viewed as an effort by covert forces to disrupt the intersection between the virtual electronic reality of computers and the physical world.
  2. May involve the use of computer network tools to shut down critical national infrastructures or to coerce or intimidate a government or civilian population.

3. Terrorist organizations beginning to understand the power of cyber crime even though they come from regions lacking in IT
4. Infrastructure at risk:
   a. Water treatment plants
   b. Electric plants, dams
   c. Oil refineries
   d. Nuclear power plants
B. Why terrorism in cyber space?
   1. Because cyber terrorism can attack an enemy's economy
   2. More efficient and less dangerous than traditional forms of terrorist activity
   3. No loss of life involved and no need to infiltrate "enemy" territory
   4. Can commit crimes from anywhere in the world with minimal cost
C. Cyber attacks
   1. Has the U.S. already been the target of cyber attacks?
      a. Difficult to distinguish between damage caused by hackers and terrorists
      b. First six months of 2002: financial services had received an average of 1,018 attacks per company
   2. What form may cyber attacks take?
      a. Logic bombs implanted in an enemy's computer
      b. Programs allowing terrorist to enter "secure" systems
      c. Overloading a network's electrical system
      d. Computers allow terrorists to communicate with agents around the world
      e. Vital national security systems disrupted
      f. Disruption of infrastructure computer systems (oil, dams)
      g. Attacks against financial system
      h. Recruit new terrorists
D. Is cyber terrorism a real threat?
   1. Not a single case of cyber terrorism has been recorded.
   2. Fears of cyber terrorism may be exaggerated or misplaced because:
      a. The infrastructure that would be the target of cyber attacks is not easy to hack into.
      b. Failure of such infrastructure would not cause a widespread panic.
      c. Power outages/problems with water treatment plants are not uncommon.
   3. Most likely use of cyber attacks would be in conjunction with a more traditional physical attack.
   4. Cyber attacks would cause neither death nor widespread destruction – thus, not in keeping with terrorist goals.
   5. Great fear that terrorists would hack into economic or military sites
   6. Threat is still there

IV. The extent and costs of cyber crime
   A. How common and costly?
      1. Most breaches are not reported to local, state, or federal authorities.
         a. Involves low-visibility acts
         b. Businesses fear revealing security weaknesses
      2. Overall costs due to cyber crime in the billions and rising
         a. Illegal copying: $29 billion in losses
         b. Payment fraud: $15.5 billion in losses
         c. Computer security breaches: average cost of $204,000 per breach
         d. Phishing and identify theft:

1) 57 million Americans received phishing e-mail
2) Average identity theft loss of $50,000 in 2004
   a. Lost wages between $1,820 and $14,340 per incident
   b. Expenses between $851 and $1,378 per incident
   c. Cost to the British economy of over $2 billion
e. Employee abuse of internet access privileges: 78% of employers report abuse
f. Cyber vandalism according to Symantec Corporation Internet security threat report:
   1) Online attackers increasingly using stealthy attacks on personal computers in pursuit of profit rather than for vandalism.
   2) Significant increase in attack programs using malicious codes
   3) Attackers targeting assaults more carefully and using less familiar programs.
   4) Personal computers increasingly the target of attacks
   5) 10,866 new viruses and worms during the first six months of 2005
   6) 10,000 "bots" now being launched daily (programs that provide remote control of victims' computers)

V. Controlling cyber crime
   A. General
      1. Rapidly evolving technology challenges law enforcement efforts.
      2. Congress has treated computer-related crime as a federal offense since its 1984 Counterfeit Access Device and Computer Fraud and Abuse Law.
         a. Enhanced in 1996 by the National Information Infrastructure Protection Act (NIIPA)
      3. Because cyber crime is relatively new, existing laws are inadequate.
         a. Identity theft was not a crime prior to October 30, 1998 when the Identity Theft and Assumption Act was passed.
         b. Today, all states except Vermont and the District of Columbia have passed laws against identity theft.
      4. After 9/11, the NIIPA was amended by sections of the USA Patriot Act making it easier to enforce crimes by terrorists against the nation's computer systems.
         a. Criminalizes knowingly causing transmission of a program, code, or command that intentionally causes damage to a protected computer
         b. Prohibits intentional access without authorization that results in damage but does not require intent to damage
      5. Computer-related crimes can also be charged under at least forty different federal statutes.
   B. Cyber crime enforcement agencies
      1. Creation of "working groups" to coordinate activities of numerous agencies
         a. Interagency Telemarketing and Internet Fraud Working Group
      2. Creation of specialized enforcement agencies
         a. Internet Fraud Complaint Center
            1) 200,000 complaints received in 2004 – a 60% increase
         b. New York Electronic Crimes Task Force
            1) Has charged over 1,000 individuals, since 1995, for losses exceeding one billion
            2) Has trained over 60,000 public and private justice system personnel in cyber crime prevention
   C. Local enforcement efforts
      1. Now creating special units to crack down on cyber crime

      a.   Toronto, Canada police department's child exploitation section concentrates on Internet child pornography

          1)   Estimates 100,000 children depicted in one million photos circulated on Internet

          2)   300 arrests in four years; only half in the Toronto area

          3)   Information sharing with Interpol

VI. Controlling crime using information technology

    A. General

        1.   IT now plays a significant role in law enforcement.

        2.   Crime Identification Technology Act of 1998

          a.   Provided over a billion dollars in state grants

    B. Law enforcement technology

        1.   IT has become a necessity.

        2.   Introduction of technology has been explosive.

          a.   1964: only one city had a police computer system

          b.   Today: almost every city of more than 50,000 has some type of computer-enhanced policing

        3.   Identifying crimes and criminals

          a.   IT allows for sophisticated analyses of data from various sources.

        4.   Data mining

          a   Analysis of behavior patterns to identify crime patterns and link them to suspects

        5.   Criminal identification

          a.   Computers link agencies so they can share information on cases, suspects, and warrants.

          b.   FBI's National Crime Information Center implemented in 1967

          c.   Computerized imaging replacing mug books

          d.   Computer systems now used in the booking process; allows for "photo lineups."

          e.   Emerging technologies:

              1)   Computerized, composite facial images

              2)   Digitization of photos to enable reconstruction of blurred images

              3)   Computer software to allow three-dimensional recreations of two-dimensional mug shots

        6.   Automated fingerprint identification systems (AFIS)

          a.   Widely used criminal identification process based on automated fingerprint analysis and computerized fingerprint systems

          b.   AFIS files have been regionalized

          c.   Number of searchable fingerprint records exceeds 14 million within the Western Identification Network.

          d.   Emerging national database

        7.   Crime analysis

          a.   Computerized mapping programs

              1)   Graphic representations of where crime is happening

              2)   Police detect patterns of crimes and pathologies of related problems.

              3)   36% of agencies with 100 or more sworn officers now using some form of crime mapping

        8.   Alternative mapping initiatives

          a.   Internet-based mapping systems to assist with tactical response plans during critical incidents (terrorist and emergency situations)

1) Washington state's Critical Incident Planning and Mapping System
 b. Further enhancement of 911 systems
   2) West Virginia Statewide Addressing and Mapping Board
    a. Using geospatial IT to produce maps showing a caller's exact location
9. Biometrics
 a. Automated methods of recognition based on a physiological or behavioral characteristic
   1) Voice, retina, facial features, and handwriting analysis
 b. Beneficial for all levels of the government, the military, and private businesses
 c. Four steps in the process of recording biometric data:
   1) Raw biometric data is captured or recorded.
   2) Distinguishing characteristics are used to create a biometric template.
   3) Template is changed into a mathematical representation.
   4) Verification process
 d. Currently, a number of biometric programs are in effect.
   1) Immigration and Customs Enforcement's hand geometry systems
   2) Casinos implementing facial recognition software into security systems
10. Communications
 a. Use of portable computers by police officers
11. Combating terrorism with communications
 a. Communications Assistance for Law Enforcement Act (CALEA) – 1994
   1) Aided law enforcement's ability to monitor suspects
   2) Requires manufacturers and carriers to design equipment, facilities, and services that are compatible with electronic surveillance needs
   3) Upon issue of a court order, communication carriers must be able to:
    a. Expeditiously isolate all wire and electronic communications of a target transmitted by the carrier within its service area
    b. Expeditiously isolate call-identifying information of a target
    c. Provide intercepted communications and call-identifying information to law enforcement
    d. Carry out intercepts unobtrusively
   4) Under CALEA, the government reimburses telecommunications carriers for costs of developing software to intercept communications.
12. Surveillance
 a. Closed-circuit cameras
 b. The Department of Homeland Security is providing $800 million to fifty cities for surveillance system setups.
 c. "Bait cars" equipped with technology to foil car thefts
   1) Motor vehicle theft dropped over 40% in a three year period in Minneapolis and 30% in Vancouver, British Columbia over six months.
13. Information processing
 a. Using IT to gather and disseminate information
 b. Justice Technology Information Network (JUSTNET) – website that offers police agencies IT information
 c. Many large police agencies have their own websites.
   1) Public can file complaints
   2) Contains employment opportunities and qualifications
   3) Distributes crime alerts
   4) Links to sexual offender registries
   5) Special features

C.   Court Technology
1.   Videotaped testimonies, court reporting devices, information systems, data processing systems to handle court dockets and jury management
2.   Communications
    a.   Closed-circuit arraignments
    b   Voice-activated cameras to record testimony
3.   Videoconferencing
    a.   About 400 courts have videoconferencing capability.
        1)   Employed for juvenile detention hearings, expert witness testimony, oral arguments on appeal, and parole hearings
    b.   Advantages:
        1)   Minimize delays in prisoner transfer
        2)   Cost savings through elimination of transportation and security costs
        3)   Reduced escape and assault risks
4.   Evidence presentation
    a.   High-tech courtrooms now equipped for:
        1)   Real-time transcription and translation
        2)   Audio-video preservation of the court record
        3)   Remote witness participation
        4)   Computer graphics displays
        5)   Television monitors for jurors
        6)   Computers for counsel and judge
5.   Case management
    a.   Older systems were limited and could not process complex interrelationships of information.
    b.   New IT systems handle complex case management from day-to-day operations of the courts to jury selection and financial management.
        1)   National Center for State Courts in Williamsburg, VA
        2)   Circuit Court Automation Program in Wisconsin
6.   Internet records
    a.   J-Net is the federal system's judiciary website that makes it easier for judges and court personnel to receive important information in a timely fashion.
    b.   The federal court's administrative office sends official correspondence via e-mail.
    c.   Automated library management system developed in 1999 that allowed judges to access a web-based virtual law library.
    d.   2002: Eleven federal courts announced they would allow Internet access to criminal case files.
    e.   U.S. Supreme Court's Public Access to Court Electronic Records (PACER), allows Internet access to case information.

D.   Corrections Technology
1.   Technocorrections – use of IT within the field of corrections
2.   Locating and monitoring inmates
    a.   Federal Bureau of Prison's database
    b.   Some states have similar inmate databases
3.   Internet monitoring of offenders in the community
    a.   Kiosks for probationer, parolees, and pretrial detainees to report to their case managers
4.   IT for prison security
    a.   Ground penetrating radar
    b.   Heartbeat monitoring

    c.   Satellite monitoring

    d.   Sticky shocker

    e.   Back-scatter imaging system for concealed weapons

    f.   Body scanning screening system

    g.   Transmitter wristbands

    h.   Personal health status monitor

    i.   All-in-one drug detection spray

    j.   radar vital signs monitor/radar flashlight

    k.   Personal alarm location system

VII. Information technology, crime, and civil liberties

    A.   Some critics are concerned that IT can compromise the privacy and liberty of U.S. citizens who have not engaged in criminal activity.

        1.   Privacy concerns often focus on new surveillance technologies.

        2.   Concerns about linkage of surveillance information to data processing and storage systems, resulting in easily accessed permanent records

        3.   Problem of balancing security and civil liberties

            a.   The level of intrusion and surveillance people will tolerate may depend on their assessments of the risks they face.

            b.   How willing will people be to sacrifice civil liberties based upon those risks?

CHAPTER SUMMARY

Cyber crime is a new breed of offenses that involves the theft and/or destruction of information, resources, or funds by utilizing computers, computer networks, and the Internet. Computer-based technology allows criminals to operate more efficiently and effectively and presents a challenge for the justice system because cyber crime's rapid evolution is difficult to detect through traditional law enforcement channels. Cyber crime has grown as information technology (IT) has evolved and become part of daily life in most industrialized societies. Some of the many types of cyber crime are cyber theft, cyber vandalism, cyber terrorism, and identity theft.

The Internet has become an important mechanism for committing cyber crime. The IT revolution has revitalized the porn industry, has resulted in extortion attempts via denial of service attacks, has allowed for illegal copyright infringement, and has provided new mechanisms for engaging in securities fraud. Incidents of identity theft have increased in the United States and can destroy people's lives. Phishing is a scam making use of e-mail or websites to steal personal and financial information and has contributed to the frequency of identity theft. Phishers have become increasing sophisticated making it difficult to discern legitimate e-mail and website content from illegitimate. The Identity Theft and Assumption Deterrence Act made identity theft a federal crime. In 2004, the Identity Theft Enhancement Act increased the prison terms of convicted offenders by two years and those offenders convicted of identity theft associated with terrorism by five years.

Some cyber criminals are motivated more by revenge or malice than greed. Such cyber criminals engage in various forms of cyber vandalism. Cyber vandalism involves malicious intent and ranges from sending destructive viruses and worms to hacker attacks designed to destroy important computer networks via Trojan horses, logic bombs, and spam. Web defacement is another type of cyber vandalism.

Cyber stalking refers to the use of the Internet, e-mail, or other electronic communication devices to stalk another person. Some stalkers pursue minors through online chat rooms while others harass their victims electronically. Cyber spying involves illegally using the Internet to gather information that is considered private and confidential. Cyber spying may be committed by disgruntled individuals or by commercial businesses, including foreign competitors. Cyber espionage is cyber spying by intelligence agencies.

Cyber terrorism can be viewed as an effort by covert forces to disrupt the intersection where the virtual electronic reality of computers meets with the physical world. Infrastructure at risk of cyber terrorism includes oil refineries and nuclear power plants. Some experts question the existence of cyber terrorism, claiming that not a single case of cyber terrorism has yet been recorded, that cyber vandals and hackers are regularly mistaken for terrorists, and that cyber defenses are more robust than is commonly supposed. Aside from these criticisms, it is concluded the threat of cyber terrorism exists.

Like IT, the enforcement of cyber crime is evolving. Since 1984, Congress has treated computer-related crime as a distinct federal offense and new legislation has been drafted to protect the public from cyber crime. Identity theft became a crime 1998 and, today, all states except Vermont and the District of Columbia have passed laws against identity theft. After the attacks of 9/11, the National Information Infrastructure Protection Act was amended by sections of the USA Patriot Act making it easer to enforce crimes by terrorists against the nation's computer systems. Federal and state law enforcement agencies have created working groups that coordinate activities of numerous agencies involved in investigating cyber crime. Local police departments have created specialized units to deal with specific types of cyber crime, such as Internet child pornography.

Criminal justice agencies are using IT to increase their effectiveness with such methods as data mining, crime mapping, and computer-aided identification of suspects. Biometrics, automated methods of recognizing an individual based on a physiological or behavioral characteristic, is also being used for identification and security by law enforcement. The courts have applied communications and IT technology in such areas as video-taped testimonies, closed-circuit arraignments, court reporting devices, information systems, and data processing systems to handle court dockets and jury management. IT has also influenced the corrections field. States have used IT to locate inmates, and corrections departments are using the Internet to monitor offenders in the community. Prisons are making use of IT to maintain security.

Though IT techniques provide the opportunity to increase the effectiveness and efficiency within justice agencies, critics are concerned that IT can compromise the privacy and liberty of U.S. citizens who have not engaged in criminal activity. The level of intrusion and surveillance citizens will tolerate may depend on the risks they perceive.

STUDENT EXERCISES

Exercise 1

Go online to http://www.sec.gov/investor/pubs/cyberfraud.htm and read the document, *Internet Fraud: How to Avoid Internet Investment Scams.* Write a summary of the article.

Exercise 2

Go to http://www.fas.org/irp/crs/RL32114.pdf and read the report, *Computer Attack and Cyber Terrorism: Vulnerabilities and Policy Issues for Congress* by Clay Wilson. Prepare a one to two page analysis of the article focusing on the degree of threat posed by cyber terrorism.

CRIMINOLOGY WEB LINKS

http://www.ncsl.org/programs/lis/cip/stalk99.htm
Visit this National Council of State Legislatures website to access your state's cyberstalking laws. How does your state's laws compare to the laws of other states?

http://www.ncvc.org
This is the website for the National Center for Victims of Crime. Peruse the website for a vast array of information, including cyberstalking and what to do if someone you know should become a victim of this crime.

http://www.survey.mailfrontier.com/survey/quiztest.html
This website contains a phishing IQ test. Access this site to learn how to distinguish fraudulent emails from legitimate emails, to see phishing facts, and to become "phishing aware."

http://www.ftc.gov/bcp/conline/pubs/alerts/phishingalrt.htm
Visit this URL to read the Federal Trade Commission alert *How Not to Get Hooked by a 'Phishing' Scam*. The FTC provides tips to avoid being 'phished' and provides information about filing an FTC report if you believe you have been scammed.

TEST BANK

FILL-IN THE BLANKS

1. Cyber crime has grown because _____ _____ has become part of daily life in most industrialized societies.

2. File sharing is a type of illegal _____ _____ that allows Internet users to download music and other copyrighted material without paying the artists and record producers royalties.

3. _____ involves the creation of false e-mails and/or websites to gain access to a victim's personal information.

4. Malicious attacks aimed at disrupting, defacing, and destroying technology that vandals find offensive is termed _____ _____.

5. _____ _____ involves illegally using the Internet to gather information that is considered private and confidential.

6. Since 1984, Congress has treated computer-related crime as a distinct _____ _____.

7. Although IT techniques provide the opportunity to increase the effectiveness and efficiency within criminal agencies, critics believe they can compromise the _____ and the _____ of U.S. citizens.

8. So far there have been no reports of major widespread _____ _____ attacks in the United States.

9. Fifty-seven million U.S. adults think they have received a _____ e-mail.

10. The National Information Infrastructure Protection Act makes it a crime to access computer files without _____.

TRUE/FALSE QUESTIONS

1. T/F More than 10,000 "bots" are being launched daily.

2. T/F IT is responsible for creating a global economy.

3. T/F Computer fraud is not a unique offense but rather a common-law crime committed using contemporary technology.

4. T/F Titan Rain is a highly sophisticated, defense industry computer security program.

5. T/F When trade secrets are stolen by a company's domestic or foreign competitors, it is terms cyber theft.

6. T/F When examining trends in computer fraud, internal attacks are now outpacing external attacks at the world's largest financial institutions.

7. T/F It is estimated that the number of pornography web pages has soared during the past six years.

8. T/F A form of illegal copyright infringement involves file-sharing programs that allow Internet users to down load music and copyrighted material without paying the artists and producers their rightful royalties.

9. T/F The Nigerian 419 scam refers to a type of cyber vandalism.

10. T/F E-tailing involves the use of the Internet for cyber stalking and/or cyber spying.

11. T/F The National Information Infrastructure Protection Act makes it a crime to access computer files without authorization.

12. T/F Data mining is biometrics process used to identify criminals and terrorist suspects at the nation's airports.

13. T/F Thousands of cyber crimes occur each year and the majority of these breaches are reported to either federal, state, or local enforcement agencies.

14. T/F New computer software is being created that allows the recreation of two-dimensional mug shots on a three-dimensional basis.

15. T/F Crime mapping allows police to detect patterns of crime and pathologies of related problems.

MULTIPLE CHOICE QUESTIONS

1. A program that is used to gain unauthorized access to and control over computers that it infects is called a/an:
    a. "droid"
    b. "roto"
    c. "bot"
    d. "e-spy"

2. The theft and/or destruction of information, resources, or funds utilizing computers, computer networks, and the Internet is termed:
    a. cyber crime
    b. cyber theft
    c. cyber mining
    d. cyber spying

3. Which is a criminal benefit of cyber theft?
   a. It offers far less competition from other offenders.
   b. It offers a much wider number of potential victims.
   c. It offers the assurance of a light sentence if arrested and convicted.
   d. It offers the assurance of nonarrest.

4. In this type of computer fraud the criminal skims small sums from the balances of a large number of accounts in order to bypass internal controls.
   a. salami slice
   b. warez
   c. "one-off kamikaze"
   d. "crack and rip"

5. This happens when webmasters forward traffic to another porn site in return for a small per-consumer fee.
   a. "porn-ponging"
   b. "loser-shifting"
   c. "fee-forwarding"
   d. "mouse-trapping"

6. Operation Digital Gridlock targeted:
   a. cyber syping
   b. Internet securities fraud
   c. illegal file sharing
   d. cyber stalking

7. "Shoplisting" is a tactic used in what type of cyber crime?
   a. Internet securities fraud
   b. E-tailing fraud
   c. Cyber stalking
   d. Phishing

8. Computer viruses and worms are types of:
   a. malware
   b. spyware
   c. botware
   d. timeware

9. In 2005, Allan Eric Carlson, a dissatisfied Philadelphia Phillies fan, received a four-year sentence for:
   a. carding
   b. phishing
   c. spamming
   d. e-tailing

10. Content analysis of web page defacement indicates that about _____% are pranks instituted by hackers while the rest have a political motive.
    a. 10
    b. 30
    c. 50
    d. 70

11. Cyber _____ can be viewed as an effort by covert forces to disrupt the intersection between the virtual electronic reality of computers and the physical world.
    a. terrorism
    b. spying
    c. espionage
    d. stalking

12. According to some experts, how many cases of cyber terrorism have been recorded?
    a. none
    b. two hundred
    c. two thousand
    d. two hundred thousand

13. According to a study of identity theft in Britain, in 2004 it took victims up to ___ hours of effort to regain their former status with banks and credit reference agencies.
    a. 100
    b. 300
    c. 500
    d. 800

14. Congress has treated computer-related crime as a distinct federal offense since the passage of the Counterfeit Access Device and Computer Fraud and Abuse Law in:
    a. 2004
    b. 2000
    c. 1998
    d. 1984

15. Identity theft became a crime in:
    a. 2004
    b. 2000
    c. 1998
    d. 1984

16. How many states have passed laws related to identity theft?
    a. only Vermont and the District of Columbia have passed laws
    b. half of the states in the U.S. have passed laws
    c. all states except Vermont and the District of Columbia
    d. all states have passed laws

17. The Toronto, Canada police department's child exploitation section estimates there are _____ children depicted in one million pictures circulating via the Internet.
    a. 100,000
    b. 50,000
    c. 10,000
    d. 5,000

18. The use of IT by states and criminal justice agencies was given a financial jumpstart in 1998 when the federal government enacted the:
    a. Justice Technology Information Network
    b. Communications Assistance for Law Enforcement Act
    c. Automated Fingerprint Identification System
    d. Crime Identification Technology Act

19. Law enforcement agencies have begun using sophisticated computer software to conduct analysis of crime behavior patterns. This process is called:
    a. crime mapping
    b. AFIS
    c. biometrics
    d. data mining

20. The FBI's _____ provides rapid collection and retrieval of data about persons wanted for crime anywhere in the fifty states.
    a. Justice Technology Information Network
    b. National Crime Information Center
    c. Automated Fingerprint Identification System
    d. Nationwide Identification Network

21. The Western Identification Network is a regionalized center for the:
    a. Automated Fingerprint Identification System
    b. Justice technology information network
    c. National Crime Information Center
    d. Nationwide Identification Network

22. Traditionally, to investigate and evaluate a crime scene, detectives relied on:
    a. photographic evidence and two-dimensional drawings
    b. forensic evidence and computerized drawings
    c. witness evidence and fingerprints
    d. photographic evidence and fingerprints

23. What combination of laser and computer technology provides law enforcement with a complete picture of a crime scene?
    a. thermal-definition surveying
    b. high-definition surveying
    c. digital-definition surveying
    d. molecular-laser surveying

24. What computerized technique offers police graphic representations of where crimes are occurring in their jurisdictions?
    a. high-definition surveying
    b. high-definition mapping
    c. crime surveying
    d. crime mapping

25. Fingerprint identification, voice-recognition, iris-scanning, and handwriting analysis are all types of:
    a. bioidentification
    b. biomapping
    c. biometrics
    d. bioforensics

ESSAY QUESTIONS

1. Explain the concept of cyber crime.

2. Discuss the problem of Internet pornography.

3. Explain phishing and the various ways phishers attempt to obtain information.

4. Discuss cyber terrorism and its criticisms.

5.   Explain how the criminal justice system is making use of IT.

MATCHING

1.   _____   Biometrics
2.   _____   "Mousetrapping"
3.   _____   Malware
4.   _____   Warez
5.   _____   E-tailing fraud
6.   _____   Logic bomb
7.   _____   File-sharing
8.   _____   Illegal touting
9.   _____   "Free credit report"
10. _____   Computer worms

A.   Similar to viruses but uses computer networks or the Internet to self-replicate
B.   Also called a *slag* code; it is a type of delayed-action virus that is set off when a program user unwittingly inputs a specific command or makes an inputting error
C.   Occurs when individuals make securities recommendations and fail to disclose that they are being paid to disseminate their favorable opinions
D.   A malicious software program
E.   This happens when web surfers try to close out a window after visiting an adult site and are sent to another web page automatically
F.   Automated methods of recognizing a person based on a physiological or behavioral characteristic
G.   A term computer hackers and software pirates use to describe a game or application that is made available for use on the Internet in violation of its copyright protection
H.   A cyber scam involving the use of the Internet for both illegally buying and selling merchandise.
I.   A form of illegal copyright infringement
J.   A common phisher scam

CHAPTER 14 ANSWER KEY

Fill in the Blank Answers

1. information technology
2. copyright infringement
3. phishing
4. cyber vandalism
5. cyber spying
6. federal offense
7. privacy liberty
8. cyber terrorism
9. phishing
10. authorization

True/False Answers

1.	T	6.	T	11.	T
2.	T	7.	T	12.	F
3.	T	8.	T	13.	F
4.	F	9.	F	14.	T
5.	F	10.	F	15.	T

Multiple Choice Answers

1.	C	11.	A	21.	A
2.	A	12.	A	22.	A
3.	B	13.	B	23.	B
4.	A	14.	D	24.	D
5.	D	15.	C	25.	C
6.	C	16.	C		
7.	B	17.	A		
8.	A	18.	D		
9.	C	19.	D		
10.	D	20.	B		

Essay Questions

1. Page 468
2. Pages 469-470
3. Pages 473-474
4. Pages 478-480
5. Pages 482-492

Matching Answers

1.	F	6.	B
2.	E	7.	I
3.	D	8.	C
4.	G	9.	J
5.	H	10.	A